My
Mother,
That Stranger

Pre-publication reviews of *My Mother, That Stranger*

"To tell the truth in an autobiographical text is immensely difficult if it goes beyond the superficial and I feel that Alborg's memoir confronts several truths (as her other texts that I know and admire have done). The marvelous force of love that reconciles us with everything (even to live at war and hungry), the fragility of every-thing, of deception and disappointment, the difficulty of leaving one's country, creating a profession and more. The found letters serve as a mechanism to rewrite the past, as a revelation and as a catastrophe. In this case there is the added beautiful mystery of why they were hidden and the final theory is convincing and moving. The form in which the author presents the letters, in a critical acad-emic analysis of sorts, works very well, since it organizes the themes and allows us to perceive the reactions of the narrator/researcher (to name her this way). Through the letters she reconstructs not only her mother's life, but the epoch. It is magical." Randolph D. Pope, Ph.D., Emeritus Professor, Commonwealth Professor of Spanish and Comparative Literature, University of Virginia, Charlottesville, VA

"*My Mother, That Stranger* is a moving book. I particularly liked the first part, the one dealing with the war years. I think I fell in love with Conchita, that young, strong woman, happy and determined. And the love and separation relationship told is frightening and beautiful at the same time. I liked the references to the letters so much that I wanted to read all eight-hundred of them. Luckily, the author includes some of them in complete form, which is impor-tant, since we can't read them all." Inés Alberdi, Catedrática de Sociología, Facultad Ciencias Políticas y Sociología, Universidad Complutense de Madrid

"It almost goes without saying that the book is of considerable interest for several reasons. Of course, the vital historical events lend interest to anything written in the Civil War period. To that may be added the complex relationship between the author's parents as well as her father's prominence as a major intellectual figure in 20th century Spain. A lot of the book is the author's reporting what she took from the letters rather than the letters them-selves. Her direct quotation of the letters is always good, because that lends the narrative a particular authenticity. I enjoyed the fact that she included a lot of the Spanish original, because if one has even a limited knowledge, the original has a particular charm and individuality." Francis W. Hoeber, Author of *Against Time: Letters from Nazi Germany 1938–1939*. Philadelphia: American Philosophical Society Press, 2015

"The author realizes that few readers will be familiar with how the Civil War affected Spanish civilian life. They are even less aware of the post-war period, in which physical poverty and chronic food shortages made life a struggle for most Spaniards. In addition, Francoist Spain experienced an oppressive political environment in which liberty of expression was non-existent. Deviation from the nationalistic, Falangist platform of women's social roles as Catholic mothers, whose place was at home, subordinate to their husbands was punished. Alborg does a wonderful job in presenting this background and context in which she observes the lives of her mother and family evolve. Indeed, the "Stranger" of the title becomes less so as Alborg scrutinizes the daily letters written to each other by her mother and father." Paul C. Smith, Ph.D., Professor Emeritus, University of California, Los Angeles

"During the preparation and drafting of this book, the author has discovered an unknown facet of her mother and the relationship of her parents. However, for the readers this is a testimony of a fundamental time in Spanish history — the three years of Civil War and the immediate postwar — from the intimacy and the enthusiasm of a young couple who was anxious to start the experience of a shared life. Through this interchange of ideas and confessions between a woman and a man in love, by means of the epistolary genre, their customs, wishes, prejudices, uncertainties, painful and tragic life experiences, but also happiness and hope for a better future are disclosed; a future that was aspired to as well by thousands of Spaniards, but that was truncated by the nonsense of the fratricide and dramatic consequences of this war. The authenticity of Concha Alborg's prose, in a confessional style, submerges us in the thought and life of her parents and, at the same time, of an entire epoch." Ángeles Encinar, Ph.D., Professor of Spanish Literature, Saint Louis University, Madrid Campus

The Cañada Blanch / Sussex Academic Studies on Contemporary Spain

General Editor: Professor Paul Preston, London School of Economics

A list of all published titles in the series is available on the Press website. More recently published works are presented below.

Concha Alborg, *My Mother, That Stranger: Letters from the Spanish Civil War.*

Peter Anderson, *Friend or Foe?: Occupation, Collaboration and Selective Violence in the Spanish Civil War.*

Germà Bel, *Disdain, Distrust, and Dissolution: The Surge of Support for Independence in Catalonia.*

Carl-Henrik Bjerström, *Josep Renau and the Politics of Culture in Republican Spain, 1931–1939: Re-imagining the Nation.*

Darryl Burrowes, *Historians at War: Cold War Influences on Anglo-American Representations of the Spanish Civil War.*

Andrew Canessa (ed.), *Barrier and Bridge: Spanish and Gibraltarian Perspectives on Their Border.*

Kathryn Crameri, *'Goodbye, Spain?': The Question of Independence for Catalonia.*

Pol Dalmau, *Press, Politics and National Identities in Catalonia: The Transformation of La Vanguardia, 1881–1931.*

Mark Derby, *Petals and Bullets: Dorothy Morris – A New Zealand Nurse in the Spanish Civil War.*

Francisco Espinosa-Maestre, *Shoot the Messenger?: Spanish Democracy and the Crimes of Francoism – From the Pact of Silence to the Trial of Baltasar Garzón.*

María Jesús González, *Raymond Carr: The Curiosity of the Fox.*

Helen Graham, *The War and its Shadow: Spain's Civil War in Europe's Long Twentieth Century.*

Arnau Gonzàlez i Vilalta (ed.), *The Illusion of Statehood: Perceptions of Catalan Independence up to the End of the Spanish Civil War.*

Xabier A. Irujo, *GERNIKA: Genealogy of a Lie.*

Mandie Iveson, *Language Attitudes, National Identity and Migration in Catalonia: 'What the Women Have to Say'*

Angela Jackson, *'For us it was Heaven': The Passion, Grief and Fortitude of Patience Darton – From the Spanish Civil War to Mao's China.*

Gabriel Jackson, *Juan Negrín: Physiologist, Socialist, and Spanish Republican War Leader.*

Nathan Jones, *The Adoption of a Pro-US Foreign Policy by Spain and the United Kingdom: José María Aznar and Tony Blair's Personal Motivations and their Global Impact.*

Xavier Moreno Juliá, *The Blue Division: Spanish Blood in Russia, 1941– 1945.*

David Lethbridge, *Norman Bethune in Spain: Commitment, Crisis, and Conspiracy.*

Antonio Miguez Macho, *The Genocidal Genealogy of Francoism: Violence, Memory and Impunity.*

Carles Manera, *The Great Recession: A Subversive View.*

Nicholas Manganas, *Las dos Españas: Terror and Crisis in Contemporary Spain.*

Jorge Marco, *Guerrilleros and Neighbours in Arms: Identities and Cultures of Antifascist Resistance in Spain.*

Emily Mason, *Democracy, Deeds and Dilemmas: Support for the Spanish Republic within British Civil Society, 1936–1939.*

Soledad Fox Maura, *Jorge Semprún: The Spaniard who Survived the Nazis and Conquered Paris.*

Martin Minchom, *Spain's Martyred Cities: From the Battle of Madrid to Picasso's* Guernica.

Olivia Muñoz-Rojas, *Ashes and Granite: Destruction and Reconstruction in the Spanish Civil War and Its Aftermath.*

Linda Palfreeman, *Spain Bleeds: The Development of Battlefield Blood Transfusion during the Civil War.*

Fernando Puell de la Villa and David García Hernán (eds.), *War and Population Displacement: Lessons of History.*

Rúben Serém, *Conspiracy, Coup d'état and Civil War in Seville, 1936– 1939: History and Myth in Francoist Spain.*

Gareth Stockey, *Gibraltar: "A Dagger in the Spine of Spain?"*

Maggie Torres, *Anarchism and Political Change in Spain: Schism, Polarisation and Reconstruction of the* Confederación Nacional del Trabajo, *1939–1979.*

Dacia Viejo-Rose, *Reconstructing Spain: Cultural Heritage and Memory after Civil War.*

Antoni Vives, *SMART City Barcelona: The Catalan Quest to Improve Future Urban Living.*

My Mother, That Stranger

Letters from The Spanish Civil War

Concha Alborg

To Virgina, and Linda,
Because we love all
mothers, with love
Concha.

sussex
ACADEMIC
PRESS
Brighton • Chicago • Toronto

Cañada Blanch Centre
for Contemporary
Spanish Studies

Philodelphia, 12/10/2023

2 4 6 8 10 9 7 5 3 1

First published in 2019 in Great Britain by
SUSSEX ACADEMIC PRESS
PO Box 139
Eastbourne BN24 9BP

Distributed in North America by
SUSSEX ACADEMIC PRESS
Independent Publishers Group
814 N. Franklin Street
Chicago, IL 60610

Published in collaboration with the Cañada Blanch Centre for Contemporary Spanish Studies, London School of Economics.

British Library Cataloguing in Publication Data
A CIP catalogue record for this book is available from the British Library.

Library of Congress Cataloging-in-Publication Data
To be applied for.

Paperback ISBN 978-1-78976-030-9

Typeset and designed by Sussex Academic Press, Brighton & Eastbourne.
Printed by Independent Publishers Group, Chicago.

Contents

Contents

Contents

The Cañada Blanch Centre for Contemporary Spanish Studies

In the 1960s, the most important initiative in the cultural and academic relations between Spain and the United Kingdom was launched by a Valencian fruit importer in London. The creation by Vicente Cañada Blanch of the Anglo-Spanish Cultural Foundation has subsequently benefited large numbers of Spanish and British scholars at various levels. Thanks to the generosity of Vicente Cañada Blanch, thousands of Spanish schoolchildren have been educated at the secondary school in West London that bears his name. At the same time, many British and Spanish university students have benefited from the exchange scholarships which fostered cultural and scientific exchanges between the two countries. Some of the most important historical, artistic and literary work on Spanish topics to be produced in Great Britain was initially made possible by Cañada Blanch scholarships.

Vicente Cañada Blanch was, by inclination, a conservative. When his Foundation was created, the Franco regime was still in the plenitude of its power. Nevertheless, the keynote of the Foundation's activities was always a complete open-mindedness on political issues. This was reflected in the diversity of research projects supported by the Foundation, many of which, in Francoist Spain, would have been regarded as subversive. When the Dictator died, Don Vicente was in his seventy-fifth year. In the two decades following the death of the Dictator, although apparently indestructible, Don Vicente was obliged to husband his energies. Increasingly, the work of the Foundation was carried forward by Miguel Dols whose tireless and imaginative work in London was matched in Spain by that of José María Coll Comín. They were united in the Foundation's spirit of open-minded commitment to fostering research of high quality in pursuit of better Anglo-Spanish cultural relations. Throughout the 1990s, thanks to them, the role of the Foundation grew considerably.

In 1994, in collaboration with the London School of Economics, the Foundation established the Príncipe de Asturias Chair of Contemporary Spanish History and the Cañada Blanch Centre for Contemporary Spanish Studies. It is the particular task of the Cañada Blanch Centre for Contemporary Spanish Studies to promote the understanding of twentieth-century Spain through research and teaching of contemporary Spanish history, politics, economy, sociology and culture. The Centre possesses a valuable library and archival centre for specialists in contemporary Spain. This work is carried on through the publications of the doctoral and post-doctoral researchers at the Centre itself and through the many seminars and lectures held at the London School of Economics. While the seminars are the province of the researchers, the lecture cycles have been the forum in which Spanish politicians have been able to address audiences in the United Kingdom.

Since 1998, the Cañada Blanch Centre has published a substantial number of books in collaboration with several different publishers on the subject of contemporary Spanish history and politics. An extremely fruitful partnership with Sussex Academic Press began in 2004. Many of the titles deal with the Spanish Civil War. Along with the history of medicine during the war and the role of the International Brigades, an area covered frequently by the series has been violence behind the lines during the war and the post-war Francoist repression.

The series' examination of various aspects of the Spanish Civil War takes a dramatic turn with the extraordinary volume *My Mother, That Stranger: Letters from the Spanish Civil War*. Its sheer originality derives from the fact that it is based on a collection of more than eight-hundred letters constituted by the correspondence between a young man who is a soldier in the Republican army fighting the Francoists and his fiancée. The young Concepción Carles was a secretarial student living in Valencia, waiting and hoping to get married. The story built on these letters is about someone who was typical of women who were educated and given wide-ranging rights under the Second Republic only to have those rights snatched away by the Franco dictatorship. The work is a significant contribution to the literature of ordinary lives in wartime.

Guest Series Editor's Preface by Antonio Feros

My Mother, That Stranger: Letters from the Spanish Civil War is a unique book in more than one sense. First, because of the range of topics it deals with, but also because it manages to strike that elusive balance between scholarly analysis and personal reflection. This is not a work of history, or literature, nor is it a memoir, strictly speaking. It is an interdisciplinary book, and, moreover, one replete with subtle analysis of complex lives and times.

In the Introduction to his powerful work, *The German War: A Nation Under Arms, 1939–1945*, Nicholas Stargardt explained that what he wanted to accomplish when studying Germany during the Second World War was not so much to describe the great battles, or to analyze the ideologies that helped shape the Nazi regime. His main goal was to understand "how people judged and understood events while they were unfolding around them and before they knew the eventual outcome." To do this, he felt the need to make use of a large number of collections of letters "between lovers, close friends, parents and children, and married couples," as a way of penetrating worlds conceived as private, but which offered a window onto the social and military events of the period. One of the conditions that Stargardt imposed on those sources was that "both sides of the correspondence are preserved and [...] continued for several years at least, so that it would be possible to see how the personal relationships between the correspondents — their principal purpose in writing at all — developed and altered over the course of the war."

I mention Stargardt's work not to suggest that *My Mother, That Stranger* and *The German War* are very much alike. Unlike Stargardt's, Alborg's work is not the story of how a people understood, or tried to interpret, the violent world produced by war, in her case, the Spanish Civil War. However, they do share some common elements. Like Stargardt's, Concha Alborg was also able to draw upon a large collection of letters (a total of 822) exchanged between her mother, Concepcion Carles, and her father, Juan Luis Alborg. This correspondence, which survives in its entirety, lasted from 1937 — the year Alborg's parents became engaged — until the end of the Civil War in early 1939. Conchita Carles, the "stranger" of the title, spent almost the entire war in Valencia, her hometown and the capital of the Republic from the end of 1936 until the end of 1937. Her father, Juan Alborg, was mobilized by the Republican government at the beginning of 1937, and spent nearly the whole remainder of the conflict on military fronts in the southeast of the peninsula. Conchita had studied to be a secretary, and her work for the Republic was related to this professional training. When he was mobilized, Juan Alborg was studying Philosophy at the University of Valencia.

Among the great pleasures awaiting the reader of *My Mother, That Stranger* are precisely Concepcion and Juan Luis' reflections on the war, its course, their own hopes and fears, the need to understand the conflict and its duration, and how a violent struggle of this kind affected the lives, and above all the hopes for the future, of the young people of the period. It is striking, for instance, that the feelings of Conchita and Juan Luis towards the war would have been more informed by their personal circumstances than by political considerations or ideological assumptions, feelings very similar to those expressed by young married or engaged couples written about actors who were not ideologically committed during the great conflicts that afflicted Europe in the 1930s and 1940s. In her letters, Conchita Carles — who served the Republic in a variety of administrative posts — commented on the situation on the home front, while Juan Luis made observations from the front line, which was sometimes quieter, if only because Valencia was the object of numerous and often deadly bombings during the Civil War.

Yet the letters — and the author only includes a few of them in full, although in the text she cites from and comments on many others — contain much more than reflections on war. They also reveal a great deal about Conchita Carles's and Juan Luis Alborg's personal motivations, the knowledge they deemed important and the practicalities of learning in wartime (for instance, the books that Juan Luis Alborg wanted to acquire and read even though he was serving the Republic in a military capacity, but also those that he asked his girlfriend Conchita to read, and that he hoped would shape her as a woman and an individual), family relationships, love and heartbreaks, hopes and fears, male-female relationships, and family stories hierarchies. As a result, this book reveals not only the microcosm of the two protagonists, but also the macrocosm of the Civil War, and Spain in the 1930s.

Fortunately for the reader, the book is also the discovery of the mother, that stranger, by the author, after many years in which the protagonist of all their lives had been her more famous father — Juan Luis Alborg, celebrated literary critic ever since the publication in Spain of *Hora actual de la novela española* (1958, winner of the National Prize for Literature the following year). Her mother, Conchita Carles, lived in her spouse's shadow during all but the years of the Civil War itself. These letters helped Concha Alborg to better understand the complexity of her mother's aspirations, thoughts, and personality. A process of discovery that is also a process of self-discovery. The reading of more than eight hundred letters, and subsequent reflections on her mother and father, the relations between them, life after the war, and emigration and life in the United States, helped the author Concha Alborg to discover herself, and not only as an Alborg, but also and especially as a Carles as a student of Spanish literature like her father, but also as a woman, daughter, wife, and mother as Conchita Carles.

Concha Alborg was born in Valencia, the city of her parents, studied in Madrid, and in 1961 emigrated with her family to the United States. She completed her doctoral studies in literature at Temple University. Upon earning her Ph.D. she became a professor of contemporary Spanish literature at Saint Joseph's University in Philadelphia, where she still resides. She has published numerous scholarly articles on the Spanish novel after the Civil War, and is the author of several novels, as well as a memoir, *Divorce after Death: A Widow s Memoir* (Shorehouse Books, 2014). Many of us hope that she will finish her next project, a complete edition of her parents' wartime correspondence, which will not only afford a deeper understanding of Conchita Carles and Juan Luis Alborg, but will also give us a more complex and complete vision of how Spaniards experienced and thought about a conflict that still affects us all.

ANTONIO FEROS
Philadelphia, August 2019

Preface by Antonio Feros

Antonio Feros
Chair Department of History
Rose Family Endowed Term Professor of History
University of Pennsylvania
208 College Hall
Philadelphia, PA 19104
http://www.history.upenn.edu/people/faculty/antonio-feros

Acknowledgments

I do not subscribe to the notion that writing is a solitary occupation. On the contrary, it takes a community of family, friends and colleagues to finish and publish a book such as this one. Each of these persons has read the manuscript or offered suggestions, made useful comments and recommendations, written reviews, corrected mistakes and has encouraged me to keep on working on this challenging project. To all of you on both sides of the Atlantic, I am much indebted: Inés Alberdi, Philip Bertocci, Aránzazu Borrachero, Peter Conn, Carmen Croce, Eileen Cunniffe, Helen Cunningham, Linda D'Amico, Diana Day, Ángeles Encinar, Cheryl Fedyna, Adriana Galanes, Alberto Gil-Peralta, Tom Goodman, Hernán Guaracao, Francis Hoeber, Ana Laguna, María Belén Molina, Susan Perloff, Carlos Pérez Sámano, Randolph Pope, Nathaniel Popkin, Ether Recio, Juana Sabadell, Paul Smith, Noël Valis, Ricardo Vivancos and the Philadelphia Athenaeum Writers Group. To all of you I express my sincere appreciation. I also owe gratitude to my relatives in Valencia and Madrid — in particular my cousins Elena Carles Martí, Inma Carles Pantoja and Juan Miguel García Alborg — who have shared stories about their parents during the Spanish Civil War, corroborating and enlightening mine. Special thanks are due to Dwayne Booth, who designed another beautiful cover and illustrated this book; to Jane Day Rasmussen, who took the author picture, making it look easy; and to Antonio Feros, who wrote such an inspiring prologue. I am most grateful to Paul Preston for including my book in the Cañada Blanch Series. Anthony Grahame at Sussex Academic Press was a model of efficiency and professionalism. It takes a village, indeed!

Hablar de nuestras madres es hablar de nosotras mismas, definirnos en la congruencia o la diferencia, responder con una proyección a esa otra individualidad que alguna vez se proyectó en nuestras conciencias para quedar grabada a fuego.

To speak about our mothers is to talk about ourselves, defining us in the similarities or the differences, answering with a projection to that other individuality that sometimes was projected on our consciousness to remain forged by fire.

Alejandra Rojas "Mujeres de palabra," *Salidas de madre*
("Women of Their Word," *Emerging from our Mothers*)

We spend most of our adulthoods trying to grasp the meaning of our parents' lives; and how we shape and answer these questions largely turns us into who we are.

Phillip Lopate "The Story of My Father,"
Portrait of My Body

Finding the Letters

In preparation for a symposium commemorating the centenary of my father's birth, the books from his libraries in Spain as well as in the United States, had been catalogued, packed, and shipped to the University of Málaga. In the summer of 2013, I went with two Spanish colleagues to my father's summer home in El Escorial, near Madrid, to make sure that all the documents and books had been properly picked up. At one point the doorman interrupted our visit, reminding us that there was a storage unit in the attic and that he had the key. I remembered storing my children's crib and toys there. On that day, there were small household items in the attic, together with a few large cardboard boxes and an imposing picture of Cervantes that eventually ended up in Málaga as well. The boxes seemed to contain miscellaneous documents.

José Polo, one of my accompanying sleuths who is a serious bibliophile, was wearing a blue librarian's smock and white gloves in order to protect our findings. In the very last box to be opened, under some class notes, Ángeles Encinar alerted us about some unusual documents. There they were, obviously hidden; more than 800 letters carefully separated into small bundles and in perfect condition, thanks to the dry climate and high altitude in that region of Spain. I recognized my father's energetic handwriting immediately, but the ones signed by Conchita were not written in my mother's typical cursive handwriting. They were written in traditional calligraphy, similar to what I had been taught by the French Ursuline nuns at Our Lady of Loreto School in Madrid. At first, I thought I had found letters between my dad and an aunt, also named Conchita, with whom my father had an affair before my mother's death, a liaison that caused no end of turmoil within my entire family. I recreated those letters in my novel, *American in Translation: A Novel in Three Novellas* (2011), and this book also caused all kinds of grief.

No, this Conchita was my mother, writing in a different script for a reason I could not yet fathom. Finding these letters was a very emotional, pivotal moment for me. I knew immediately I had to bring them home to Philadelphia, where I currently live, rather than ship them to Málaga with the rest of my father's documents. I purchased a carry-on suitcase and I have not been separated from this evocative treasure-trove since. All of the 822 letters are sitting on my dining room table, arranged in chronological order in two neat files. My father's letters, although they are practically the same in number as my mother's, occupy almost double the space; my mother always let her husband have the last word — and then some.

My mother was born in Valencia on June 21, 1916. She was named Concepción after her mother, a name that traditionally becomes Conchita and Concha, just as I started my life as Conchín to become Conchita during my school days in Madrid and, later, Concha throughout my life in the United States. Naming children after their parents and using a diminutive form was commonplace in Spain and, despite their liberal political leanings, my family was traditional in that respect. Whenever anyone asked my mother about her family, she always started by saying that she was the oldest of seven with four brothers and two sisters who came after her in short succession. She was equally fond of each of them and often remarked proudly how handsome her brothers were, with full heads of wavy hair until well into their advanced age. She was, however, the most striking of them all; small in stature, with auburn hair and beautiful green, smiling eyes.

Her parents lived in Valencia, close to the Ruzafa Market, in a modest flat similar to the one I remember visiting often as a young girl. José Carles, my grandfather, was a loving man who doted on his children, my mother in particular. He worked as an accountant at a bakery near the city harbor, easily reachable by trolley from their home. Despite being the third largest city in Spain, Valencia, with its 380,000 inhabitants in 1936 was, and still is, very much a provincial city, walkable and easy to navigate. When my mother finished secretarial school, she started working for the telephone company to supplement the family income and her siblings followed suit as soon as they were old enough to work.

The Spanish Civil War, which started with General Francisco Franco's coup on July 18, 1936, broke the routine of my mother's family as well as that of the entire city. By November 1936 Valencia became the capital of the Republic with the established legal government of President Manuel Azaña. The battle lines were mainly drawn geographically: Valencia, Barcelona and Madrid staying on the Republican, Loyalist side (also called "Red") of the Socialist Government, while the South, Castile and the North, with the exception of the Basque region, were allied with the Nationalist, fascist Falange movement (with their blue shirts) under General Francisco Franco. Some families found themselves in the deplorable situation of having relatives, even siblings, fighting against each other just because they lived in different regions of the country.

My mother had just turned twenty years old when the war broke out. At first, everyone thought that it would be a matter of months before the conflict was settled and for a person like her, life still seemed normal enough. She was gregarious, had many friends and loved to go to the beach. She did not have a formal boyfriend at that time, but I have seen pictures of her at parties, wearing costumes, laughing gaily as if she did not have a care in the world. On New Year's Day 1937 she went to a party with her theater group and was introduced to a lanky, reserved, serious university student with thick, black-framed glasses. Juan Luis Alborg could not have been more different than Conchita Carles.

At that time, the man who would become my father was completing his studies in the humanities at the University of Valencia. He lived a few blocks from my mother's family with his uncle, Miguel Alborg, who never married and ran the family cheese import business, his sister Teresa Alborg (who would become my godmother) and his stepmother, Teresa Monserrat. After his mother passed away, my grandfather soon remarried and had a daughter from his second marriage. As the son of a widow and a university student, there was a question as to whether my father could be drafted to fight in the war, but he was called just a few months after he met my mother. My parents wrote to each other almost every day between July 1937 and the end of March 1939; no one in my family, including me, had any idea that their letters had survived and still existed.

There are scores of histories and memoirs that have been written about the Spanish Civil War, from the all-time classic *Homage to Catalonia* by George Orwell (1938) to one of my favorites, *Doves*

3

of War: Four Women of Spain by Paul Preston (2016). But this memoir is unique because it is based on the complete, intimate letters between my parents and focuses on my mother rather than my well-known father. My mother's life was exemplary of the women who were formed under the liberal Spanish Republic only to be silenced during Franco's repressive dictatorship (1939–1975). This book differs from other works presenting a women's perspective. *Women's Voices from the Spanish Civil War* edited by Jim Fyrth and Sally Alexander (1991), for example, focuses on the narratives of foreign women who were deemed to be more objective. *Memories of Resistance. Women's Voices from the Spanish Civil War* by Shirley Mangini (1995), emphasizes the narratives of political and literary figures because of their prominence or accomplishments. In several respects my book is a microhistory of the Spanish Civil War as seen by individuals who illuminate the official story told in history books. My mother's personal narrative adds to the understanding of this significant time because she showed us how a family lived in the midst of war. Accounts such as these are generally relegated to footnotes in traditional history books. According to Mangini, "The Spanish memory texts of war and its consequences are women-woven texts, fused together to form a historical quilt" (56). I would like to add my mother's story to this memorial quilt, since she "has provided us with such insights into the lives of Spanish women and the impact of the Spanish Civil War" (65).

Reading my parents' letters, I realized that I did not know my mother well, thus the "Stranger" in my title. Writing about her has truly been a journey of discovery. The mother I grew up with was not the same woman portrayed in my parents' letters. After marrying my father, under his tutelage and living in Francoist Spain, she changed from a liberal young woman to a watchful mother. The patriarchal society overwhelmed her Republican upbringing by far.

In addition to discovering my mother, as Phillip Lopate expresses in his epigraph, the process of writing this memoir became a journey of self-discovery as well. I realized the degree to which I am like my mother and how I differ from her in other ways. Immigrating to the United States, for example, was something that she did not fully accomplish, emphasizing the differences between us. Nevertheless, the impact of my mother's legacy is significant, not only on myself but on others members of my family. As part of my mother's rich legacy, I have included some of her favorite recipes in an appendix. Her cooking is a way in which she expressed herself and her Spanish culture.

The 2014 symposium turned out to be fortuitous for me, since I found my parents' letters, but I shall always wonder why my father hid these letters and, even more puzzling, why he never mentioned them to me. He followed my writing career and knew of my interest in his stories about the Spanish Civil War, which I included in my first work of fiction, *Una noche en casa* (A Night at Home, 1995). There is not a chance that he had forgotten about these letters that were so carefully kept; he had a sharp mind until the very end. It is very possible that he hid them during his second marriage to keep them safe from his wife, who was jealous of my mother and had removed all of her pictures from the house. Another explanation as to why he did not tell me about the letters could be that he did not really want me to write about this part of his life, although he encouraged me to write about him as a Don Juan character. He often told me of his adventures after my mother died, urging me to take notes; his only request was that I not call him José Luis as I did in some of my works, but Juan, appropriately, his real name.

It is very ironic that I would be the one to find these letters, and not only because I am a writer. When I arrived at his apartment, several of my dad's students and some of his paramours had been through the entire place, cataloguing and taking inventory. My brother lives only a few kilometers from El Escorial and he was always good at keeping an eye on our parents' possessions. Also, my father's third wife had made this place her home and still spends vacations there. In fact, the attic was full of her belongings. What is truly coincidental is that in 2006, right after my second husband died, I also found correspondence with his lovers, which proved that, unbeknownst to me, he had a hidden life too. I wrote about this dramatic event in my memoir, *Divorce After Death: A Widow's Memoir* (2014). Granted, that separated by some seventy years, my parents' letters were in an attic in Spain, while my late husband's letters were on a laptop in the United States. But poetic justice does, indeed, seem to exist and I was meant to write about my family's past, proving that sometimes one can find out more about people post mortem than when they were alive.

At first, I was going to write a memoir that focused on my father's long, peripatetic life and illustrious career but, upon reflection, I decided to write about my mother's quieter and shorter life, albeit an equally fascinating and meaningful one. I trust that there will be other works written about my eminent father, but probably none about my not-so-well-known mother. Had I rushed to finish this project, I would have written the wrong book. Like my mother, I was married first to a man who also fought in a war and, later, to a wandering husband. As her daughter and as a mother myself, I am the ideal reader of her letters. I trust that, given my academic expertise on contemporary Spain — history, culture, literature and language — I will also be the ideal writer to interpret the letters and put them in the appropriate context for English-speaking readers. I have translated direct quotes from the letters into English and used parenthesis with the exact dates given, even though I did not write about them chronologically. Although this family memoir is not intended to be strictly an academic study, I have included textual notes and a bibliography to elucidate historical facts alluded to in my parents' letters and to clarify historical points. Likewise, this book is not meant to be read as a history of the Spanish Civil War, which serves mainly as the background of the story.

MIGUEL ALBORG VILAPLANA
SUCESOR DE JUAN ALBORG

COMISIONES
REPRESENTACIONES ESPAÑOLAS
Y EXTRANJERAS

GENERAL SANMARTIN, 10

DIRECCION TELEGRAFICA:
"ALBOVILA"
TELEFONO 12122
···

QUESOS HOLANDESES
LA MARCA MAS ACREDITADA DEL MUNDO

AGENTE REGIONAL

TRADE-MARK
PATRONAGE
"LA CARRETILLA"

Valencia 4 de Junio de 1937.-
(España)

Queridísima Conchita:

Supongo que a la hora en que te escribo habrás dado los primeros pasos para la instalación de tu nueva residencia. Me imagino lo atareada que estarás y daría cualquier cosa que estuviese pronto por poder ayudarte y conseguir así dos cosas que deseo con toda el alma: quitarte trabajo y estar contigo. Por desgracia no puedo alcanzar ninguna de las dos y aquí me tienes con una morriña metida en los huesos que me quita hasta las ganas de hablar con nadie. Anoche llegué a casa cuando ya estaba cenando mi familia, y pretextando todavía cierta molestia por la inyección de tifus, me negué a cenar. Después de muchos ruegos hice un simulacro de cena y me marché a la cama; necesitaba estar solo para mi unión con calma mi disgusto que no sé cuando podré echarme de encima; y hablando con franqueza lo deseo de veras pues en tal estado de ánimo soy hombre al agua.

Esta mañana me he pasado una hora exacta (de 8 a 9) en el balcón de mi casa por si te veía pero como no te he visto supongo que habrás cogido el tran-

Conchita's Letters

Reading my mother's letters has been a very moving experience for me. Sometimes I would find myself laughing out loud, other times my eyes would fill with tears and I had to take a break. In some ways I could hear her crystalline singing voice as I remember it. But most of the time I felt that I really did not know her well. She was obviously young, but resourceful and clever, and so in love with my dad. Yet I know that she became embittered with him because of his never-ending need for female attention. In these letters, I discovered that she was the one in control, assured of her power over him, teasing him, knowing full well that he was infatuated with her. What she did not know is that he would repeat this pattern time and again with other women. But I get ahead of myself.

In my mother's first nine letters my dad was not yet away at the front lines of the war. She had left Valencia for a small town in the mountains of Llombay, with her three youngest siblings, Fina, Salvador and Toni, "The Three Musketeers" as she called them. It is obvious that my grandparents were worried about their children's safety and the scarcity of food in Valencia that would only get worse as the war wore on. But my mother did not like Llombay, which she called "diabolic Llombay" (June 11, 1937). She had to cook inside the house because it was so windy on the patio. Food was as scarce as it was in Valencia to the point that, on a good day, she could only find a half dozen eggs and she needed to stand in line every evening to get drinking water. At one point she asked my father to bring her some olive oil.

According to the envelopes, my father's letters during those few weeks were sent to Luis Cardona with my mother's name in parentheses. This man probably was a family friend who took them in to help out. The envelopes are meticulously typed; my father was always a fanatic about writing addresses clearly. Amazingly, the forty-five centimes stamps with the Spanish Republic seal are also intact. More importantly, the envelopes were from the family's cheese import business with the logo "Cheeses and Butters, The Most Prestigious Brand from Holland, with Premium Warranty." My paternal grandfather changed the family surname, Alborch, to the more European sounding Alborg, in order to give a better accreditation to the cheese business. I know that my mother was a practical woman, and the fact that my father had the family business to fall back on, must have been very reassuring to her, regardless of my father's literary studies and ambitions.

During their first separation, my father took a bus and made day trips to Llombay on Sundays. My mother's letters were written in the school-girl cursive that I mentioned earlier and have spelling mistakes that I am sure my father pointed out, since she often called him "my professor" and said: "go ahead and correct me" (June 13, 1937). She turned out to be a quick study, though, because in later letters there were practically no spelling errors. In fact, her style became expressive and self-assured very quickly. In the letter of June 9, 1937, she wrote: "You are a grand thief, because you have taken away my heart, my sleep, my peace and quiet, which is one of my biggest treasures."

While she was staying in Llombay, my mother could talk on the phone with her mother daily, despite the poor connection, since my grandmother worked at Telefónica, the Spanish telephone company. It surprised me to see my mother so irritated with my grandmother, trying to convince her to let her go back to Valencia in order to be near her boyfriend. But my mother was very close to her mother. As the oldest of seven siblings, she helped with the household chores in every way and practically ran the house when my grandmother was sick and needed surgery, keeping her company at the clinic and worrying endlessly about her. I do not know what kind of surgery my grandmother had; it was probably an OB/GYN issue, because my mother mentioned some heavy bleeding. Of course, my dad could never talk about "those" issues and when I looked through his letters to find out more information, there was no clarification.

All of my parents' letters were written by hand most of them on small, plain paper of about 6 x 9 inches. It is incredible, despite the poor quality of the paper, that all the letters are intact, with hardly a mark, ink stain, or rip of any kind; especially given the fact that my dad carried some of them around for months. I know that he left my mother's letters in Valencia the few times that he had a leave from the front. I wonder if my father already had any inkling about their literary value. How fortunate for his curious, literary-minded daughter! My dad's letters were much longer than my mother's. His were usually about six or seven pages long, but there are many that are eleven pages or longer, while hers tended to be three or four pages. For this reason, his letters occupy almost double the space than hers. My father's nervous, sharp handwriting can be difficult to read, but my mother did not seem to have a problem with it. She could read his letters as easily as if they were printed and she could not understand why his family had a hard time reading them (August 3, 1938). He often wrote in a very small script, always on both sides of the page to save paper and urged my mother to do the same.

My mother's letter of July 15, 1937 is the first one she wrote with her rounded, distinctive handwriting that I recognized immediately. She was afraid that it looked more masculine than the cursive she learned at school and asked my dad: "Am I masculine perchance? No one can answer that better than you." My dad liked her characteristic handwriting better and she never used the school calligraphy again. I can only imagine the effect that my mother's "feminine" tactics must have had on my dad. Although my parents' letters were chaste by today's standards, it surprised me to see this seductive side of my mother. When I was growing up, it was my father who was the seducer, constantly charming her while she played hard to get.

Despite my father's complaints, my mother was the ideal inter-locutor and recipient for my dad's letters. She often told him to write more about his feelings and how much he missed and loved her — as if he needed any encouragement. One of my father's favorite authors was Juan Valera, a master of the epistolary genre, something that I learned from my dad when he tutored me as a young girl. My mother may not have known as much literary theory as my dad, but she was a great reader and she knew how to urge him on and how to read him: "I will read your letters with the eagerness that a thirsty person drinks water" (July 7, 1937).

No sooner had my mother and her siblings returned to Valencia, my father was called to serve, despite their expectation to the contrary. Right away the rumor that he would be allowed to come back circulated among family and friends and this false hope was very detrimental to his adjustment to their separation. Just before his departure, they had a serious argument and almost broke up; they both referred to this incident as a reminder that their relationship had to endure until my dad returned from the war.

My mother expected a letter every day and when she did not get one, she was in a bad mood, "humor perruno," (doggie humor) as she called it (June 6, 1937). She could also describe it in more poetic terms: "When I don't have a letter it's as if I lack air to breathe well. Believe me, I have a weight on my chest that doesn't allow me to breathe with liberty and calm" (March 16, 1939). If there is something repetitious in her letters, it is the constant count of how many days she had missed a letter and how many he owed her. Never mind that they were writing during times of war. On the few occasions that she was angry with him, she sent him a handshake instead of a loving goodbye: "I'm not angry, you know? When you feel like it, you'll write . . . Good night and until the next time. A handshake for today from your Conchita" (March 30, 1938). Sometimes she admitted that, although she was upset, she wrote to him anyway for selfish reasons; she felt worse if she did not write: "Does this happen to you as well?" she asked my dad (April 26, 1938).

My mother usually wrote in the evenings when everyone else in the household was asleep; oftentimes at 1:00 a.m. or even later. Her family was large and boisterous and she needed peace and quiet. She kept paper and envelopes in a cardboard box that served as a desk on her lap. Sometimes she wrote to him under the threat of an air raid, but she did not care and continued writing (December 12, 1937). My grandfather worried that my mother was not getting enough sleep and ordered her to stop writing. She wrote to my dad: "I've had two warnings already, at the third he will turn off my light and lecture me," (December 15, 1938). Even the dark would not stop my mother from writing. On more than one occasion, she wrote by candlelight because they had lost electrical power.

It is surprising that neither my mother nor my dad were concerned about the imminent Christmas holidays during their first year apart. The only special dates for them were the day they met, January 1, 1937, and the 24 of each month, since they confirmed their commitment on June 24 of the same year. Only on her Saint's Day, did my mother receive special greetings from my dad and small gifts from her friends and colleagues at work. My father mentioned during the approaching Christmas of 1938, how he wished that they would not have to spend more holidays at war.

The Saints' Day used to be as important as birthdays in my family. Traditionally, in Spanish culture children were named after a saint from the liturgical calendar; my mother and I shared the Feast of the Immaculate Conception on December 8. I know that their families were not religious, but they did observe this custom. When I was growing up, my family always celebrated this day, which was a national holiday, with an open house. Relatives and friends would stop by and my mother would serve her special "rollitos," anisette cookies that I still make to this day during the Christmas holidays.

As the war dragged on, there was a shortage of paper and my mother had to scramble to get it from her office and send it to my dad, as well as stamps and envelopes. Inside the letters there are several tiny notes written on scratch paper, which have also miraculously survived. The first time I read the letters, I panicked thinking that some were missing, only to find out that my dad had been on leave for a few weeks from June 13–20, 1938 and August 10–31, 1938, for example. It seems that my mother wrote four or five letters at the end of the war that my dad never received. More about that later.

At first, my mother said that she would not go out to the cinema or for walks when my father was away, but soon she was making plans to see her friends and relatives. After all, she told him, she did not need to have a boyfriend just to go out to the movies as she had always done that by herself. I am sure she had grander expectations in mind, like marriage and a family. She told him clearly only a month after his departure: "When I am Alborg's wife . . . " (August 2, 1937).

There was an interesting exchange between my parents about my father's wish to have in my mother a girlfriend, mother and sister, all in one. In a very modern concept, he told her that his ideal woman would be his best friend. My dad did not feel loved by his stepmother; in fact, he always felt like an orphan despite evidence to the contrary. I noticed that my mother often referred to my dad in her letters as "mi niño," (my child). She described a picture that my father had given her in which he was a young boy, holding a wooden hoop, posing for a formal portrait. Describing the snapshot, she said: "My child who hasn't grown up yet and is looking straight at me, with the small hoop in his hand" (July 15, 1937).

At moments like this, I was moved to tears. I have this same picture framed in my bedroom and my dad definitely looks serious and forlorn for a four or five-year-old. He is wearing a short black pantsuit with lace cuffs and collar, sporting a black pork pie hat leaning to the right that gives him a formal stance. His shiny black shoes and high, white crocheted socks show off his well-shaped legs. I looked on the back of the picture to see if there was a date or a note, but the only visible mark is the Valencian photographer's seal. Thus, I know that I have the original photo, in perfect condition, probably the same one that my mother owned, and that has survived for over eighty years. Knowing how my mother loved children, I am certain that this picture must have moved her as much as it does me today. Interestingly enough, my father always called my mother "Mamá" and never used Conchita as he did in his letters.

My mother's health was a recurring subject already in the early letters. She complained of a backache, neck ache, and headaches. My father brought her some vaccines and urged her to see the doctor to have them administered. Unfortunately, I remember her often being sick when I was a little girl. She suffered from chronic liver disease and had recurring flare-ups that kept her in bed for days at a time. She most likely contracted hepatitis when she served as a blood donor during the war and was never completely cured. Sadly, she did not live the forty more years that she told my dad to expect in her letter of June 17, 1937.

During my dad's absence, my mother kept in close contact with his family. She liked Teresa, her future sister-in-law, and the two of them met often to mail letters at the Central Post Office. She also visited his two elderly aunts, Isabel and Vicenta. They must have moved to Valencia about that time from Salem, the mountain town where the Alborchs came from originally. I remember them very well, they always spoke in Valencian, the regional language. They never married, were always dressed in black, mourning for one relative or another. They both wore their yellowish hair in small, tight buns in the back of their heads. They stayed in the same house in Valencia where I was born after we moved to Madrid in 1953. My mother wrote to my dad almost every day and expected him to do the same in return, which he did faithfully. Since his family did not receive as many letters from him, my mother had the perfect reason to visit them and share news. She liked to go out every day, often with a young sibling in tow.

It is obvious that my mother missed my father terribly and her letters showed more tender feelings once he left Valencia. Her family teased her constantly and she practically hid from them when she was writing to my dad. One evening, when she was writing in bed very late, her mother told her playfully "not all crazy people are in Leganés" (June 25, 1937). Leganés was the renown psychiatric hospital in Madrid. Despite it all, my mother continued going out as much as she could, including to the movies, while my aunt Teresa decided not to see another film until her brother came back from the war. My mother loved *Cristina de Suecia* (*Queen Christina of Sweden,* 1933) with Greta Garbo, and my dad, who also managed to make it to the movies, even while on the front lines, raved about *Entre esposa y secretaria* (*Wife vs. Secretary,* 1936) with Jean Harlow.

I had to laugh when I read this. The fact is that my parents loved the cinema and my father often compared my mother to Rita Hayworth, particularly when she wore her beautiful hair down, as he liked it. One of my favorite memories of my youth in Madrid was going to the movies with my parents. My father would tutor private students at home until 10:00 p.m., often getting a quick bite to eat afterwards, and then rush with my mother to the 11:00 p.m. screening at the Tivoli Theater in our neighborhood. If I had all my homework finished, I would be allowed to join them, unbelievably on a school night. Besides, my brother did not come and I would have my parents all to myself, one of the rare occasions when this happened. I remember seeing *La Strada* (The Road, 1956), and *The Nights of Cabiria* (1957) with Giulietta Masina and other films by Federico Fellini, one of the Italian directors that my father admired. As an act of rebellion, we did not see Spanish films that were full of apologetic military stories about Franco. Needless to say, I love cinema to this day.

Amazingly, my mother also managed to go swimming with her friends and her two sisters Amparín and Fina who were "like mermaids" (July 18, 1937). She described El Saler, with its pine groves, the same beach where we would later go as children. My mother always loved the beach, but my father was more adept at hunting rabbits on dry land. She would tease him because he could not swim, a skill she was proud to show off. On the pretext of narrating an outing to the beach, she described her bathing suit to my dad: "I wore my new bathing suit that fits me like a glove. Too bad that you are not here to see it! (July 15, 1937). She was equally flirtatious when she told him that her aunt had made her a dress that emphasized her shoulders. She really was quite a coquette describing her clothing to him; she was also planning to have a navy-blue dress made and bought a navy purse to match her ensemble. Accessories were always one of my mother's favorite things, as they are mine.

During the war, she had a jasmine plant on her balcony and sent him pressed flowers in her letters regularly. These have been lost, but I can almost smell them hidden in this treasure-trove. I remember when we lived in Valencia, every Sunday morning we would take a walk in the Botanical Gardens behind Turia Street and we would stop by the flower shop for my mother to choose a colorful bouquet. Most families went to church on Sundays, but my family was not religious and I do not remember going to church except for christenings or our First Communion that my brother and I celebrated together, since we were close in age. Likewise, there were no religious thoughts mentioned in my parents' letters. There were no prayers, no faith evoked, not a single mention of God, even in everyday expressions.

Once my father was away in Valdepeñas on the Southern Front, he started worrying about their letters being censored. At first my mother said that she would censor herself, so that some old bearded man would not read the sweet nothings they wrote to each other but, in the same letter, she changed her mind and continued as usual "because the old goat would have been young too and he would understand" (July 13, 1937). I recognized this fearful attitude immediately, especially from my dad. When we moved to Madrid, he worried that having fought against Franco during the war would make him stand out in the capital. He was afraid that he would be labeled as "un rojo" (a Red, a liberal) or that he would be asked to sing the Falangist hymn, "Cara al sol con la camisa nueva" (Facing the sun with a new shirt on) as he had seen during demonstrations at the university. In all the years he lived in the United States, he was concerned that his telephone line might be tapped and refused to talk politics during my calls. He never became a citizen, although he had a green card and was in the United States legally, he still feared the government and was suspicious of its power.

Interestingly enough, at the bottom of my mother's letter of January 29, 1938, I noticed a paragraph written in a different handwriting, with darker ink. It took me a few minutes to figure out that a censor had indeed intercepted her letter. His message to my dad said: "Comrade, when you answer this comrade, tell her that censors have a very high concept of the moment in which we are living and that, therefore, they abstain from touching anything in the letters, I salute you." No wonder my father was always paranoid about censorship!

My mother often felt sad when she was writing her letters. Actually, her moods rose and fell easily. But she said: "No soy llorona" (I'm not a crybaby), (July 13, 1937). It is true; I do not remember my mother crying much in my life. She complained about her poor health regularly, but crying, hardly ever. When I read her letters, I was amazed that she knew herself so well at such a young age. When my father complained that her letters were not as long as his, she answered with a clever comment: "Love is not measured by the number of pages it takes to write about it" (June 11, 1937). It surprised me that my mother was the one who suggested that they number the letters, which has been so helpful for me in organizing and keeping them in order. With each of the places where my dad was deployed, there is a new set of numbers. My mother maintained a close account of the letters she wrote and received and would get upset if my father missed a day or the letters were delayed in the mail. On one occasion, my dad had not written because he had a sore knee from playing soccer and she wrote back saying that she did not know he wrote with his feet. Then, she finished the letter with her characteristic sense of irony, saying she was going out for a walk and hoped not to fall, suggesting that if she hurt herself, she would not be able to write either (December 22, 1937).

When I read about my father playing soccer, I remembered that he and my brother loved playing and we had a cultural misunderstanding because of this when we lived in the United States. It happened in West Lafayette, Indiana, where my dad taught at Purdue University. My parents rented a house for one summer that had a beautiful front lawn. As soon as my dad made friends among the faculty, he started a soccer team. It was very hot in the American Midwest, but they played religiously on weekends. By the time summer was over, the lawn had turned into a dirt field. When the owners saw it, they were very upset with the immigrant family who had ruined their lawn. My dad could not understand

17

why they were angry. Why else would they want such a lovely green field!

Each time that I read my mother's letters, I find a new bit of information I had missed before. I love spending time with her, getting to know her in such an intimate way. When I have to put them down, they stay in my head and I miss her if several days go by and I cannot get back to her letters. It is like reading a favorite novel and missing the characters when we finish reading it. I am so aware of the magic and the good fortune in finding these letters and I do not forget it for a minute. How amazing it is that there are no letters missing, that they are in such excellent condition given that my father carried some of them during entire months of the war, that they were saved, hidden, and that I would be the one to find them after almost eighty years.

Queridísimo:

Termino de recibir tus cartas 23 y 24.

Me doy por enterada sobre lo que me dices de la transfusión advirtiéndote que no olvidaba lo que te prometí y por lo tanto eres innecesaria tu advertencia, que, por la forma en que lo has hecho me ofende.

Si como dices no me escribirás hasta que no recibas ésta carta, no esperes tampoco a

Two Visions of the Spanish Civil War

Since Valencia, along with the Levantine region of Catalonia, stayed loyal to the Republican Government, my father was drafted by the Spanish Republican Army, fighting against Franco's troops, which had the air support of the Third Reich and the Italian Fascist forces. He was stationed with the infantry on the Southern Front in Valdepeñas, a region in Castile-La Mancha that is particularly well known for its wine. My father was never engaged in any direct combat. He carried a rifle and had guard duty but, given his high level of education and poor eyesight, after some basic training, he was granted a special dispensation and was assigned to the rear-guard. Later, he served as a radio operator in the support forces as well. A lot of southern towns, including Valdepeñas, had been evacuated by the time my father's battalion arrived, so the soldiers took over people's homes and lived in small groups rather than in barracks. In my father's letters there was practically no reference to any battle or specific information about the war; he did not even mention Franco, for example, or any other leader by name. In part, I am sure, because of his concern of censorship.

The living conditions were far from comfortable and food was hard to find, particularly in the winter months. During the spring and summer, the soldiers would eat whatever fruits and vegetables were available in abandoned fields. My father had a straw mattress to sleep on in the house where he stayed and sometimes had to make do by rolling his blanket on the hard ground if they were in reconnaissance or away from the town for other reasons: "My bones have rights too, they are the ones who miss the mattress the most" (January 25, 1938).

Because my father was the son of a widow, he could have been excused from serving altogether. In fact, for the first few months on the front, he was sure that his family would be successful in getting an exemption for him and he would be allowed to return to Valencia. This never happened, although it played a significant role at the end of the war as we will see. There were several mentions of how frustrated he was, hoping to be sent back. He felt that it would have been easier to adjust if he had never had that false hope: "The fact is that I'm impatient to the max; since I had hoped to see you very soon, I'm so restless that I can't sleep or eat in peace." (July 31, 1937).

My mother, waiting for her fiancé in Valencia, was very aware of the seriousness of the situation: "Estamos en guerra," (We are at war) she wrote early on and reported regularly about air raids in Valencia (September 5, 1937). Richard Rhodes in his book *Hell and Good Company: The Spanish Civil War and the World it Made* describes these raids by German airplanes as "bombs falling like black pears" (54). By November 1936, the Republican Government had moved its offices from Madrid to Valencia where they were better protected, surrounded by regions loyal to the Republic, although according to Paul Preston in his book *The Spanish Civil War: An Illustrated Chronicle 1936–1939,* this move was controversial, since it left the capital of the country without a government (87). Arturo Colorado Castellary points out in his book about the Prado Museum and the Civil War that even the artistic treasures from the Prado Museum were moved from Madrid to Valencia for safekeeping (11–12).

At that time, El Grao, the harbor in Valencia, was particularly hard hit by the fascist ship, Canarias, in order to cut off supplies arriving by sea. One of the first mentions of air raids was in my mother's letter of July 7, 1937, when the building where my grandfather worked was bombed and about seventy houses were destroyed. It happened on a Sunday and my grandfather was not in his office; otherwise he could have been injured or killed. Nevertheless, he was not able to go back to work right away, which aggravated the family's financial situation. My mother often gave the exact location and estimated damage caused by the bombs. When the Viveros Gardens and Zoo were attacked, she wrote wondering if the animals were hurt and when Campsa, the oil refinery, was hit, she described thick smoke that obscured the sun (January 19, 1938).

At first, my mother and the smaller children would go down to the shelter when the alarms sounded. My grandmother was particularly frightened. But soon they all stayed at home, especially at night, although my mother went to bed with her clothes on, just in case. She slept in the same bed with her sister Amparo, who was a teenager during the war, but Toni, the youngest, climbed in bed with them as well when he was afraid. The description of how my mother covered Toni's head with a pillow so he would not hear the planes was very touching (July 7, 1937). It seemed that Toni, who was only five years old when the war started, was the one who suffered the most. On another moving occasion, the young boy asked if he would be able to eat sweets again when the war ended. Just hearing this simple wish made my grandmother cry (January19, 1938).

On New Year's Day of 1938, my mother saw a Republican plane come down in a spiral from her balcony. Her brothers ran over to see it, but she did not, although it was obvious how upset she felt: "They took out the pilot in pieces," she wrote, wondering why the parachute did not open. According to Richard Rhodes, Valencia's civilian population was not targeted as much as in Madrid, but nevertheless, "Nationalist aircraft bombed the rest of Spain with near impunity" (52). The number of civilians killed from bombings alone was 100, 000 and, of those, 10,760 were children (209). In July 1938, there was a major attack on Valencia and my mother wrote about it several times. Her entire family experienced a difficult time when Pepito, one of her paternal uncles was wounded in action and was moved to the military hospital in Castellón, north of Valencia; another uncle, Rafael, died of a heart attack on December 27, 1937.

Although my mother tried to stay positive and did not like to tell my dad about the horrors of the war in Valencia, she shared with him an awful scene she witnessed on her way home from work in one of her most graphic descriptions:

> I saw some wounded people and some dead ones . . . the bombing was in The Grao, but they bring them here (I'm horrified). As I walked on the sidewalk, I saw a cycling brigade in charge of transporting the wounded . . . the two first ones were carrying a boy of about thirteen, I figured it out by the length of his body, which was covered by a blanket. His head was uncovered a tad, that's how I

know it was a boy. I was even more horrified when I saw a small lump on the next stretcher, and I don't have any doubt that this was a limb of this unfortunate child. (April 25, 1938)

She ended the letter by apologizing to my dad for upsetting him and told him that she could not even eat that day.

My mother listened nightly to the official war report on the radio and every time she heard news about the southern troops she trembled, fearing that my father was under enemy fire (September 29, 1937). When I read letters like this one, I could not help but think of the Vietnam War when, as a new mother with a baby daughter who was only weeks old, my husband was flying an F-4 Phantom over North Vietnam. Unlike my mother, during the fourteen months of his absence, I had to stop watching the evening news and reading the daily newspapers. I could not bear to know how many jets had been shot down or how many American casualties there were on a given day. I remember the Tet Offensive of January 1968, just a few weeks before my husband's scheduled return date, as a particularly tense time. Then I knew that if anything had happened to him, I would receive a house call by a Marine Corps Chaplain or an officer. I feared the doorbell as much as my mother and her siblings must have feared the air raid alarms.

Fortunately, I knew the date my husband was scheduled to come back from Vietnam; not knowing how long the Spanish Civil War was going to last had to be disconcerting for my parents. One of my mother's family's biggest worries was that the two oldest boys, Pepe and Vicente, would be called to serve. As the war continued on, their fears came true and Pepe was called, thanks to "this macabre lottery" as my mother called it (July 13, 1937). Pepe was lucky in that he was stationed near Valencia and could visit home frequently. He could also talk with my grandmother when she was at work at the telephone company's office. Pepe was engaged to be married and my mother often commiserated with Elena, his girlfriend. This aunt became my resource for family information after my mother passed away. Of course, I had not found these letters yet and I never spoke to her about the war. Since then, oftentimes I call my cousins in Spain to share stories with them and ask questions.

In the winter of 1938, as soon as Vicente turned eighteen, he had to leave as well in what would be called "la quinta del

24

biberón" (the baby bottle brigade). Richard Rhodes wrote that they were "innocents, untested adolescents between sixteen and twenty years old . . . many had never shaved" (227). My cousin Inma, Vicente's daughter, corroborated the story that my mother described. My Uncle Vicente left with espadrilles for shoes only to find out that there was snow on the ground when his battalion reached Cuenca, north of Valencia. The family had to scramble to find boots to send to him. My mother also sent him a sweater she was knitting for my dad who did not need it as urgently in the warmer South.

Finding food during the war years was one of the biggest concerns for my mother's family in Valencia. With a paternal uncle and aunt who also lived with them, there were eleven people to feed. My mother did the daily shopping before going to work in the morning and often stood in line for basic staples like bread, sugar, potatoes and milk. She mentioned several times how far outside the city she had to go, taking public transportation, to find vegetables or eggs. Instead of coffee, something my mother loved, they drank chicory. When my mother started working in a government coop-erative, it helped a lot in getting the necessary coupons to buy whatever was available on any given day. Shirley Mangini in her book *Memories of Resistance* states that "women were also hero-ines even in the smallest tasks, such as food shopping in the midst of constant shelling" (73).

My mother wrote a funny story about her siblings eating a paella cooked with rabbit, only to find out that it was a cat that had been skinned. Vicente got sick when he found out and Toni cried. There was hardly any meat or fish. Horse meat was a staple in Valencia as well as on the front lines, but neither one of my parents would eat it. In fact, horse meat was still for sale when I was a little girl in Valencia. I remember that my brother saw a dead horse hanging in the butcher shop and he refused to eat any kind of meat for a long time.

When I think of my mother's family during the war years, I really cannot imagine what it must have been like to feed that many people on a daily basis. As is the norm in the Spanish cultural tradi-tion, the main meal was served around two in the afternoon and supper was quite late, after 10:00 p.m. or so, around the time of the evening war broadcast. The small children were fed earlier in a separate shift, which made sense because the dining room in my grandparents' house was not that large. I am certain that the lack of proper nutrition had a negative impact on my mother's health.

In fact, the biggest consequence of the Spanish Civil War at the personal level was my mother's delicate health and, ultimately, her early death. Having a social conscience moved her to volunteer as a blood donor. She told my dad that she had "universal type IV blood" and hoped that he would not mind, "because it breaks my heart knowing that there are people dying for lack of blood and, since mine is good for everyone, I will donate whenever I can" (April 15, 1938). She often fasted because she heard bombings at night and suspected she would get a call from the hospital in the morning. According to Richard Rhodes, many scientific advances made during the Spanish Civil War, were incorporated extensively during World War II, blood transfusions was one of them. "The system was called *autoinyectable rapide* (fast autoinjectible) and, as adapted by Duran Jordà, it stored the donated blood under low pressure, pushing it into the patient being transfused just as the donor's blood had been suctioned out" (42). Although the biggest danger of using contaminated needles lies with the patient, it is very possible that my mother contracted hepatitis during one of the transfusions.

In her letter of September 7, 1938, she complained of being sick for days, vomiting whenever she ate, having a fever — that she blamed on the fact that a truck almost ran her over on her way to work — and she did not work for days. We all know that having "almost been run over by a truck" does not cause a fever, but hepatitis does. Don Enrique, the visiting physician, recommended bed rest. I have read this letter word for word to Dr. Alberto Gil-Peralta, a Spanish physician who is familiar with the practices during the Civil War, and the unsanitary conditions of the Spanish hospitals at that time. He corroborated my suspicion that my mother probably contracted hepatitis during one of her blood dona-tion visits and was not properly cured. Paul Preston in his book *Doves of War: Four Women of Spain* states that in the hospitals "Hygiene was abysmal" and that Nan Green, one of the women who volunteered in Spain during the Spanish Civil War, "was appalled by the gory conditions that she found" (2264). Priscilla Scott-Ellis Pip, a nurse also profiled in Preston's book, contracted liver disease while volunteering in Spain and had to go back to England to recuperate (943, 1026).

I remember my mother being sick in bed ever since I was a little girl, with bouts very similar to the one she described in her letters. Years later she was treated at the Mayo Clinic in the United States for liver disease, probably caused by untreated hepatitis and she died in 1975 at 58 years of age. My father, who often tried to curtail my mother's desires and decisions, was being prudent when he forbade her to ever give blood. In his letter of September 30, 1938, he warned her that if she ever volunteered for a transfusion again, she could consider their engagement broken: "I have decided not to write to you again until you agree formally with me." I am sure my mother already knew how apt my father was to carry out his threats and she agreed, but it was probably too late for her by then. Nevertheless, she was offended by the tone of his request and wrote a very curt letter back: "If as you say, you won't write to me until you receive this letter, do not hope for me to write until I receive your answer to this one" (October 5, 1938).

Despite her health concerns and lack of proper nutrition, my mother continued to work full time. In addition to the daily food shopping, sewed clothes for her siblings, and knitted sweaters, vests and scarves for my dad and her two brothers when they were drafted. It sounds like they had some help with the laundry and heavy cleaning, but my mother often mentioned that she had to wash the clothes, which I am sure was done by hand; I do not remember ever seeing a washing machine in my grandparents' home. It is evident that my mother gave her paycheck to her parents, because she mentioned that they would give her 100 pesetas (about one dollar) for her personal expenses; I suppose it was per month and not per week.

As Hugh Thomas wrote in his iconic book, *The Spanish Civil War*, in the fall of 1937, the official Republican Government moved from Valencia to Barcelona (773). My mother was offered a better salary to move there with the office of the Sub-Secretary of Propaganda in the Ministry of State. But, since she once got into trouble with my dad when she started a new job without asking him, she explained it to him in great detail and practically begged him to let her go. She was not only a good girlfriend but a very good pupil and she knew how to convince him. Her family was not keen on the idea either, but they were in a difficult financial situation, especially since Pepe had been called to serve and they had lost his salary. They arranged a place for her to stay with friends and she accepted the job. At this point, there was a lot of suspense in her letters because the Ebro River was flooded and the trains were not running. For anyone who knows about the Spanish Civil War, the mere mention of the Ebro is upsetting in itself, since some of the bloodiest battles were fought there. Finally, after weeks of anticipation, my mother and her co-workers took a bus for the twelve-hour trip. My mother only lasted a couple of weeks in Barcelona; she missed Valencia and was farther away from my dad. When she caught a cold, she returned to Valencia and her old job. Although she did not stay in Barcelona, the fact that she was willing to go there in the midst of war and, despite my dad's and her family's wishes, serves to show what a determined young woman she was. Barcelona was seriously bombed as soon as she returned to Valencia. The house where she stayed was later destroyed and her former host and boss, Mr. Tena, was killed (March 23, 1938).

Despite her many responsibilities, my mother was seemingly undeterred to go out every day and not just to work. Although she often said phrases like " . . . if the fascist planes don't get me first," or " . . . if a bomb doesn't kill me first," she went to the movies and visited friends and relatives. She mentioned that her younger siblings played near the shelter during the day in case the alarm sounded, but she ran around Valencia doing errands and enjoying her relative freedom, having as much fun as possible on the home front.

By 1938, all the young men walking in the city had to have a "salvoconducto," a special dispensation stating why they were not at the front. It irked my mother to see young men about and she wondered if they had a proper permit. Seeing couples together was even more upsetting to her. One afternoon she saw a man reading to his girlfriend, like my father used to do with her, and she had to turn around and walk on another street because she could not bear to see them again (January 31, 1938). One of my mother's best friends, Conchita Guillén, whom I remember from my childhood, got married and was later awaiting her first child during the war. In this case, my mother felt happy for her friend, embroidering a tablecloth as a wedding present and knitting baby clothes when she was expecting. Just the way she wrote about the expectant mother showed that my mother was thinking about starting her own family:

The baby boy (that's what she wants) will be born when we are already at peace, no? At least that's what I hope. I don't know how long this infernal war is going to last. When I'm dying for it to end! The truth is that I can't imagine what it will be like having you next to me forever: so much happiness will seem unreal. And I don't want to dream anymore . . . I am anguished and afraid. (March 21, 1939)

It is surprising to me that my father's letters had much less information about the war than my mother's letters, since they were existential and philosophical in tone. Granted, my father was not fighting in the trenches and that he was very concerned about the letters being censored. "It so happens," he wrote in his expressive style, "that the bitter lemon of my military life is squeezed only for you: the only drops of fresh juice fall in your letters lost in the curse of my everyday hours," (January 5, 1938). His letters were mostly an obsessive rendering of his love for my mother and how much he missed her, with all sorts of instructions as to what she should and should not do, which we already know she disregarded as much as possible. This is all in direct opposition to the way it was at home when I was growing up. My father would talk incessantly about the horrors of the Spanish Civil War and my mother would remain silent. I did not know any of her stories until I read these letters.

It seems that my father was frustrated and bored at the same time to be at war, not being part of the action; he wrote: "Boredom is an enemy who doesn't use a rifle, but is also to be feared," (October 30–31, 1937). Nevertheless, my father had friends on the front lines and one of them, Seseña, was killed in action, which obviously was a sobering experience. On one occasion he mentioned that a soldier in his brigade had a day off and came into town and told my dad that life in the trenches was not so bad. He went on to say that this young soldier was from Granada and witnessed the uprising against Franco in the streets of this city: "He has been three months on the front lines: a hero" (September 5, 1938). I wonder if my father knew at the time that the poet García Lorca was executed in Granada during those first days of the uprising. People in Spain had to wait until after Franco's death to confirm that Lorca's body would never be found.

From Valdepeñas my dad was moved to Andújar, in the province of Jaén, a region of Andalucía in southern Spain, where he started a short training program in radio transmission and became a radio operator. From the end of September1937 to January of 1938, he was stationed in Arjona with the Second Company of the 89th Brigade. He described Arjona as "an eagle's nest atop a mountain range" and he went on to say: "Across Arjona, and also on the top of the nearby mountains, is Porcuna, the first fascist town. One feels a certain emotion the first time one makes out enemy territory, knowing that those against whom we are fighting so insistently are so close" (September 26, 1937). He repeated this unnerving concept of being so close to enemy lines: "It's hard to imagine that in invisible burrows, there are thousands of men lying in wait, with savage-like hate in their souls" (December 18–19, 1937).

In Arjona my father was lucky enough to be able to stay in a private residence. I remember hearing as a child how kind the lady of the house, Doña Carmen, had been to him. She was a great cook, so important in my dad's priorities. She had a small child and my mother knitted an outfit for him. It was very endearing and old-fashioned when my father wrote that he had started to call her Carmen, without the formal "Doña," and that he almost used the familiar "tú" with her. The following year, as the Republican front retreated to Arjonilla, my dad complained that he had to go back to eating the war rations. He made the eight-kilometer trek on foot to Arjona several times just to spend a few hours with Doña Carmen and her family.

Although my father was stationed on the Southern Front, where it was not as cold as in other regions of Spain, he often complained about being uncomfortably cold. I remember how sensitive he was to low temperatures. When my family moved to Madrid in the early fifties, one of his biggest concerns was how much colder it was than Valencia, where he could ride his bicycle to the university. In Madrid, he rode a scooter that helped with the longer distances, but not with the continental climate. Only a few months before we immigrated to the United States in 1961, we were able to own a car, a true luxury in those hard times of the Spanish postwar years.

Nevertheless, my father was not the only one suffering from the cold during the war. Manuel Azcárate in his book, *Derrotas y esperanzas. La República, la Guerra Civil y la Resistencia* (Defeats and Hopes. The Republic, the Civil War and the Resistance), mentions that the cold in battles like the ones in Teruel and the Ebro River was the biggest enemy of the Republican soldiers, who were not prepared, trained or outfitted to deal with the natural elements

(143). He tells the story of Miguel Hernández, the renowned Spanish poet, who was fighting in the snow, wearing only espadrilles, the identical situation that my mother described when her brother Vicente was drafted with the infamous "baby bottle brigade."

In my father's letters, his obsession with the weather was quite amusing. I laughed when he complained for two entire pages about how he felt: "Believe me if I tell you that I'm frozen" (December 13–14, 1937). First, he confessed that his long introduction had a purpose. He wanted my mother to forget about the scarf she was knitting him since he already had one, and for her to make him some wool socks: "calcetines tobilleros," which could be translated as ankle socks. Then, he described, in great detail, that the stitch should be very tight and the wool very fine in order to be as warm as possible and still fit inside his boots. I can only imagine my mother's reaction, who was an expert knitter, and the last thing she needed was my dad's instructions. Knitting is one of several things I did not learn from my mother that I wish I had. It is one of my "asignaturas pendientes," an expression difficult to translate into English, a failed subject, perhaps. I do, however, like to sew and made most of my clothes and my daughters' clothes as well while we lived on military bases during my first marriage. To this day, I make bibs for friends' children and grandchildren; the proverbial apple did not fall far from the tree.

As the war dragged on, both of my parents wrote less about the everyday, practical needs of food and clothing and more about the philosophical issues of their future happiness together. My mother asked herself if future happy days would make up for the sadness she felt. She answered her own question with these moving words:

No matter how happy I might be later, I will never forget these bitter hours. I will be doubly happy, because we will know how to savor better our own happiness, but even so, I won't forget these sad and precious hours of the best of our wasted forever youth and no matter how hard we try we won't be able to ever recuperate. (February 8, 1939)

It is difficult to say who echoes whom because I remember reading similar sentiments in my dad's letters and I had to double-check the dates. Sure enough, on February 2 of the same year, my dad had expressed similar sentiments: "I have regretted a hundred thousand times the precious time that we are wasting now when the full faculties of youth would make it highly profitable." I assume that my mother had received my dad's letter, but in any case, by then my parents were in perfect harmony. Now it is my turn to be sad.

Sometimes the desperate tone of my mother's letters reminds me of Mercé Rodoreda's protagonist in *La Plaza del Diamante* (The Diamant's Plaza) when she was living in Barcelona during the Spanish Civil War:

> Each day is a heavier burden. I don't know if other people feel this way, but days are never-ending to me. When I go to bed I say 'another day has passed already, one less day left of war,' and the same every day, but the war doesn't end and each day I feel more frightened. (March 8, 1939)

As time went on, my mother seemed to be traumatized by the constant suffering. She mentioned that she never used to remember her dreams, but she remembered her nightmares all day then (December 23, 1938).

By the end of the war, the tone of my mother's letters was more and more dark. On three occasions she mentioned that she wished she would die. I can only imagine how depressed she must have been to write that to my dad. She wondered if they were ever going to be able to make up the lost time. She regretted being a Spaniard in such hard times "with this terrible and bloody war" (January 30, 1939). The bombings were more frequent and severe then too; if there was an air raid while she was at work, she would go down to the shelter, something she had stopped doing. The gas lines had also been hit and she wondered how they were going to cook and feed everyone since they did not have charcoal or wood either. They would have to eat bread with olive oil and go to bed early (February 8, 1939). A coworker, Amalia, died of pneumonia in just a few days; bombings were not the only thing killing people — malnutrition and poor health conditions were killing them too.

Of course, she did not know then that the war was almost over and that, despite all their suffering, my dad and her two siblings would return home without any physical wounds; the term and the concept of post-traumatic stress disorder did not exist yet. She also did not know that when the war ended, and after having been detained in the bullring for weeks, her two brothers, like most of the soldiers who fought against Franco, had to re-enlist into military service to the dictator's government. Pepe and Vicente would waste three more years of their youth. My father, thanks to his tremendous insight, was spared being drafted again after the war. Obviously, this part of the story is not in his letters, but he would tell it to my brother and me when we were young.

My father's last letter was dated March 28, 1939, three days before the official end of the war. At that time, he was stationed in Casas de Utiel, a small town about 80 kilometers from Valencia. Although there was no mention of this in his last letter, my father must have been keenly aware that something serious was about to happen. Each day, trucks carrying the defeated troops left the front, driving them to Valencia. My father feared that they would be jailed or even killed for having fought against Franco. When his turn to get into one of those trucks approached, he went into hiding. He hid during the daytime and walked under the cover of darkness towards Valencia. In addition to some books and his meager possessions, he was carrying my mother's latest letters. In order to get something to eat, he traded his blanket and his uniform pants and jacket for food. He did not want to call any attention to himself. Wearing a sweater my mother had knitted and other civilian clothing, he arrived in Valencia at night, exhausted, hungry and scared; but he waited patiently until morning when his building front door opened. He ran up the three flights of stairs and rang the doorbell. His sister Teresa opened the door and yelled the endearing diminutive she used for him, "Juanito," crying uncontrollably. My father would tell my brother and me, finishing like the gifted storyteller he was: "I washed up, shaved and, without going to sleep or getting anything to eat, I ran to your mother's house to let her know I was home safe and sound."

My father's suspicions were correct. The trucks delivered the defeated Republican soldiers to the Valencian bullring where they waited for weeks and even months to be processed. Many were jailed and score more were killed. Most, like my two uncles, were drafted immediately and, wearing their new Falangist uniforms, were sent to North Africa to serve three years of military service in Franco's army. Since my father was the son of a widow and her only legal support, he was finally granted a dispensation and did not have to serve again. He enrolled at the University of Valencia when it reopened and finished his doctorate as soon as he could.

Valencia fell to Franco's forces on March 30, 1939. Unlike other regions of Spain, such as the Basque Country, which fell earlier during the war, the people in Valencia did not have a chance to be evacuated or to flee the city by ship to other countries. Hugh Thomas describes how people in the city were parading, making the fascist salute: "Women and children ran forward to kiss the hands of the conquerors, while roses, mimosas and laurels were flung from balconies of the middle class" (914-915). I am certain that neither my father nor mother, nor anyone in their families were part of such fascist celebrations.

According to Hugh Thomas, those killed in action on both the Republican and the Nationalist sides, the murders and executions behind the lines, as a result of tribunals and in prison camps, in addition to those who died of malnutrition, "Spain may be supposed to have lost nearly 800,000 people in the Civil War, including the flower of the new generation" (926–927). Shirley Mangini emphasizes the scores of women who were imprisoned during Franco's regime and the deplorable condition in which they were treated. In Madrid's Ventas jail alone, there were between 14,000 to 10,000 women prisoners (101). No wonder I never heard my mother speak about the war; she must have been afraid to be jailed herself. After all, we know that she supported the Republican cause, worked in a government office and she donated blood while, according to Mangini, women were imprisoned for such small infractions as carrying a gun or wearing overalls, the "Milicianas" (Republican women soldiers) uniform (100).

By Hugh Thomas' account, a conservative estimate of those who permanently emigrated from the country is about 300,000 (927). My parents, my brother and I were only four of those not counted, since we did not leave Spain until 1961.

momentos en que te recuerdo con más
ahinco y entonces al pensar que te tengo tan
lejos se me hacen amargas y pesadas las horas. Si no te recordase tanto sería más feliz.—

Perdóname que me ponga un poco
cursi por una vez y te envíe una seguí-
dilla que viene como anillo al dedo. Es
de Concha Espina y dice así:

"Es amor en la ausencia
    Como la sombra,
Que cuanto más se aleja
    Más cuerpo toma...
Amor es aire
Que apaga el fuego chico
    Y aviva el grande.—

Hasta la cuenta de que te he escrito
yo (desde luego íntimamente te he sentido)
y sobre toda explicación de mi estado
afectivo actual para contigo.—

A Pygmalion Story

As spunky as my mother was in regard to my father's orders and suggestions, and as brave as she acted in the face of war, when she met my father, she was no match for his superior education and intellectual development. As we have seen, they met on January 1, 1937, at the party of a theater group that my mother belonged to. Ferri, a mutual friend, introduced them. Manuel Azcárate explains in his book how in Valencia, during the first months of the Spanish Civil War, youth organizations were formed under the auspices of the Socialist government to promote culture in order to recruit the young population: "The JSU (Juventudes Socialistas Unificadas / Unified Socialist Youth) organized recitals, theater, film projections, all kinds of activities that could have a great impact on the morale" (125). Given my mother's gregarious nature and committed attitude, it was not unusual for her to belong to a theater group, which shows that she was interested in the arts before she met my dad. But it was out of the ordinary for him to go to a party, since he was essentially anti-social. Although he already had a girlfriend at the time, it seems that he attended the party alone and broke up with her as soon as he started courting my mother.

At that time, the University of Valencia was still open and my father was enrolled there in the School of Philosophy; he had five courses left to finish his Ph.D.: Modern World History, Contemporary World History, Geography, Archeology and Epigraphy. This is ironic, since his first book was *Manual de Historia Universal* (World History Manual). In fact, my father had arrived at the university well prepared because he had an extensive education in Classics at the Jesuit Seminary where his Uncle Miguel had enrolled him after my grandfather died in 1929, when my dad was an adolescent. I believe that my dad's anti-religious sentiment was an outgrowth of his difficult years in the Seminary. Nevertheless, academically he benefited from a superior education. I remember hearing his sad stories of rigorous studies and cruel discipline, when he could only leave school for a few weeks in the summer. He spent those short vacations in Salem, a small town in the mountains of the province of Valencia, where the Alborchs (the old family name) were from originally.

A few years ago, I had the opportunity to visit Salem, the place of my ancestors, for the first time, and I was shocked to see such a small, isolated town and could imagine how restricted my dad's life must have been as a young boy. Nevertheless, one of his uncles was the Mayor of the town and his family was one of the most prosperous. During my visit, some people, all named Alborch, came to greet me and several of them remembered my dad fondly. Now there is a street named after him, their most illustrious son, and he figures in Salem's official history book, *El poble de Salem I la foia de les fonts* (The Town of Salem and the Valley of the Fountains). Thus, to a certain degree, my mother was worldlier, if one can consider Valencia in the 1930s as worldly. But she had not even finished high school, which she left to attend secretarial school, a more practical option with better opportunities for employment. When my parents met, she was a very resourceful young woman and an essential bread-winner in her large family. I am sure that my dad was also attracted to her because she was strong and, in some ways, a challenge for him, he would not have fallen in love with her if she had been meek and compliant.

As I have mentioned, my mother's first letters, written in the old-school longhand had frequent spelling mistakes. It is obvious that my father tutored her during the six months before he was called to the front since she called him "my dear professor" and he referred to her as "my dear and adored pupil" (July 13, 1937). My mother was a quick study and, not only are there no spelling errors in future letters, but her style grew in sophistication and her handwriting became more mature and beautiful. Her biggest transformation, however, was her intellectual growth. Guided by my dad, she read extensively and grew in self-assurance and intellect. Undoubtedly, like Pygmalion, my father excelled at the job of a sculptor carving the figure of his beloved in his image and expectations; granted that my mother would often surprise everyone, including herself.

In the very first letter that my mother wrote to my dad when he left for the front, she said: "I'm dying to be your secretary" (July 7, 1937), and she became that and much more. When the university closed, she took it upon herself to go there time and again, trying to find out when it would reopen and exams would be scheduled. Of course, she hoped that for that reason my father would be allowed to return to Valencia, which, no matter how hard she tried, did not materialize. Her determination was evident: "No pienso dejar a ningún bicho viviente hasta que no lo sepa" (I don't plan to leave any stone unturned until I find out, September 29, 1937). When she heard that the university might open, she volunteered to go in his place, since she had his identification number, and take notes for him (October 10, 1937). She kept all this information from her family and even his sister Teresa, although they were getting close, undoubtedly because she did not want anyone to change her mind.

Evidently, upon his departure, my dad had left some homework for my mother, because she was already reading Juan de Valdés, the Renaissance Spanish humanist, known for his *Diálogo de la lengua* (Dialogue of the Spanish Language), a treatise on the rules of phonetics, vocabulary and grammar. My poor mother; I know exactly what she must have gone through. I too was tutored by my dad on these matters and there was no room for error. No wonder I ended up teaching Spanish literature; I learned it from a master. My mother refrained from making comments on Valdés, but told my dad how much she loved reading because she could see him in the books (July 13, 1937). How is this for being a loyal and smart pupil? When he recommended that she read *El origen del pensamiento* (The Origins of Thought) by Armando Palacio Valdés, (no relation to the earlier Valdés), she replied ironically, that she should read *El secreto de Barba Azul* (Bluebeard's Secret).

I guess that my father's teaching also included moral values, since my mother was reading *Las siete columnas* (The Seven Columns) about the seven capital sins by Wenceslao Fernández Flórez, who had won the Spanish National Prize in 1926 for this novel. It is interesting to point out that my father's career catapulted when he also won the same prize in 1959 for his essay *Hora actual de la novela Española* (Present Hour of the Spanish Novel). She liked *El niño de la bola* (The Child with a Ball in His Hand) and *El escándalo* (The Scandal) by the novelist Pedro Antonio de Alarcón, also a Spanish classic (July 17, 1937), but a very accessible one for his use of humor and romantic plots. Likewise, she enjoyed *Tristán o el pesimismo* (Tristán, the Pessimist), a novel of manners also by

Palacio Valdés. It is not lost on me that my mother did not write that she enjoyed Juan de Valdés, very honest reader that she was.

I am not suggesting that my mother was a cultural novice before she met my father. She had at least a basic education because she used literary terms when she described a film, "*Una chica de provincias* (Small Town Girl), was like a romance novel" and she called my father "Don Quijote" when she found out that he went hunting with a friend (July 7, 1937). Incidentally, Adam Hoschchild in his book *Spain in Our Hearts: Americans in the Spanish Civil War, 1936-1939*, states that the first edition of *Don Quixote* was sent to Valencia from Madrid for safekeeping during the war (72). My mother also mentioned Freud when my dad forgot to date a letter, which she interpreted as covering up for skipping a day without writing to her (July 12, 1937), although she probably was already under my dad's spell by then. Of course, he did not miss a beat, teasing her in return: "Since you are a psychologist now . . . " (July 27, 1937).

The height of my mother's daringness was evident when my father sent her a beautiful love poem by Concha Espina, in "seguidilla" form (a seven-line poem, with rhyme in the second and fourth, and fifth with seventh lines), which he quoted by heart:

> Es amor en la ausencia
> Como la sombra
> Que cuánto más se aleja
> Más cuerpo toma.
> Amor es aire
> Que apaga el fuego chico
> Y aviva el grande.

(Love in a separation / is like a shadow / the farthest it is away / the largest its body. / Love is like air / that blows out a small fire / and enlivens a large one), adding that he could have written it himself, because it expressed exactly how he felt about her (September 28–29, 1937). My mother responded by saying that he was wrong, correcting the last stanza and asking him what Freud would say since my dad claimed to share the same feelings for her (October 2, 1937). The first time I read my parents' letters I thought that she was going to be in deep trouble for this answer. It was never a good idea to correct my dad about poetry form and with the reference to

Freud in the mix, even less. I was right, his lecture was forthcoming, telling her how unfortunate and wrong her comments were since she obviously did not know what "seguidilla" form was and he did not get the reference to Freud (October 6–7, 1937). Needless to say, my mother agreed with him as soon as she had the chance: "You were right about the 'seguidilla'" (October 9, 1937). Of course, I had to find out for myself if my father was correct.

Thanks to the Hathi Trust digital library, I did not have to leave my desk. This poem is at the end of *Dulce nombre* (Sweet Name), a novella by Concha Espina and it is exactly as my father remembered it. In all fairness to my mother, however, they could have both been right, because "seguidilla" is also a musical form and that is probably the version my mother knew by heart.

My mother loved classical music and often mentioned in her letters what she was listening to on the radio while she was writing. She enjoyed *Cavallería Rusticana*, Granados' "Oriental" and "Andalucía" and wished he had been there when she heard Bizet's *Carmen* (September 30, 1938). She wrote that she felt sad when the operetta *La princesa del dólar* (*The Dollar Princess*) was playing, although it was happy music (December 23, 1938). Surprisingly, my mother had promised my dad that she would study music when the war ended. This was a promise she did not keep; I never heard about this until I read their letters. But I do remember clearly my mother singing tangos in her mellifluous voice with the complete lyrics, which I still can repeat from hearing her. Now I wonder if my mother learned to appreciate classical music from my dad and whether the popular songs she sang came from her carefree youth before she met him.

Classical music was the only kind of music we heard at home when I was growing up. My dad brought home all of Beethoven's symphonies as soon as he purchased our first family record player. I have a fond memory of listening to Khachaturian in my father's study and being allowed to stay up in recognition of my mature taste. During my dad's stay in Valdepeñas, he managed to go into one of the abandoned homes and listened to Schubert on the gramophone, a composer he never used to like but that, under the circumstances, made him feel "romantic" (December 21-22, 1937). It is hard to know who was influencing whom. I recognize my dad's terminology when my mother complained that a film she saw was "una españolada" (a bad Spanish film, without tambourines or bulls) and "una americanada" (a bad American film, without gun shots, January 15, 1937). At times, she admitted that she was using his very words: "Tell me the truth 'monada' the truth, Alborg's phrase" (August 7, 1937). Also, at a later date: "If I were as suspicious as you, I would say that your laziness has won over your heart (Alborg's words)" (February 28, 1938).

As soon as my father got paid, he sent a money order to my mother so she could start buying books for him. In a pattern that would repeat itself for the duration of the war, he gave her lists advising her which ones, among those books, she could and could not read. He was forever grooming her. The list is extensive and varied; I will leave future Juan Luis Alborg scholars the task and enjoyment of analyzing it. For now it is worth pointing out some titles in order to show the diversity and breadth of my father's knowledge and curiosity at such an early age, considering that he was then only twenty-three years old: *Los trabajos de Urbano y Simona* (Urbano's and Simona's Works*) and *La pata de la raposa* (The Fox's Paw) by Ramón Pérez de Ayala, a Spanish philosopher; *Guía de la mujer inteligente* (*A Guide for an Intelligent Woman*) by George Bernard Shaw, author of the famous *Pygmalion* and with whom my dad shared so many traits; *Calle Mayor* (*Main Street*), the American classic by Sinclair Lewis; *El círculo de familia* (*Family Circle*) by André Maurois, the French liberal author who, like my dad, left the family business to pursue his literary interests; *Canguro* (*Kangaroo*) by D.H. Lawrence, the then controversial English writer; and the complete works of Miguel de Unamuno, the quintessential Spanish philosopher, among many others. It really is uncanny how many connections there are between these authors and my father's future ideas.

My mother went from bookshop to bookshop looking for and ordering his books. She ended up knowing the booksellers by name and received a discount in some places, such as Maraquat & Pont. At first, she was glad he was buying books with his salary; later she became concerned that the books were getting expensive and he would run out of money. My dad suggested that she buy the paperback editions since they cost less. The complete works of the philosopher José Ortega y Gasset, for example, cost 75 pesetas (less than a dollar) and Thomas Mann's *La montaña mágica* (*The Magic Mountain*) was only 25 pesetas. My mother enlisted the help of Ferreres, a friend of my dad's, who had come back to Valencia because he had failed his physical exam. Otherwise, she was up to the task alone. It turned out that she bought many first editions from Labor Publications for a mere few pesetas and now they are among the most valuable and rare books in the collection of my father's books housed at the University of Málaga. My father relished getting these books and arranged a library in the barracks: "Que ya me ha proporcionado agradables ratos de lectura," (Which has already provided me with pleasant reading moments, December 20–21, 1937).

At one point, my mother suggested that she should not buy any more books, because they were getting so hard to locate. But still I found several more eclectic lists of titles that my father ordered: *Los pueblos* (The Villages) by Azorín, a Generation of 1898 writer; *Los monederos falsos* *(The Counterfeiters)* by André Gide, the French moralist; *El artista adolescente* (*The Portrait of the Artist as a Young Man*) by the Irish modernist James Joyce; *La decadencia de Occidente* (*The Decline of the West*) by the German historian Oswald Spengler; *La incognita del hombre* (*Man, the Unknown)* by the French physician Alexis Carrel; *Las obras completas* (The Complete Works) by Rubén Darío, the Nicaraguan poet, even though Ferreres, my mother's helper, said that my dad did not like poetry (February 26, 1939). The list is endless. Every time I reread the letters, I find more books my dad had requested and each time they are more esoteric; how he could keep up to date while being away at the front is unfathomable! No wonder my mother asked him if she should read these books, when she found them (April 8, 1938). She must have felt overwhelmed.

It is significant to mention the books that my father ordered specifically for my mother. For example, he wanted her to read *Lucía Miranda* by Eduarda Mansilla, a Latin American novel that tells the story of the wife of Sebastián Hurtado, a Spanish soldier from the 1500s settlement in Argentina's Río de la Plata. Lucía is captured and remains faithful to her husband, suffering a horrible death for her loyalty. I will not play psychologist, as my mother would, but this novel is completely different from the books my dad was buying. Probably he thought she would enjoy something more romantic with a woman protagonist. It could be that he was familiar with this popular legend, which had several other versions. After all, my dad's Ph.D. dissertation topic was the chronicled writings of Latin America and this narrative was included in one of the earliest accounts by Ruy Díaz de Guzmán's in 1612 — more fodder for future scholars.

My father also recommended for my mother *Guía de la mujer inteligente* (*A Guide for an Intelligent Woman*) by George Bernard Shaw, which does not need to be analyzed in Freudian terms to figure out my dad's intentions. *The Magic Mountain* by Thomas Mann was also one of the books he suggested for her. Again, the parallels between the protagonist, who is an orphan with a family member who was ill with tuberculosis, and my dad are evident. El *círculo de familia* (*Family Circle*), the novel by André Maurois was also a suggestion for my mother. Not only is this book appropriate for its innovative ideas about family life, but Maurois is the one who says: "Without a family, man, alone in the world, shivers in the cold," which was one of my dad's themes to be explored later. It is worth noting how up-to-date my father was as this book was translated into Spanish in 1935 (Editorial Juventud) and my father was acquainted with it already by 1937.

Likewise, it is important to see which books interested my mother. She was reading for a second time *La esfinge maragata* (The Maragata Sphinx) by Concha Espina (the same author of the infamous "seguidilla"). She loved this novel, which is much more realistic and without a happy ending than the romantic ones suggested by my dad. She also enjoyed *Tiempos felices* (Happy times) by Armando Palacio Valdés, that sported a white cover and my mother commented that it should have been pink since it was about love (December 3, 1938). One of her favorite books was *Arrowsmith* by Sinclair Lewis, which illustrates her increasing sophistication. It is not hard to see why she saw similarities between the protagonist and my dad. She was comparing him to Martin Arrowsmith because, like him, he believed in love at first sight or perhaps she liked the happy marriage, uncharacteristic in Sinclair Lewis' novels. Nevertheless, this is what she said in her amateur literary analysis:

> I have already read *Arrowsmith*. It is one of the novels I've read that has impressed me the most. I do find similarities between the protagonists and us; you and him are more alike than her and me, although we are pretty much alike. However, I wouldn't allow you to spend days and nights without coming home. Is it not enough what we are going through now? Leora is a better person than me in this regard.

A Pygmalion Story

I believe, nevertheless, that if she found herself in my place, she would feel the same. I'm really looking forward to be able to discuss this novel with you (and not in writing, huh?). (April, 26, 1938)

It makes me very sad to think that my parents had almost a full year left to wait for the war to end.

There are at least two books that my father wanted my mother to read that she did not comment on: *A la sombra de las muchachas en flor* (*In the Shadow of Young Girls in Flower*) by Marcel Proust, the second volume of his *In Search of Lost Time;* and *Madame Bovary* by Gustave Flaubert. I really wonder what she thought of those modern heroines and how she related to their stories of adultery and betrayal. At times, my mother lamented that she did not have as much time to read as she used to with all of her responsibilities. I know that she continued to appreciate my father's suggestions and endless thirst of knowledge, because I remember her always reading while we lived in Valencia and, later, in Madrid.

During my father's absence, my mother also managed to go to the theater, although most of the time she did not like the performances. She went to The Ruzafa Theater to see *Las de Villadiego*, a popular Spanish musical, and she labeled it as being "stupid" and "silly" (December 20, 1938). She did not care for *El niño de oro* (The Golden Boy) either because it was an Andalusian farce (January 1, 1939). Her taste seemed to be more serious and discerning since she enjoyed *Los intereses creados* (*The Bonds of Interest*) by the Nobel laureate Jacinto Benavente, which she went to see with her siblings (January 10, 1939).

When my father left for the front, my mother had not met his stepmother yet nor had she visited him at his house, just to give an idea of how formal the courtship relations were in those days. Teresa, my dad's sister, and my mother became good friends and they both used to meet in the evenings to mail letters to him. There is a very touching episode when my mother went to my father's house for the first time and Teresa showed her his room: " . . . thought for a moment that you would be there and you were going to scare me. I saw your desk and library and I felt so sad not being able to see you there" (November 10, 1937). I had a similar experience when my husband was away during the Vietnam War. On Christmas Day 1967, I visited my in-laws with my baby daughter and in the late afternoon we went upstairs to my husband's old room to take a nap. I remember smelling his English Leather cologne on the pillow, seeing his books, his photos, and his horseback riding trophies on the shelves under the eaves, and feeling very close to him and yet so distant. I picked up a familiar photograph of him on his college graduation day and I showed it to my little baby, saying to her: "Look it's your daddy; give him a kiss."

On another occasion, my Aunt Teresa and my mother looked at family pictures and my mother commented on the one of my dad holding a hoop that I have already describe and another of an even younger little boy whom she loved. My dad was dressed in a white coat, again wearing a pork pie hat, sitting on a black wooden horse. She felt like kissing his picture, but was embarrassed to do so in front of his family: "I hope to kiss him some day . . . when you arrive, we must look at the pictures together," she wrote (September 29, 1938). From then on, she often returned to my dad's home after work where she knitted, meeting his family members as they stopped by to visit. Once my father knew that she was going to his house, he must have told her to look for some of the articles he had already written and she commented that she liked the literary one better than the one on film and theater (November 1, 1938). I have not been able to locate those early writings of my dad's, undoubtedly some of his first works.

Having been tutored by my dad I can imagine how my mother felt; it was like a mixture of exhilaration and exhaustion. He was an excellent teacher, clear and humorous. I would make me laugh, for instance, with his comments about Isabel II, the Queen of Spain, who was not a good constitutional monarch because she had sexual relations with her ministers, despite being married. He always added details that were not in school books. He taught me geography, history, French, Classical Greek and Latin, subjects that I later excelled in, probably thanks to the paternal foundation. I also had a private tutor for algebra and mathematics, which I failed consistently. Once I was punished and had to stay in Madrid, missing out on a summer vacation, a story that I fictionalized in *Una noche en casa* (A Night at Home). The fact is that my father had to take over with my mathematics as well and only then was I able to pass the dreaded State examinations. As my reward, I was allowed to read *La Regenta* (The Regent's Wife), the story of Ana Ozores and her adulterous affair with a parish priest by Leopoldo Alas, a book

I treasured and love to this day. I wonder what my mother thought of my dad's parenting skills.

But even my father made mistakes, despite his exceptional literary mind. In one of his early letters to my mother he quoted Oscar Wilde, which is in itself interesting, since I have not seen this author's name mentioned in any of my dad's book lists. He must have had it memorized: "Oscar Wilde said that women inspire the desire to execute great works, but they always prevent us from executing them" (June 10, 1937). Wilde was only half right about the great works part, but he could not have been more wrong about my mother. My father might have been like Pygmalion, grooming my mother and opening her mind, but she was much more than his "adored pupil," she became his muse, as we will see in upcoming chapters. She inspired him, allowing him to concentrate on his work by tending to their children and creating the family he so intensely craved.

da estos días por la seguridad de
tus escritos.

Al mediodía es cuando casi
siempre tengo tus cartas. (El ascensor
casi hace dos meses que está estropea-
do,) bien, pues yo subo de dos en dos
los escalones y cuando llego... mi
"aperitivo" luego la prosaica y nece-
saria comida; luego el trabajo,
luego otra vez el "aperitivo" (vuelvo
a leer tu carta cuando vengo)
y luego... ya no te doy más la
lata, que me voy a dormir.

Quiéreme mucho, mucho,
y mucho y si algún día fla-
queas, avísame: yo no te avisaré
nunca porque te quiero hasta
lo infinito

Conchita

11-112-

Terms of Endearment

In an article about love during the Spanish Civil War, Iker González-Allende states that "La guerra es amor y el amor es la guerra" (War is love and love is war). He goes on to say that during the Spanish Civil War the extreme circumstances that the country was suffering provoked people to live love in a more intense way (528). Ultimately, he proves that the girlfriend character in Concha Espina's novels represents the suffering and patriotic commitment to the mother country. Although we know that my mother read Concha Espina's early novels, I do not think that she embraced the Falangist ideals that this author displayed in her later works.

However, my parents' love story was undoubtedly fueled in part by the long separation caused by the war. My father, in particular, expressed his sentiments on this issue in beautiful letters like this one:

> There are moments, believe me, in which I truly lament to have fallen in love at this time. For temperaments like mine, without a happy medium, all nerves and exaggeration, that when they love, love completely, love is the biggest torment if it's met with difficulties. And now there are many. However, I think that perhaps Fate has wanted for it to happen this way in order to show me a great passion that I would probably have not known in "easier" times. (November 20–21, 1937)

To a large degree, there was a process of seduction led by my father, who was more of an expert in matters of the heart. My mother's style and perhaps her own feelings grew in intensity as time went by and she echoed his passion. When she was telling my dad about her brother Pepe's relationship with his girlfriend, she said with great flair: "Now that I'm taking the pen through the gardens of love

49

and since all this is not rose-colored, let's allow the thorns to speak to us of more serious matters" (February 22, 1938).

My dad addressed my mother as "Conchita de mi alma," (Conchita of my soul); "chatita," "chatísima," (little pug-nosed one); "inolvidable," (unforgettable); "queridísima," (my dearest); "adorada" (adored one); and any combination of the above. She favored "queridísimo," "cariño" (beloved); and she often called him "feísimo" or "mi chato feo" (my very ugly one or my ugly pug-nosed one). My dad was in no way pug-nosed, since he had a consider-able-size nose. She told him on one occasion: "You can't imagine a little pug-nose girl crazier for a big-nosed guy than I am" (August 23, 1937). Also, I know for a fact that my dad grew tired of my mother telling him how ugly he was, even if it was in jest. He did not feel ugly, on the contrary. Once he got used to life on the front lines, he told my mother that he had a good appetite, that he felt strong, that he was tanned and even handsome: "The mirror in the room where I sleep says very good things about me" (September 28–29, 1937). It surprises me that my father would call her "monada" (cutie), which I never heard my dad use and I thought it was a more contemporary word, while she used "miquito" (little monkey), that is approximately as negative as "feo."

Although my mother told my dad how much she loved him, she often teased him, playing hard to get, particularly during the first year of their separation. I recognize this trait in her and I am sure it is related to some insecurity she felt, despite my dad's passionate expressions of love. Her letter of January 25, 1938, is a good example: "I love you more each day, so don't tell me any-more that I took some days off [from writing to him] . . . You know full well how much I love you, but you like to pull my leg. But be careful because I could bite you." In later letters, her tone is more loving: "Feísimo, I love you too much, if it wasn't for this, I would be at peace, but this way I don't have a second's peace" (January 30, 1939).

In some ways it became more difficult for them to be apart after my father's few visits to Valencia. My mother wrote after one of them: "I am writing in the dining room, but I don't want to sit in my place, because I look at the mirror over the buffet and I don't see you next to me like the last few evenings. Good night, I am sad and I feel like crying. Always, always yours, Conchita" (November 12, 1938). I understand my mother's feelings completely; I remember how I felt after R & R (Rest and Recuperation) in Hawaii with my husband during the Vietnam War. Having been with him made me miss him even more; it was as if I had forgotten what it felt like to be married to him.

The letters' farewells are obviously full of passion in my dad's case and are often written in jest from my mother. Here are some examples: "Until tomorrow, chatísima. Love me as much as possible, because with the head start I have you are not going to catch up. A kiss, only one kiss! But very long, very long and on the lips. I adore you, Juan" (September 28–29, 1937). One more memorable farewell: "A million kisses which will go in express mail to your mouth. Always yours, Juan" (June 10, 1937). Here are her less effusive versions: "Until tomorrow, silly goose. (I'm angry at you). Always, always yours, Conchita" (September 13, 1938), and " . . . all my thoughts and love are yours, Conchita" (September 24, 1937). And one farewell that I treasure: "Love me, love me lots, lots and lots and if one day you lose heart, warn me; I will never have to warn you because I love you infinitely, Conchita" (May 9, 1938).

Sometimes my father's declarations of love seem excessive and obsessive and I wonder if one of the reasons he did not tell me about the existence of these letters is because he was aware of his exaggerated romanticism as a young man and he guessed that I would be skeptical. In fact, I invented some letters written by him included in my novel *American in Translation: A Novel in Three Novellas* years before finding these letters and they share the same boundless passion. In any case, just when I think that I have to take a break from reading his letters, he comes out with an endearing thought and I am enthralled again. In his letter of October 30, 1938, when he was daydreaming about a short visit with her in Valencia, he told my mother: "I was remembering in particular the moment when we said goodbye: these two times that I have kissed you in front of other people taste like heaven to me because this seems to make you more mine and I don't wish anything more than having you be mine forever." Such a modern man, practicing public displays of affection or PDAs as my daughters call them.

Despite the great passion between them, my parents' letters were chaste, certainly by today's standards. There was never an off-color joke or expression, nothing in bad taste. Granted they were concerned about the censorship, although it is obvious that their letters were never confiscated, since I have all their letters, not missing a single one. My father's kisses on the mouth were as daring as he got. She was less apt to give away her kisses and even less on the lips. It is very endearing when she sent him kisses and said that they were from her little brother: "Kisses from my brother Tonín (I don't dare say from me). Always yours, Conchita," (May 3, 1938).

There was only one instance when my mother was sexually suggestive and I wonder if she meant it that way or if she was being innocent. My mother gave my dad a little wooden charm to take to the front lines. I have kept this little treasure in one of my trinket boxes, without knowing its origin. Only when I read these letters did I realize its history. The little bear has a red body and arms with green pants, orange socks, and black shoes. His ears are made of brown leather and he has prominent open, red lips. A tiny safety pin is attached to its head with a clear thread. On one occasion, my dad told my mother how he slept with it and she clearly stated how she wished to be in bed with him too! "Feísimo, in yesterday's letter you told me that the little bear sleeps with you and the bed that he has now is very hard; well, you tell him that sincerely I am envious of him. You have no idea what I would give to be in his place" (September 8, 1938). How is this for being a forward, sexy girl-friend? It is interesting to note that she was writing this letter at 2 a.m., a very good time for a nighttime reverie, but at the end of this letter she added a parenthesis saying that my grandmother had her forty-seventh birthday that day. It is almost as if she did not want to end with such a daring thought. The little bear reappeared in some letters as a subterfuge for her: "Kisses to the little bear and . . . his owner" (February 21, 1939).

We already know my father's affinity for love poems, although he promised her that this one by Gabriel y Galán, the renowned Spanish modernist poet, would be the last one, since he thought that it was corny to quote love poetry, obviously by heart:

> . . . porque un querer derechero
> Como el querer te ablande
> Es igual que un agujero:
> ¡cuando más le hurgas más grande!

(. . . because a rightful love / if it softens your loving / is like a hole / it gets bigger if you poke at it! September 30, 1937). Not as romantic as the one by Concha Espina and the seguidilla that caused so much disagreement between my parents, but a prosaic simile nevertheless to show that although my father may not have used his rifle while serving in the rearguard, he had lots of arms in his arsenal. Interestingly enough, these lines belong to a long love poem titled "Un Don Juan" (a Don Juan) — more about this iconic figure and how it relates to my dad later. Also, when I went back to the trusty Hathi Trust digital library, I found that my dad's recollection was not exactly right and that a couple of words had been modernized by him. Unfortunately, since my mother is not here to correct him, I have to do it in her place.

Jealousy was experienced very differently by my parents. My mother definitely was more sensitive and caring. On two occasions, she ran into my father's ex-girlfriend and was jealous for a minute, but soon felt sad for her when she noticed that she had started to cry because she still loved my dad. My mother referred to her as "la agujita," (the little needle), presumably a thorn in her side (July 8, 1937). My father, on the other hand, was sarcastic and transparent in his feelings of jealousy. There was a telling episode during my mother's short stay in Barcelona. Tonico Llorca, a colleague at work, walked with her to the office and showed her around the city. My mother went to great lengths, undoubtedly to pacify my dad, explaining that this young man was engaged to be married and how in love he was with his young girlfriend, a seamstress. My dad answered that he did not need so many explanations:

Chatita mía: the only powerful argument is if you truly love me; that's the only thing that convinces me . . . Examine your conscience and tell me with your hand on your heart how is the account. And if you really love me, stroll about with Tonico as much as you want and I will be reassured. You don't need to tell me how old the girlfriend is or if she is taking sewing courses; I'm not planning to have a housecoat made. (November 26–27, 1937)

Fortunately, he redeemed himself because he ended this letter with one more declaration of his never-ending love: "Remember that I love you like a real fool (this is not a joke, you deserve it), but I want your correspondence and not only in letters. Always yours, Juan."

Special days such as the anniversary of the day they met, January 1, and on the 24 of each month, since they became engaged on that date, served to recommit their relationship and to express their love for each other. My mother mentioned it every month and was especially warm on January 24, 1938, their first anniversary, despite her usual "feísimos:"

> Feísimo, a year ago today we stopped being friends to love each other much more, do you remember? Exactly at this time a year ago we were at the entrance of the Tyris [a movie theater], waiting for our friends, do you remember as well? I remember it all as if it had been a short time ago and, here we are . . . it has already been three hundred sixty-five days . . . Since at twelve months of our relationship we haven't been able to be together, let's see what thirteen has in store for us. More tomorrow, Feísimo. All my love for you once more. Your, Conchita

My dad, always more passionate and expressive, told my mother on the same date: "On the first year of our relationship I send you all my love, which is enormous, with the most passionate kiss I'm able to give you" (January 24, 1938). On their second anniversary, my dad was able to be in Valencia on leave and neither one of them wrote much about it in subsequent letters. My father also sent a heartfelt felicitation to my mother on her Saint's Day:

> I would want my felicitation to be so warm that you would realize through it the immensity of my love, but all the words seem dull. If I were next to you perhaps just a look would be worth more than all I could tell you. But if Fate has wanted for us to be so far today, let's hope that long days overflowing with love and happiness will make up for these sad days, which are only worthwhile because they serve as proof of my love that will be yours forever. Chatita mía, receive today the tightest hug and the most felt kiss, which I will give to your portrait since I can't give it to you. (December 8–9, 1937)

From very early on, both of my parents made references to how happy they were going to be and what a wonderful, loving life awaited them. Obviously, having each other and the promise of a happy future made the months first and, later, more than one year of separation bearable. It is interesting to note how these feelings developed chronologically in a crescendo. My father remembered the kisses they shared during the last days they spent together with a literary metaphor: " . . . at least the hope of future days sustains me and the excitement of kisses like those are only a paltry prologue of the gigantic work of love that we are going to live" (December 22–23, 1937). As we have seen before, it is difficult to see who echoed whom; my mother said: " . . . if you feel the same way about me, we will be a model marriage someday" (May 15, 1938). On another occasion, my mother expressed her feelings with these beautiful words: "Here behind the glass panes of the back porch, looking at this gray afternoon, I'm thinking of the days full of light, peace and happiness that we will spend together, but they seem so far away still . . . " (December 11, 1938). A few months before the end of the war she said: " . . . I hope that we will be very happy; if it wasn't for this dream that is my life, I don't know what would become of me" (January 30, 1939).

My parents had no way of knowing when the war would end. My mother must have written several more letters up to the day it ended on April 1, 1939, but the last letter my father received was dated March 21, 1939 and, therefore, the last one he carried home and that I now have. On that date my mother was anticipating the war's end, thinking of marriage and even children:

> I see that you are sad and worried; you will see how good I'm going to be so that you won't remember these bitter hours. We are going to be so happy . . . Conchita Guillén has already ordered her baby. I congratulated her; I suspect that the baby boy (that's what she wants) will be born in peace time, no? At least that is what I hope. I don't know how long this infernal war is going to last when I'm so eager for it to end! The truth is that I can't imagine having you next to me forever; so much happiness seems unreal. And I don't want to dream anymore I feel anguished and afraid.

In fact, my father had already proposed marriage to her a few months earlier in his prolific and detailed style:

> If Destiny grants us life and health, we have to get married as soon as possible. As long as we have some sure means to earn a living, at once. Without waiting to acquire many of the traditional things; those will arrive later little by little. This will undoubtedly be inconvenient, but we will be happy in exchange and it will be a dream to make our home in concert with our happiness. It's necessary to recover the time that fate has made us lose now and not dally

because we lack some detail here and there. Tell me what you think of this project, chatísima. (December 23, 1938)

Traditionally, in Spain, middle class couples waited to get married until they had purchased or rented a place to live and had furnished it completely with all the "details," as my father mentioned. I remember friends of my own generation, including my cousins, spending months decorating their homes before their weddings. My mother's answer was true to her personality, practical and short: "About what you tell me about our marriage, I'll tell you that I would be very happy to, why not? And, of course, we will take advantage of all the time for us since unfortunately now we can't" (December 28, 1938).

I suggested earlier that my parents were communicating through the books they were reading. My father let my mother know what he was thinking, what his values were, what was important to him, and in matters of the heart, this was no exception. We know they both loved *Arrowsmith* and they saw themselves reflected in the literary characters of Martin and Leora. My father, in particular, was a lot like Sinclair Lewis' protagonist, impulsive and quick to fall in love. In the very first letter he ever wrote to my mother, which he hand-delivered to her less than a month after they met, he told her that he was in love with her and he had broken up his prior relationship (January 23, 1937). When my mother did not take the bait and asked for more proof, my dad appealed to Apollo in one of his original images, since after all "Apollo was a god in love" (December 26, 1937). Despite my mother's acceptance of my dad's proposal of a marriage without the traditional trappings, he went back to this issue as it related to Martin Arrowsmith. His long explanation was very telling:

> It has enchanted me again in an inexplicable manner that part of Martin's life when he marries Leora before finishing his studies and then they both work together with their soul full of dreams. I repeat one more time that those are my same problems; Martin's doubts and his concern about the future, his conflicts between following his studies and his slow-to-realize plans or to sacrifice everything to get married quickly to Leora, which would change his life completely. That's why I told you that if *Arrowsmith* is not my real life, is at least my possible life . . . Like Martin, the necessity to tend

56

to the maintenance of a home for the two of us will be a concerted delay of my most dear plans . . . after you, don't be suspicious. I don't know either to what degree you are like Leora . . . Keep in mind that a lot of what Martin became is because of her and the same dream gives me breath. (February 18, 1939)

This time my mother did not take the bait and refused my father's proposal in no uncertain terms: "I would like to speak to you about your little paragraph in today's letter; I'm referring to your probable future life. I warn you that I am not suspicious, but if I were to be an obstacle to see your literary career started, from now on I would stop being your girlfriend to be your best friend or your second sister" (February 23, 1939).

At this point I had to confess that I could not understand my mother's reaction, which seemed to be contrary to her earlier acceptance. I realized then that I needed to communicate with her in the same language and I had to read *Arrowsmith* myself to find out what had triggered her anger, aside from my father's patronizing tone. I was most surprised when I read it, since it is such an American novel. Much of its plot deals with university life, including fraternities and there is so much about medicine and life in the Midwest, which must have been so foreign to my parents. I wonder if my dad's desire to emigrate to the United States was born then. The most surprising twist is that Martin and Leora eloped and had to live apart until he finished his medical studies. I then understood my mother's reaction. What she was suggesting to my dad was that she may not object to postponing some of the traditional details of a wedding, but in no way was she interested in eloping, regardless of his future career, good reader of the novel that she was. I have to admire her, standing up to my dad and holding her ground on his own literary turf.

Interestingly enough, according to Kathryn Hughes' review of *The Victorian and the Romantic. A Memoir, a Love Story, and a Friendship Across Time*, "There is a continuing literary trend in which (usually) female narrators twine their own life into that of a classic author" (18). This is exactly what my father seems to have done with Martin Arrowsmith. Not only was my dad the same age as Martin, but they were both disillusioned with the times, their families and people in general as we will continue to see in succeeding chapters.

The two photographs I have of my parents' wedding day on December 26, 1942, speak for themselves. One was taken outside of the church, which is not surprising; despite not being religious, all weddings in Franco's Spain were celebrated in the church with the civil part of the ceremony held inside the sacristy right after the wedding. The priest, dressed for the cold with a full-length coat with a cape and a traditional *cappello romano* hat, is standing among a large group of people. On my mother's side of the family, I recognize my grandmother, quite formal wearing a mantilla; my mother's two youngest brothers, Salvador, looking dapper with a coat and tie, and Toni, too young at eleven years of age to get dressed up, is wearing a sweater. Perhaps Pepe and Vicente were still in the military serving under Franco, although it was the day after Christmas and they should have been home on leave. My mother's two sisters, Amparo and Fina are not in this photo either. On my father's side of the family, I only recognize his Uncle Miguel, the patriarch who ran the family business and the short great-grandfather who lived to be 103 years-old. My parents are in the middle of the picture with the Valencian sun shining brightly on their faces on that winter day. My mother looks radiant and stylish, wearing a white coat and a black hat with matching gloves (black was the color for brides in those days). She carried a large bouquet of white flowers and had a big smile on her face. My dad, on the other hand, looks sheepish with his hands folded in front of his dark, heavy coat. He had a rather strange rule that one should not smile in pictures, because it made one look silly. I am glad my mother was not following the rules on that day and her beautiful teeth showed in her full smile.

In the other photograph, everyone is serious; sitting around the dining table in my father's family home are my grandmother and Uncle Miguel, who must have been the godparents and standing behind, my dad's stepmother and his sister wearing a fancy lace apron. Some hot chocolate and sweets are on the table. I remember my mother telling me this was the only thing served when we looked at these pictures together so long ago. I am certain that there was no formal reception because Spain was still reeling from the Civil War and that would have been considered wasteful. In *Textos para la historia de las mujeres en España* (Texts for the History of Women in Spain), María Laffite, despite being the Countess of Campo Alange, describes her wedding reception in very similar terms, calling it a "tea" (381). Nevertheless, in the photograph of my parents' wedding, there are fancy silver serving pieces on the table and on the buffet, along with some art pieces on the furniture and on the walls. My mother still has her white coat on, but it is open to reveal the black dress, a string of pearls and a fancy pin. My father looks just like I remember him as a child, professorial and serious with thick black-framed glasses. I really do not know how many details of a formal wedding they skipped, but they certainly did not elope the way Martin and Leora did. My mother had won that battle! Some twenty years later, in 1964, I went to Madrid to marry my first husband on the same wedding date as my parents.

For obvious reasons, this chapter about my parents' love story has been hard to write; it makes me sad to read how in love they were, knowing that their marriage did not have a happy ending. I wonder when their passion started to wane. I remember them being loving with each other up to the early sixties when we already lived in the United States. There was a sunny day in Seattle, when my mother was sitting on our front porch, and my father was taking endless pictures of her long reddish hair. I glimpsed them in bed together on another occasion later in Lafayette, Indiana, when I arrived home unexpectedly. Certainly, my mother's illness took a toll on their relationship. My father was not cut out to be the care-giver and she was not an easy patient, with frequent complaints. Perhaps I have to think like my mother to better understand their relationship. Just as she said that love is not measured by the length of the letters one writes, a marriage or love should not be measured by how many years it lasts.

esto Aunque no vendrías tan
pronto como había imaginado, de.
jo para entonces lo de mi crisis.
Seguramente los de Miró Ra.
dio saben que te escribo y quieren
ponerme buena música. Perdón
por mi filarmonía pero la ver.
dad es están tocando cosas muy
buenas.

Cariñet bara vit y hasta
demá. Vol com ella a Riu a la Peña

Conchita

Valencia 2 de Mars de 1938
14 vit

nº 65,

Linguistic Style

The Franco Regime (1939–1975), consistent with its nationalistic, fascist policies, systematically repressed Spain's regional cultures. As a result, it was forbidden to speak or study the Basque, Catalan and Valencian languages. I grew up hearing my father speaking Valencian at home in defiance to the dictatorship, while my mother always answered him in Castilian Spanish. She was fearful that someone would turn my father in and he would end up in jail, but my father never stopped speaking Valencian at home. My brother and I never learned to write Valencian since it was not taught at school, although we could understand it well; our bilingual, schizophrenic upbringing was quite common, particularly while we lived in Valencia. A few years before his death, my father told me with great glee that a Catalan colleague in the department at the University, Pep Miquel Sobrer, stopped by regularly and they spoke in the regional language — Catalan and Valencian being so similar. I was probably one of my father's last interlocutors in that language. Whenever I visited him in Bloomington, Indiana, up until the time he died at almost ninety-six years of age, he would still speak to me in Valencian.

It is worth noting that in my parents' letters, with regard to the use of the regional language, the dynamic was the complete opposite. My intelletual father usually did not express himself in Valencian, while my mother's letters were full of terms of endearment and other expressions in that language, along with an obvious affection for the city of her birth. These characteristics show the extent of the repression they suffered while living under Franco. My mother did not feel as free to speak her native language as she did in her letters; my father showed his defiance all of his life, until well after Franco's death in 1975 and the rightful return of the regional languages under the democratic government. My mother's love of the Valencian culture, along with prolific usage of popular sayings, and her ironic twists, including some repetitions that she copied from my dad, helped give her letters a charming, personal linguistic style.

"Che!" is a symbol of Valencian identity. It is used to express surprise or a simple greeting like Hey! "Che!" migrated to Latin America, Argentina and Uruguay, in particular. (Ernesto) Che Guevara, the Argentine Marxist revolutionary, got his nickname for his frequent use of this expression. My mother used it repeatedly, giving her letters a colloquial tone: "Che! Estic feta una chanca" (Hey, you, I am a wreck, June 18, 1937). Other Valencian expressions she used were: "Chiquet" (Little one, June 1, 1937); "Anem tirant" (Feeling so so, January 17, 1938); "Se fa tart" (It's getting late, January 19, 1938). When she transcribed messages from my father's Aunt Isabel, who always spoke in Valencian, my mother did it literally: "Ella te vol molt y també vol que li escrigues" (She loves you a lot and she wants you to write to her, January 17, 1938).

Oftentimes my mother liked to use affectionate phrases at the end of her letters in Valencian, as she did on January 29, 1938: "Cariñet: te vols mes que may, la teua, Conchita" (Little darling: I love you more than ever, your, Conchita). She even wrote her name in the regional language on occasion, which gave her letters an intimate tone:

Cariñet bona nit y hasta demá. Vol com ella a tú a teua,
Concheta
Valensia 2 de Mars de 1938, 11 nit

(Little darling, good night and until tomorrow. Love her as she loves you, your, Conchita. Valencia, March 2, 1938, 11 at night). And less than a month before the end of the war, my mother asked my dad: "Bueno, cariñet, me vols? Yo a tu en tota le neua anima" (Well, Little Darling, do you love me? I love you with all my soul, March 4, 1939).

Although my father did not use Valencian nearly as much as my mother did in his letters, there is always the exception that proves the rule. He wrote a clever saying on the day he received a package and three letters from my mother all at the same time: "Día de molt, vespra de res" (Day with lots, eve with nothing, January 27, 1938). In one of his frequent comments about the weather, he told my mother this metaphorical saying, in case she had not heard it:

"Si la Candelaria plora, iver fora y si riu, ya ve el estiu" (If the Candelaria cries, winter is out and if she laughs, summer is coming, February 5, 1939). This means that the cold weather is over in early February; whether it rains on February 2, the day the Candelaria Virgen is celebrated, or even if it is sunny on that day. In other words, it is a Valencian version of the American Groundhog Day. He also confessed that while he was on the front lines, he liked to speak Valencian with comrades from his city because he was getting tired of all the Andalusian slang (December 27–28, 1937).

My mother loved Valencia, I remember how difficult it was for her to leave her city and her family when we moved to Madrid in 1953. During the war, when she went to work in Barcelona, she only lasted a few days, complaining that she did not feel well there. She did not like to have to take trolleys and subways to get around and missed not being able to walk everywhere as she did in Valencia (November 21, 1937). In her letters, even in the midst of war, the love of her city was evident: "Valencia without bombs is charming" (January 25, 1938), she wrote. My mother relished describing her strolls through the city, naming the streets: "I walked home along Pascual y Genís Street, crossing Colón and I went by where you used to live" (October 23, 1938). On one occasion she met her mother after work at the Telefónica building and went up in what must have been one of the tallest buildings in the city then. Looking through the windows she remarked: "I had never seen Plaza Castelar at night and raining as it was, I saw it from there, with a bird's eye view, and I liked it, you know?" (September 27, 1938).

It seems that there often were air raids very early in the mornings and she called it in her typical ironic style, the "Despertá," a Valencian word that means the wakeup call: "The wakeup call was at five o'clock and it lasted until seven" (January 22, 1938). The "despertá" refers to the first fireworks during the city's famous holiday of Las Fallas when it celebrates one of the most famous holidays in a country known for its festivities. Saint Joseph, the carpenter, is the patron saint of Valencia and every year in March there is a week-long celebration of spring in which huge, up to five story-high, wooden and paper mâché monuments are erected in each neighborhood to be burned at midnight on March 19. Each "falla" has a sarcastic theme about local, national or international events depicted with exaggerated caricatures of life-size "ninots," or dolls. During an entire week there are daily parades, flowers' offerings to the Virgen de los Desamparados (Our Lady of the Forsaken), and fireworks in an endless bacchanal, which mixes the sacred with the profane, very much in Valencian style. A significant part of Las Fallas celebration consists of wearing the regional dress, both men and women. Entire families, particularly the young girls, dress up in elaborate costumes with their hair braided, wearing "peinetas" (hair combs), mantillas, embroidered skirts, and ornate jewelry.

As part of Franco's repression of the regional cultures, Las Fallas used to be low-key, but they came back with a vengeance after his death. I do not remember Las Fallas growing up in Valencia, but I went religiously with my relatives from Madrid as I got older. For some reason, my parents never went back on this holiday. I suspect that my father, who hated loud noises, vetoed the idea. However, I have a formal portrait of my mother taken in a studio, wearing the regional Valencian dress. She looks stunning despite the sepia tone of the photograph that does not show the bright colors of the costume. I have an idea when this photo was taken; she looks young, but it does not predate her marriage to my dad, since she is wearing her wedding ring. My mother is seated, with a serious demeanor — proof that my father was not far behind, since he did not like anyone to smile in pictures. Aside from the elaborate jewelry, embroidered dress with lace sleeves, and the hair comb, my mother's perfect features are striking. Every year a "Fallera Mayor" (Miss Las Fallas) is chosen and she could have been the queen any year, as far as I am concerned.

Unlike my cousins, I never had a regional dress made to wear during the holidays; I guess that my parents thought it was a needless expense since we no longer lived in Valencia. Whatever the reason, it was one of those things that immigrants have to remedy and in 1982, during a visit to Valencia, my Godmother Teresa took me to a photographer to have my portrait taken. Of course, despite the photographer's perplexity, I insisted that it be sepia like my mother's. I do not look as fair as she did, with my brown eyes and dark hair, but this is the closest I came to being a Valencian beauty. This story has legs, because I was able to talk Jane, my youngest daughter, into having her portrait done wearing the Valencian regional dress and she does look like her grandmother, since she is fair and has my mother's side of the family's good looks. Not one to call it quits, I have in mind to take my twin granddaughters, the fairest of them all, to have their portraits done as well!

One of the reasons my mother appreciated the city of her birth was her love of the sea. I remember summers when we were children going to El Saler or to Playa de la Malvarrosa (Malvarrosa Beach), where we rented a cabana to spend the day. My mother was a good swimmer and used to tease my dad because he had never learned how to swim. I was not surprised to read that my mother would have liked to live by the sea when she married my dad, although I had never heard her say it:

> When the war ends, I want to go live in El Cabañal, where my aunt Carmen used to live, but more toward the beach, by the street with the trolley, where you and I went on January 17, remember? I had always wanted to go to the beach and live close to it . . . if it's possible and the war allows us to end up alive. (February 9, 1939)

The love of the sea is one trait I have inherited from my mother. Today, for example, I am writing at the Jersey Shore; it is not the summerhouse we owned in Ocean City when Peter, my second husband, was still alive. It is a rental, but it is comfortable and beautiful, with an expansive view of the ocean, the dunes, and the green marshes full of birds: red winged black-birds, cardinals, sparrows and finches. During storms the gulls, plovers and sandpipers come up too. Early in the mornings on the trail to the beach I look for foxes scurrying about looking for birds' eggs and at night I can see Atlantic City in the distance, full of neon lights that dwarf the old Absecon Lighthouse.

Another linguistic trait in my mother's letters in the Valencian language was the use of the possessive to refer to her siblings, "mi Pepín" and "mi Vicente" in particular. This is an affectionate use that showed how close she was to her family: "Today my Vicente left and we don't know where to; he agreed to let us know when he arrives and he will tell us what town he is in. It's eleven p. m. and he hasn't called yet" (April 29, 1938). Coincidentally, my cousin Inma, Vicente's daughter, sent me a photo of my mother with those two brothers when I told her I was writing this book. I had never seen that picture, probably taken in Madrid in front of El Retiro Park, when my mother's family lived there for a short time due to my grandfather's work. My mother's loving face is full of determination and her pose is indicative of her protective role in the family when she must have been only seven or eight years old. In the photograph she is wearing a short skirt with a contrasting jacket, Mary Jane patent leather shoes, gloves, and a huge bow on top of her head. Her left arm is resting on her brother Pepe and she looks as if she might be saying "Here is my Pepín." Vicente is on the other side wearing a beret as is his brother. What I like most about this picture is that, in the few photos I have from my childhood, I look exactly like my mother. I will write more on this issue later.

As I read my mother's letters, I am always amazed at how wise she was for a mere twenty-one-year old woman and how sure she was of herself, particularly when it came time to stand up to her overpowering fiancé. I am certain that her position within her family, as the oldest of seven siblings and the arrival of the war, contributed to her maturity. One way in which she expressed her wisdom was by the use of sayings or proverbs. Luis Iscla Rovira in his book *Spanish Proverbs: A Survey of Spanish Culture and Civilization,* states that "Spain is the country of proverbs," (9). He has cataloged almost three thousand proverbs with their corresponding literal translations in English, by itself commendable, but he neglected to find their English counterparts, which, to me, is the most difficult task as we will see.

To show how much my mother missed my dad, for example, she repeated a very common saying "Estoy más sola que un hongo" (I'm lonelier than a mushroom, June 11, 1937). Who would think of mushrooms as being lonely? My mother must have meant that she missed my dad because she was hardly alone in the midst of such a large family. When my father called my mother "stubborn," she answered with another popular saying that incorporates antonyms: "Cabeza dura, corazón tierno" (Hard head, tender heart, July 20, 1937). Many Spanish sayings use rhyme: "Mi gozo en un pozo" (My joy in a well, August 4, 1937) is one of them, which my mother used, meaning that she thought she would receive a letter, but did not. Another rhyming saying is "A lo hecho pecho" (What is done, is done), which she wrote when she was embarrassed for having asked my father for a hug, hoping that the censors would not read that letter (January 13, 1938). "Salir el tiro por la culata" (To fire from the butt of the gun) is another way in which she expressed the unexpected disappointment of not being able to visit my dad on the front as she was planning. Her father was adamant and said: "I won't allow my daughter to go," despite all my mother's schemes (December 21, 1937). She also expressed her frustration with another saying when she could not write to my father because they were in the midst of an air raid, the alarm was sounding, and they had lost electric power: "El que manda, manda" (He who is boss decides, January 17, 1938).

In one of the frequent letters my mother wrote counting how many she was missing and complaining that she had not received the daily letter from my dad, she told him: "El que todo lo quiere todo lo pierde" (He who wants it all loses it all, January 7, 1938). The meaning is clear, but finding an equivalent saying in English is another story: Greed will make you lose it all, perhaps? What is also evident is that she was using it as a threat; if my dad did not write enough, she would stop writing to him or maybe even break up with him. This double-edged sword of her wisdom is something I remember very well. My dad's sayings were funny; my mother's were not. In fact, my dad interpreted this saying as a threat as well and was angry with her: "You finish your little paragraph with a saying in quotes and all: 'He who wants it all loses it all.' This saying is almost always inexact, but that is not important now; what do you mean by this?" (January 11, 1938).

Sometimes I still hear my mother's voice and the sayings that she repeated all her life. I have to admit that I did not always appreciate their exact meaning and, even less, the double *entendres* in which she imbued them. For example, she would threaten me with "Ya encontrarás el zapatito de tu pie" (You'll find the little shoe that fits your foot), which has little to do with its apparent English counterpart, "If the shoe fits wear it." My mother's version was a lot more menacing; it meant that sooner or later I would find someone to treat me as poorly as I was supposedly treating her at that moment. I had my own, sunnier interpretation of this malevolent shoe; I liked to think of Cinderella's fairy-tale glass slipper that Prince Charming was bringing for me to try on, but that was not meant to happen either.

On one occasion, when my dad had been bragging about his conquests with southern women, she warned him: "De tanto estirar la cuerda al fin se rompe" (When one pulls on the string too much, it finally breaks, July 17, 1937). One of my mother's shortest letters was dated April 18, 1938, written in beautiful, cursive handwriting. She told him in no uncertain terms that whenever she did not get a letter, she would not write that day either because "Amor con amor se paga," (Love is paid with love); "Tit for tat" or "One good turn deserves another" as we would say in American English. I am not surprised to find that my mother also used Valencian sayings: "Sempre plou cuant no ya scola" (It always rains when there is no school, April 2, 1938).

My father used sayings as well, although his were more for entertainment purposes than to admonish. In *Don Quijote de la Mancha*, Miguel de Cervantes' masterpiece, Sancho, his squire, is famous for saying a proverb for every occasion. Accordingly, my dad said that he was in a "Sancho" mood that day and strung these two sayings together when he wanted my mother to do something: "Quien no llora no mama" (He who doesn't cry doesn't get the tit), which does have a counterpart in English: "The squeaky wheel gets the grease." Although he knew not to ask too much since "La avaricia rompe el saco" (Greed will break your bag, June 16, 1937)). When my mother complained that my dad's letters were short (nothing could be further from the truth), he answered her with: "Dijo la sartén al cazo: ¡Quita allá que me tiznas!" the Spanish version: of "That's the pot calling the kettle black." Again, he tied it with another saying: "Dime de que alardeas y te diré de que careces," "It takes one to know one" more or less, since he liked to win every point (November 3–4, 1937). A funny saying that I remember well is: "No está el horno para bollos" (The oven is not ready for pastries), meaning that it is not a good time to do something. My father used it to tell my mother not to come to the front lines to see him, as she was ready to do, that it was temerity (January 8, 1938).

In those years, he actually worried about her as much as she did about him. We have already seen that my dad was concerned about her health and urged her to see the doctor before it was too late: "Más vale remendar una gotera que una casa entera" (It's better to fix a leak than the entire house, January 21, 1938). Consequently, he did not hesitate to lecture her when he felt that she was not following his rules. When my mother took a government job at the Ministry of Propaganda, he was very upset that she did it without asking his permission first, taking advantage of the situation. He reprimanded her with the graphic saying "Hacer de tu capa un sayo" (To turn one's cape into a long coat): "I am very upset with you because in the first chance you had to satisfy me in something important, you have turned your cape into a long coat" (September 19–20, 1937).

Not surprisingly, when I speak Spanish, I like to use sayings too. The ideal one for describing my mother's edgy style is that she used to give "Una de cal y otra de arena" (One swipe with lime and another with sand), which roughly means to say something nice followed by something less pleasant. It is something similar to a backhanded compliment in today's parlance. My all-time favorite saying is "Una golondrina no hace verano" (One swallow does not a summer make). I found out that Cervantes' Don Quixote used it. It sounds so poetic in Spanish and I love swallows. Besides, I remember fondly the swallows in San Juan Capistrano in Southern California. Each March 19, Saint Joseph's Day, instead of celebrating Las Fallas, the swallows arrived all at once in a black cloud of chirping birds that obscured the sun. I went to see their arrival during the year I lived in San Clemente while my husband was stationed at Camp Pendleton Marine Corps base. I wondered where did these American swallows fly from, South America perhaps. In Spain, swallows did not have a set date to arrive and they came from North Africa, which made them even more exotic to me.

I remember arguing with my mother about the meaning of this saying. She always warned me that things were not what they seemed, not to expect the best or I would always be disappointed, to restrain my hopes. According to her, just because the swallows had come, it did not mean that summer had arrived. The closest counterpart in English I can come up with is the "Don't count your chickens before they hatch," which somewhat parallels the bird motif. But, despite all of my mother's admonitions, I have never been good at waiting and I have been counting chickens all my life, anticipating more swallows to arrive. Frankly, I disagree with my mother on this issue; it is not a mistake to count chickens. Even if the events of my life do not end as I would wish, even if I suffer disappointments, I have already enjoyed imagining the best. Which takes me to another of my mother's sayings: "Que me quiten lo bailado," something similar to a Spanish *carpe diem*, impossible to translate. Literally it means to let them take away from me the dances I have already danced, which is something I can thoroughly agree with.

"Mal de muchos consuelo de tontos" (Bad for many, consolation for the dumb ones) is an easy saying to figure out: "Misery loves company," it is not literal in Spanish, but it, too, has an edge. My dad used it to complain about the mail since all the soldiers had the same problem (January 2, 1938). Another one of my favorite sayings is the rhyming one "Las cosas de palacio van despacio" (Courtly matters take a long time). Basically, it means "Bureaucracy takes so long" as my mother said when she was finally paid four hundred pesetas, although she still did not know her full salary (August 4, 1938).

Even when my mother did not use sayings, she often had a piquant edge to her expressions and she could be quite humorous too. For example, she kept in touch with Ferreres, my dad's friend, who did not pass his physical exam and spent the war years in Valencia. Cleverly, my mother had enlisted his help with my father's book orders. She wrote about him:

> Our friend Ferreres is very thin, he looks like spaghetti. If it weren't because he is always weighted down (with books under his arms) I think he would have already blown away. The wind is known to perform tricky jokes sometimes. (January 24, 1938)

As the war dragged on and they had to eat horse meat, my mother wrote that she would not eat it because she did not want to start kicking (December 19, 1937). She described the wedding of a girlfriend, Visita, when the air raid alarm went on during the ceremony, writing "this is an alarming sign, no?" (September 10, 1938).

As we know, one of my mother's specialties was threats. She was quite short, barely five feet. My dad must have teased her about her stature, because she sounded defensive when she told him that she had grown a little, but if she grew any more, she would have to break up with him to find a taller man than him (July 24, 1937). When he told her that he felt strong, she answered: "If you are as strong as steel, be very careful, this material is highly sought after now" (September 7, 1937). In the same vein, when my father said that he was eating well and putting on some weight, she stated:

> If you continue to eat that way, you will get fat and then you will be a bigger target for the enemy. So, be careful because I wouldn't like

70

to be made a widow before it's time and I warn you that black makes me look great (if I may say so myself). (December 28, 1937)

In some instances, my mother imitated my dad's style. He liked to repeat things two or three times, "repeating like a cicada from sunset to sunrise: come back, come back, come back" (June 22, 1937) and particularly in his closings: "Now, good night since I'm going to dream about you. Yours, yours, yours, Juan" (November 3–4, 1937). If she was in a good mood, she would repeat the same thought: "Te quiere mucho, mucho y mucho" (I love you lots, lots and lots, July 29, 1937). Often, she imitated him, but with a twist: "Hasta mañana, feísimo, ya sabes que no te quiero nada, nada y nada" (Until tomorrow, feísimo, you know how I don't love you at all, at all and at all, December 28, 1937).

It is worth noting that my mother's sayings were markedly more frequent in her earlier letters. As she gained confidence in her epistolary style, she did not rely as much on them. Her thoughts were more personal and original, possibly inspired by my father's sophisticated style. To describe the bombs during an air raid, she used ironic images, calling them "una lotería macabra" (a macabre lottery, July 13, 1937) and also "lluvia de bellotas," (rain of acorns, January 16, 1938). She could be funny as well, like when she said that she was "playing the piano" instead of washing the dishes (July 7, 1937). My mother always loved sitting in the sun to get some color and, even during war time, she would go up to the roof of her building to read. She said in a beautiful letter with lyrical flair: " . . . I have been on a magnificent terrace from where I could see the sea and the neighboring mountains. I have been sitting in the sun and he, always so loving, has left on me his bronze footprints" (February 12, 1938). I liked it when she made a play on words with her own name, a seashell, comparing the conch shell to a "pearl" (December 29, 1937).

When she was not so obsessed with counting the letters she had received, she could be quite poetic and loving. On July 12, 1938, she told my dad "if the airplanes allow me, I will dream about you in my sleep, when I'm awake I always dream about you." One of my favorite letters is one in which she described a night she was writing and he had arrived for a visit:

Valencia, July 13, 1938
Queridísimo,

It is very late, it's already 1 a.m. I haven't written before because I was waiting to be alone and at peace. The moon is coming through the balcony all the way to the dining room and it arrives all the way to where I am. It's as beautiful a night as when you came and that's why perhaps I have been waiting for you this evening. Now I know that you won't be arriving this evening . . . it's so much like the other that I thought I saw you turning around the corner like the time before . . . When will we in nights like this one go to the sea? I can see it shining from here. I would go so happily, holding your arm...Do you remember the night of the 13th last month? What joy to see you anew! That day this dining room was so animated until so late, tonight everyone is sleeping. To complete that night so much like this one, I can also hear the airplanes. And now I'm really leaving you. I'm going to see if sleep loves me and I can leave with him.

Always and more than ever, your,
Conchita

There were some puzzling expressions that my mother used frequently in her letters: one was "¡Qué poncho!" I have never heard this exclamation that has nothing to do with the piece of clothing. At times like this I wish some of my mother's siblings or some other older relatives were still alive so I could ask them. I checked with one of my cousins in Madrid and he explained to me that he had not heard of ¡Qué poncho! either, but that women of my mother's generation would use meaningless expressions like this one instead of stronger expressions, which were reserved for men only. Then ¡Qué poncho! could mean "qué porra" or "córcholis." In her case, it meant "What the hell!" since she used it as a means to express frustration as in her letter of October 19, 1938, when she was angry at my dad because she had not received a letter in three days: "Until this evening [when I will write again], silly goose. Say hi to the little bear and for you a pull of your ears ¡Qué poncho!" On another occasion she said: "¡Poncho! I really would like to see you. You too? Perhaps all those things that you tell me about thinking about me and that you want to see me and I don't know what else are stories, no?" (January 19, 1938). Here ¡Poncho! could mean Damn!

72

"Mecachis la mar" (Shoot) is another strange expression, but this one I have heard. It is similar to ¡Qué poncho! since it hides a stronger meaning that my mother did not dare write (Shit, January 25, 1938). When she was upset with my dad which, as we have seen, was not a rare occurrence, she said that she was saying goodbye "a la francesa" (in French style), which meant that she was taking leave without a proper goodbye, certainly without any sweet nothings: "And I'm saying goodbye French style, although I feel as Spanish as ever," (February 15, 1938).

Another puzzling expression my mother used, particularly in the last months of the war, was to call my father "calamidad" (calamity). This word is easy to translate, but hard to comprehend. When it is used for a person literally it can be quite offensive. According to the *Spanish Urban Dictionary*, it means "good-for-nothing," "useless," although it really depends on the tone in which it is used. I think my mother must have used it in jest and as a sign of their intimacy. As she grew surer of herself, she would use a word like this, meaning that she understood him and loved him so, whether he was ugly or not, as is the case here:

> At the end of your letter from the 23rd you asked me if I love you enough to feel reciprocated. Well, have you perhaps doubted it, feísimo? Do I love you? Of course, I do, calamidad! More than you love me, the truth, the whole truth. (July 28, 1938)

The word "calamidad" is also characteristic in the vocabulary of Carmen Sotillo, the protagonist of *Cinco horas con Mario* (Five Hours with Mario) by Miguel Delibes, the Spanish postwar writer. She used it with the same sense of frustration.

It is obvious that my mother became increasingly frustrated and worried after being apart from my dad for so many months and this emphasized her less patient side. The war was taking a heavy toll on every aspect of her life and she often expressed it openly to him. She ended the same letter of July 28, 1938, saying that she was afraid and highlighted the word "m-i-e-d-o:" "And now I'm going to bed although not to sleep because I am a-f-r-a-i-d!"

As we have seen, translating sayings into English is easy to do, but to grasp their meaning and to find a counterpart is another story. "Hacer de tripas corazón" (Turning your guts into a heart, July 22, 1937) is one of them. It would be similar to making lemonade out of lemons in contemporary terms. My mother used it when she wrote my dad a letter, although she had not heard from him that day. I have to agree with James Michener when he said that "Spain is a mystery and I am not at all convinced that those who live within the peninsula and were born there understand it much better than I do" (Quoted in Iscla Rovira, 28).

los ojos lánguidos esperando que llegue el momento en que los convierta en vestidos o blusas en ropa interior: en cualquier otra cosa, podría si no tuviese este mi carácter pasarlo bien y no no hay manera. —Me levanté a las siete esta mañana: cosí el pantalón de Joaquín le terminé a Vicente unas cuantas cosas. Hice la comida, le serví, fregué, barrí puse las sillas en orden me planché el vestido que me venía corto (me lo he alargado como te prometí) y me acosté una hora. Y después de esta hora de medio té escribo. Pienso, cuando termine de escribirte, terminarme un camisón que comencé anteayer y ponérmelo hoy mismo desde luego. Después le comenzaré la montería a Lau-

Discovering My Mother

Reading my mother's letters has been a journey of discovery. Despite growing up in a small, close-knit family, I realized that I did not get to know her as well as I knew my father. In part, this had to do with my father's dominant personality and the fact that he lived such a long life in comparison to my mother. I was surprised to discover, for example, that as a young woman she was employed full-time and, even more surprising, my grandmother worked as well, with seven children at home. I grew up during Franco's dictatorship and the Sección Femenina (Women's Section) formed and run by Pilar Primo de Rivera. She was the sister of José Antonio Primo de Rivera, the founder of the Spanish Falange, the fascist party that was the base for Franco's doctrine and principles. The Sección Femenina taught us that men were superior, that women had to be subordinate to them, that women's roles were as wives and mothers, raising strong children under the traditional mores of the Catholic Church. In the words of Pilar Primo de Rivera herself: "The only mission that Spain assigns to women is the home" (Quoted in *Historia de las mujeres: El Siglo XX,* The History of Women: The XX Century, 217).

It is important to note that my mother did not grow up under Franco. She was formed during the Second Spanish Republic (1931–1939), one of the most liberal governments in the world during the1930s. Under the Republic, women like my mother could vote, divorce and have an abortion, rights that Spanish women would not recover until after Franco's death over forty years later, under the subsequent democratic Constitution of 1978. Carmen Martín Gaite, one of Spain's best known writers during Franco's years, wrote about the differences between the Republican Government and Franco's regime in her book *Usos amorosos de la postguerra española* (Love Mores During the Spanish Postwar Years):

From the pulpits, the press, the radio and the Women's Section classrooms, moderation was preached. The three years of the war had opened a chasm between the Republic, lavish with novelties, rehabilitations, and ferments of all kinds, and the threshold of this tunnel of unforeseeable duration through which people were starting to proceed. (13)

According to Mary Nash, during the Spanish Civil War women fought alongside the men on the front lines and some 20,000 women joined forces with the anti-fascist movement in all kinds of social, educational and health services (410–411). María Dolores Ramos points out that Valencia was second only to Barcelona in upholding the revolutionary principles of equality in women's salaries and other workplace issues (654). It is not surprising then, as we have seen, that during the war my mother volunteered to give blood, that she was ready to visit my dad on the front lines, or that she left her beloved Valencia to get a better salary working in Barcelona with the revolutionary government. As a young woman, my mother was a typical example of the ideal Republican woman, strong and self-sufficient. She became the oppressed woman I knew during the years of Franco's antifeminist repression. As Mary Nash points out:

> Franco's discourse about women was created from the traditional
> gender discourse in its configuration of women as wife and mother.
> The political purpose of Franco's regime reflected in the legislature,
> is the limitation of women to their domestic chores at home, the
> recuperation of the patriarchal family and the social subordination
> of women in a patriarchal androcentric order. (621)

My father, despite his liberal intellectual ideas, agreed with the conventional gender roles associated with a traditional Spain and he was instrumental in shaping my mother's image in that way.

As we have seen, my father's patriarchal views were evident. He became upset when my mother changed jobs without asking him and he threatened to break up with her if she continued to give blood, although he must have been genuinely concerned about her health. He really did not want her to work at all and told her so several times. My mother finally asked her father if she could quit her job and he answered with a curt: "No digas tonterías" (Don't say such nonsense). I am certain that there was a financial need for my mother to work and we know that she gave her salary to her parents. Consequently, my grandfather appreciated what a good daughter she was and told her that she was "Una mujer hecha y derecha" (A full grown woman, December 27, 1937). But once she was married to my dad, my mother changed from: "Soy una mujer fuerte" (I'm a strong woman, April 4, 1938) in her letters to being the typical mother I knew according to the Sección Femenina's values of marriage, children and running the house. Although my mother was planning to continue working, my father told her clearly in one of his letters that she would not work outside the home when they got married:

> I told you once before that I would only tolerate that you work at any job if it was to accelerate our union as it may happen when the war ends. Of course, you would stay at home as soon as I can provide for you on my own because I plan to give you enough work, although not the kind that you are undoubtedly thinking about now. Let's hope that, you change your mind by then. (December 23, 1938)

In addition to working fulltime at the government cooperative where she kept the books, as we have seen, my mother helped with all the chores and responsibilities of running a house with seven children. During the war, she shopped for food and stood in lines to get the family rations before leaving for the office in the morning. She cooked, cleaned, ironed, mended and sewed clothing for herself and her siblings. Here is what a day for her could be like:

> I got up at seven this morning; I sewed Tonín's pants, I finished some things for Vicente. Made lunch, served it, washed the dishes, swept, arranged the chairs, ironed my dress (I lengthened it as I promised you), lay down for an hour and I'm writing to you after this hour of sleep. When I finish writing to you, I will finish a nightgown that I started day-before-yesterday and I plan to wear tonight, of course. After that, I'm going to start the tablecloth for Conchita Guillén. I have set a schedule to finish it as soon as I can. Today I have to baste four napkins and sew the hems. It's really too bad that you are not here keeping me company. (September 11, 1938)

Not only do I remember my mother doing all these things, but I also learned to do some of them myself at her side. During my years as a Marine Corps wife I, too, made my clothes and, later, my daughters' as well. To this day, I actually iron the sheets. One of my mother's beliefs was that a woman needed to know how to do everything even if someone else was going to help at a later date. She could also crochet and knit, two things that I wish I had learned to do with her. I pointed out that she knitted sweaters, vests and socks for my dad and her siblings when they were on the front lines. We remember well that as soon as she heard that there was a new baby in the house where my father was staying, she knitted an entire outfit for him.

One of my mother's favorite pieces of wisdom was "No es más limpio el que más limpia, sino el que menos ensucia" (The cleanest person is not the one who cleans the most but the one who dirties the least). This concept I can relate to, because cleaning is not my favorite chore, while keeping things in order is one of my traits. Another strange piece of advice was "Lo que cosas en domingo, tendrás que descoser con la nariz" (Whatever you sew on a Sunday will need to be undone with your nose). This scary thought undoubtedly is a maxim left over from the Christian dogma about Sunday being a day of rest. Sewing was also present in another of my mother's sayings: "Eso es coser y cantar" (That is like sewing and singing) and it meant that it was so simple to do, a mindless task. We could summarize my mother's entire philosophy with another one of her favorite sayings: "Despacito y buena letra," something like "Proceed with caution," or "Don't upset the apple cart;" undoubtedly related to Franco's cautionary doctrines.

Amazingly, my mother also painted the kitchen and fixed radios and small appliances, hidden talents I was not aware of. I had to laugh when I read that because my brother, even as a young boy, was the house repairman. He would take apart any electronic gadget he could get his hands on, even if he did not know how to put it back together again. It was interesting to find out that he came by his talent honestly. He grew up to own a successful telecommunications company. My mother wrote about fixing an iron in a very funny letter when her brother Pepe was having a disagreement with his girlfriend. In Spanish "plancha" can mean an iron or a disappointment. Let us see if her cleverness comes through in the translation; I am sure my father relished it:

I don't know if I've ever told you that I can fix electrical irons. Yes, I do fix them and, since I can fix them, I know a bit about mechanics and, of course, I'm going to try to fix this 'breakdown' and if it turns out to be a 'plancha' I'll bring it home, they are so expensive nowadays. (February 20, 1938)

My mother was aware of her charm. She told my father how, as the war wore on, there was a car called the "kangaroo" because they picked up young people outside the movie theaters or walking in the streets if they did not have the proper dispensation for not serving on the war front or the government: "I haven't been asked yet for my documentation, probably I look like a very good person" (April 17, 1938). She knew how to take care of herself as well. When she had the night shift, she made sure to ask for a ride from an official car, begging my dad not to lecture her for having accepted her job (September 23, 1937).

A study of my mother's letters would not be complete without mentioning her cooking. Even as a young woman she could cook everyday fare for her entire family. She mentioned making a "paella," but since she wrote it in quotations, she must have meant that it was not authentic due to the scarcity of food at that time (December 9, 1937). She told my father that she would make "Popeye-like" spinach empanadas for him someday, because they were delicious (December 28, 1937). When my mother worked in a government cooperative, once in a while she had some extra food to take home. On the day that she brought home some pomegranates, she wrote that she prepared them with some sweet wine and sugar (October 3, 1938), exactly the same way that I make them; evidently, I was paying attention to her cooking without even knowing it. On a winter Sunday they had "cocido" (meat stew with rice) for the main meal, but she feared that she would not eat a lot, because she had lost her appetite although, if my father were there, she would eat a big plate (January 16, 1938).

Rice was and still is a staple in Valencian cooking. Thus, even during the war, it appeared in their meals, such as "Arroz con acelgas" (rice with Swiss chard, February 6, 1938), a soup-like dish — one of the few that I would not eat as a child and still do not like. The strangest thing is that my mother said to my dad not to worry, she would not make that for him; I take it that he did not care for it either. Another funny recipe was the one for chickpeas. My father, who did some cooking for the troops during the war, complained that he did not know how to cook chickpeas so that they were tender; she answered that chickpeas must be masculine like him and that was why they were so hard (grammatically, "garbanzos" in Spanish are indeed masculine). In any case, she gave him the recipe: Simmer them in salt water for about five hours and they would turn out as tender as a lettuce's heart (April 29, 1938).

Despite the frequent references to food, the civilian population suffered as much deprivation as the soldiers and malnutrition was one of the most serious issues during the Spanish Civil War. Enrique Moradiellos states that the two elements that caused the most anguish in the civilian population were the terror of the bombings and the acute sense of hunger (447). My mother mentioned that she had not eaten an egg in months and "even less meat and fish, that I have forgotten their taste" (January 25, 1938). My father was obviously worried about my mother's lack of proper nutrition and, after one of his visits, she listed her entire menu to show him that she was listening to him, although it hardly was a balanced meal: "This noon I ate fairly well; I had some 'hervido' (boiled vegetables), some fried onions with cauliflower, two slices of fried bread, an orange and some chicory" (February 1, 1939). My parents were coffee fanatics; I remember them roasting their own coffee when I was little. One of their biggest complaints for years after the war was the shortage of coffee and how they had to drink chicory instead.

I do not want to give the impression that my mother was only adept at domestic chores. We have already seen how eager she was to learn from her fiancé and what a great reader she was; how she found time to read is in itself an accomplishment. Also, the first chance she had, she made arrangements to learn how to type better in order to improve her salary and her chances of employment (October 3, 1937). In the same letter she bragged about her salary "Dos duros diarios" (ten pesetas everyday) and she wrote in detail about all the work she had to do in the office. She really was an exemplary daughter and a practical woman. She gave her salary to her parents and they gave her fifty pesetas, which she planned to put into a savings account, something that made her feel very proud: "As you can see my independence is going ahead somewhat" (March 4, 1938).

On Christmas Day of 1938 my mother was particularly depressed and did not want to do anything with her sisters

Amparín and Fina, who were going out to the movies together. Her mother tried to console her, but my mother felt sad that she was no longer an innocent child who could be consoled. In another reflective moment a few days later, on January 5, 1939, the eve of the arrival of the Three Kings (Spanish Christmas, when Spanish children get their gifts) my mother remembered how happy she was as a child on nights like that one. She wished that she had not grown up, although now that she was a woman, she had her fiancé as compensation.

Nevertheless, my mother fit easily into the maternal role. When my grandmother was sick, my mother practically ran the household: "This morning I took my mother's role in every way and I even did more than my mother, I washed the floor which she can't do because her legs hurt" (August 7, 1938). Sometimes she had to miss outings to the beach, as much as she liked going, because she had "to play the mother role" (August 24, 1937). We saw earlier that my father was looking for more than a girlfriend in my mother. Since his mother had died so young and he was not close to his step-mother, he also wished to find a mother figure. It is interesting to note that when we were growing up, my dad always called my mother "Mamá." He never used Conchita or Concha, although I heard some of the terms of endearment that he used in his letters, such as "Chatita."

It is not surprising that my mother, coming from a large family, would welcome the idea of having children of her own. A few months before the end of the war, she saw the movie *Las cinco cunitas* (Five Little Cribs) and a spicy exchange surged between my parents. First, she told my dad that she wondered if she could be like the mother of the five babies, but not to be frightened, time would tell (January5, 1939). His answer was immediate, he wanted to know more about how she felt: " . . . do you feel like being a mom of a large family: very well, precious one, at your command unconditionally, I hope I don't have to put a stop now to your impetus . . . (January 11, 1939). Aside from his sexual desire, I wonder if my dad said that he was willing to have several children to please my mother or if he wanted the large family he never had. My mother commented on "Five Little Cribs" one more time, thanking my dad for his obliging offer to father her numerous children, but leaving any related discussion for a later date (January 16, 1939).

My mother changed and matured during the war years. The letters served as the courtship before their wedding. She went from a young ingénue, writing with grade school cursive to accepting marriage and welcoming the idea of having a family. For me, the experience of reading her letters and writing about her has had an impact as well. I have reevaluated aspects of our relationship as I discovered traits about her personality. Like any mother-daughter relationship, we had our differences. Growing up I felt that she favored my brother, who was the first-born and a son, something very important in the Spain I grew up in. I remember hearing repeatedly how my brother and I were twenty months apart, meaning that I came very soon after him. Probably the pregnancy was not planned, but I do not want to suggest that I was in any way unwanted. Having the "parejita" (the little couple), a boy and a girl was a common ideal family then.

Unfortunately, there are no photographs of my mother with me as a baby, yet there are many of her with my brother. This is something that bothered me from the time I could ask about the situation. I was told that my parents did not own a camera and borrowed one from Uncle Miguel when my brother was born. By the time I came into the picture, so to speak, my father was not on speaking terms with his relatives and this is the reason no pictures of the new baby exist. This is a plausible explanation, since I saw my dad argue and break up with family members and friends all his life, including my brother and me when we were adults. I have a formal studio photograph of my beautiful mother flanked by her two serious and impeccable children. I also have one single picture of baby Conchín being kissed by my brother in my parents' dining room. My father's arm is visible in a corner holding me in place. In the pictures of my mother with my brother she is radiant, often wearing the same white coat she wore on her wedding day and her long hair held in a net in a *maja*-like style.

Alison Bechdel in her bestseller graphic memoir, *Are You My Mother? A Comic Drama*, also had to grapple with her relationship with her mother. She based her findings on the ideas of Donald Winnicott, the English psychoanalyst who, in his studies about mothers and their babies, concluded that a mother only needed to be "good enough" to instill a sense of security in her child, holding her baby being central to the bonding of mother and child (61). I wish I had a picture of my mother holding me in her arms, but I do not. After pestering my entire family for photos to no avail, I had to refer to anecdotes to reach the conclusion that my mother had indeed been good enough and then some. I had to create my own narrative of my mother with me as a baby; I am not a writer for nothing. As Alison Bechdel has said: "The writer's business is to find the shape in unruly life and to serve her story. Not, you may note, to serve her family, or to serve the truth, but to serve the story" (283).

My mother breastfed both my brother and me as was the custom in 1940s Spain. My favorite anecdote is that as a toddler, when I could barely walk and started talking, I would go to my mother no matter who was at home, asking her for "el postre" (the dessert) and she would oblige to the merriment of my entire family. I do not remember doing this, of course, but to my embarrassment, I grew up hearing this story until recently when I realized that it gave me a clue about my mother as a mother. Like my two daughters, I was an early talker. I must have been close to two years old when I went to my mother asking for her milk. I was a small baby with delicate health and frequent earaches. I remember my mother telling me that she continued to breastfeed me almost until I started kindergarten. I assume that my mother was surprised when she found out she was pregnant with me. She probably believed the myth that she could not become pregnant as long as she was breastfeeding her son. She must have been crazy over my brother, but I came along when he was only twenty months old and claimed my dutiful place within the family. He was the one who was left without his dessert!

Looking back, I can see that I learned how to be a mother under my mother's wing. I keep house like she did, I share a lot of the same values, and I have her double-edged humor. I wonder what she would think if she could see me now with my daughters, whom she barely got to know, and my three beautiful grandchildren who have her wavy, beautiful hair. She would love that they call me Mare, Valencian for mother. I think she would be proud of me and of my professional and personal life. She would be sad that I am a widow and that I had to endure a similar situation as hers with an unfaithful husband. I would have to tell her not to worry, that I do not even have to wear black. My mother reflected about widowhood in one of her letters. When her Uncle Rafael died, she felt great sympathy for her Aunt Amparo, commenting how she never wanted to be in her place, without a spouse, because the person left behind is the one who suffers the most (December 27, 1937). I am thankful she did not have to experience that.

I think my mother would be happy that I am writing about her and setting the record straight, not just for her, but for all the women who, like she did, grew up liberated, although they may not have called themselves feminists. In fact, I should point out that my mother's youngest sister, Fina, barely mentioned in the letters as a funny, tall teenager, also died in 1975, the same year as Franco and my mother, when she was only fifty years old. The women of their generation had to buckle down under their husbands and a repressive society during nearly forty years of Franco's dictatorship. María del Carmen García-Nieto explains: "It was a legislation obviously patriarchal, marital and discriminatory that relegated women to the private and domestic sphere." (663). García-Nieto states that 30,000 Republican women were arrested and about one thousand executed at the end of the war (664). Having worked for the Republican Government during the war, my mother must have been worried about her own situation; undoubtedly, the societal repression weighed on her to the point of not speaking in her beloved Valencian language.

If, as we have seen in an earlier chapter, my parents saw themselves reflected in literary characters, it is important to remember that my dad may have been like Sinclair Lewis' Martin Arrowsmith; quick to fall in love and eager to marry, but his real passion was his thirst for knowledge and, ultimately, his academic career. While my mother's favorite book, on the other hand, was *La esfinge maragata* (The Maragata Sphinx) by Concha Espina, which depicts the life of Mariflor, a feminist young woman ahead of her time interested in women's issues and fighting for her vindication. Mariflor believed in a woman's free will to decide for herself, without a man in her life. But, like Iker Gónzalez-Allende has said, Concha Espina in later works supported the ideals of the Falange, as it happened to other women of her generation and my mother's generation, because it promised order and social harmony, sublimating women as mothers and perpetuators of the human race (529).

Y ahora vuelvo a lo mío. Me acabo de creerme que te copiaban hasta ganas de llorar y todo porque a la salida del trabajo te acompañara tu hermano en vez de acompañarte yo. Esto es jabón también. (Entre paréntesis te diré que aunque con esa duda, y sólo de pensar que pueda ser verdad se me inunda el alma de gozo). - Pero aún en el supuesto de que no me engañes no haces nada de más: te quiero con una intensidad que no me creía capaz de alcanzar nunca. - De tanto mirarlo casi me he comido con los ojos tu retrato. - Y consta que aquí hay andaluzas para recrear la vista: me explico que San Juan fuese andaluz, porque aquí ser Juan es fácil. —

Mucho cuidado con los bombardeos aunque el Ministerio sea refugio. - Aquí

Recognizing My Father

Although I have focused on my mother, my father's charismatic personality has come through in their letters to each other. When I found them before the symposium marking the centenary of his birth, I wrote only about my dad. My essay at that time was titled "La redención del Don Juan" (The Don Juan Redemption). I analyzed then how my dad, like the Don Juan character in Spanish literature, redeemed himself through my mother's love. It is clear that my parents had talked about this libertine protagonist because there are several references to him in their letters. For example, my mother's family called her Doña Inés, who was Don Juan's lover and savior. My mother did not deny her role and wrote to my dad: "They make fun of me and call me Inés. I don't pay attention to them because my Don Juan deserves this and a lot more" (July 13, 1937). On several occasions she signed off with the literary character's name: "Until tomorrow Juan, your Inés who doesn't forget you" (November 3, 1937) and: "Well, Don Juan, your Inés takes an exit backstage. Not without notifying you one more time that she loves you with all her soul" (March 5, 1938). Her clever use of the theatrical term here served as a reminder that my parents had met at a party of the theater group she used to belong to and that she enjoyed the theater.

My father is even more direct in his references to Don Juan. In his letter of September 21–22, 1937, he wrote:

I love you with such intensity that I never thought I was capable of reaching. I have almost eaten your portrait with my eyes because I've been looking at it so much. Even though there are Andalusian women here to pleasure one's view; I understand why Don Juan was from Andalusia, because here Doña Inés is easy.

My dad was referring to the romantic play by José Zorrila, *Don Juan Tenorio* (1844), where the protagonist is from Seville and is in love with the virtuous Doña Inés. On another occasion, when my mother was making plans for my father to enroll at the university, he went so far as to quote the iconic words from the original Golden Age play by Tirso de Molina, *El burlador de Sevilla*, 1630, (The Trickster from Seville): "Tan largo me lo fiáis," loosely translated as "I'll believe it when I see it" (October 4–5, 1937). Leave it to my father to traverse easily between plays two hundred years apart.

Given my father's knowledge of Spanish literature, I do not think that it is a coincidence that some verses he quoted by Gabriel y Galán in a letter belong to a long poem also titled "Un Don Juan," 1902, (A Don Juan), (September 30–October 1, 1937). I would not be surprised if my father knew the entire poem by heart — despite the fact that it contains thirty stanzas. I do not remember hearing him recite this particular poem as a child, but he knew many and would readily oblige. "Un Don Juan" is also funny; more than a love poem, it tells in very expressive language the story of a young man who does not dare tell his beloved that he is in love and wants to marry her. My father was the exact opposite, but I can imagine him reciting this poem to my smitten mother. She used to tell me that one of the reasons she fell in love with him was in part because he made her laugh.

Knowing my father, it is very possible to see him switching from the serious to the farcical in his letters, he was always a paradoxical man par excellence. On a winter night on the Southern Front, he was complaining about the cold, because houses in Andalusia were open and drafty. Therefore, he decided to go to bed early; he excused himself from writing to his beloved in this lyrical and original way:

> This decision was almost an act of love . . . I thought that in a warmer ambiance I could better think about you and, although they were not written, the remembrances of you would be more fervent. In addition, I wanted to dream awake for a while and downstairs even my dreams were in danger to become frozen. To avoid this mishap, I took them to bed and there, with my eyes closed, with the light off, I wandered through an illusionary kingdom while the mountain wind was blowing through the streets (December 5–6, 1937).

90

My mother was well aware of my father's charm with the ladies; she warned him not to brag about being a seducer (July 17, 1937) and when their friend, Ferreres, told her that my dad was flirting with the southern women, she let him know in no uncertain terms that she was popular with men as well: "The guys here are very nice to 'chatitas' like me" (August 15, 1937). The interesting thing is that my dad did not deny his actions; he was sorry only because Ferreres had ratted on him. According to Julio Barcos, part of the liberal mores of the Republic was that there was "one and the same moral for both genders" with: "Chaste women for chaste men, or free women for free men, but never chaste women for libertine men" (Quoted in *Textos para la historia de las mujeres en España*. Texts for the History of Women in Spain, 375). My mother abided by the "rules" of the times. For instance, when my father recommended that she wear some lip balm that stayed on even while kissing, she told him to go ahead and try it, and she would do the same. She then answered him with one of her clever sayings that he should have as much fun as he wanted and that she would have the same right: "Las pintan calvas" (They are painted bald), which makes no sense at all in English, but means that it is the perfect occasion to do something (January 9, 1938). Not to leave any stone unturned, my mother warned my dad again that if he ever betrayed her, she would never forgive him (March 18, 1938), something that would prove to be prophetical.

The Don Juan motif had legs and it continued throughout their letters. My mother remembered that my dad told her that "to conquer a woman more than anything else, it's necessary to lie a lot . . . his luck is that she had already been conquered by him" (March 25, 1938). However, she did not believe him when he told her that even if she became a little old lady all of a sudden, he would love her the same; she asked him to forgive her for not believing such a beautiful lie (September 26, 1938). In the same letter, she suggested that he grow a mustache because she had seen his "double" and he looked great with a mustache. Since she could not see him, a few days later, she insisted, asking: "Are you letting your mustache grow? It looked great on your dad" (September 30, 1938). In one of her last letters, she told my dad how happy she was he had grown a mustache and that she could not wait to see it (March 17, 1939). My father would sport a chic mustache on his wedding day and for the rest of his life. My mother also wanted my dad to cut his sideburns in a fashionable way, but did not like it when he had his head shaved and called him "feote peloncho" (big ugly bald guy, July 9, 1937). This made me laugh because my first husband arrived with his hair shaved for our wedding in Madrid in December 1964 and it caused all kinds of amusement, despite the fact that he was wearing his formal Marine uniform. I had to explain that the haircut was part of his officer's training. At that time in Spain, men only shaved their head in case of a serious contagious illness like typhus or tuberculosis.

Both of my parents, my father in particular, had very strong views as to each other's physical appearance, which is related to their concept of seduction. He was particularly obsessed with my mother's long hair and did not like it when she got a perm or cut her hair short. She was aware of her power as a seductress, describing how beautiful her hair looked (December 29, 1938), and mentioning the articles of clothing she was wearing in great detail (December 4, 1938). She also promised him that she would not wear earrings or high heels until he returned (February 22, 1938). I assume in order not to appear too attractive to other men, since he warned her that if any man got too close to her, he would scare them away with his rifle " . . . because to love too much and not to eat enough are two things that make one lose their mind, and if they are both together like here now, even more" (September 6–7, 1937). Nevertheless, in the letters there was no mention whatsoever about their bodies or any explicit sexual innuendos.

In José Zorrila's version of the classic play, Don Juan Tenorio, as it befits a romantic hero, is saved by Doña Inés' love. He is redeemed by her purity and good deeds and his soul rises to the heavens in an apotheosis of love in the last act. I would argue that my father's love letters redeemed him as well. Not only was he so in love with my mother and his letters were so beautiful and heartfelt, but the fact that he knew himself so well redeemed him; it is not as if he were trying to deceive her. Early on he told my mother: "Perhaps because of my essentially anti-lyric personality, a bit dry, more apt to hurt than to praise, I will not be able to give you an approximate idea of the depth of my love for you" (June 16, 1937). He told her on another occasion:

> I was telling you in this morning's letter that I find myself somewhat
> sad and worried by this absence that promises to be long. My suspi-

92

cious and pessimist personality that you were beginning to change, without even noticing it, is coming through again for my torment. I continue to be afraid that if a lot of time goes by without seeing each other you will get used to being without me and will forget me little by little. (July 18, 1937)

Even if I did not know my mother at all, as a reader of these letters I would need to ask myself: If someone as loving and generous as her was in love with my dad, what did she see in him that the rest of us mortals did not see? In the same letter, quoted above, my father tells my mother that she has "an excellent personality, ductile and tender." My mother's love, just like Doña Inés' did, redeem her Don Juan, indeed. She really was my father's salvation, his dream, his hope, and his greatest conquest.

The experience of reading my father's letters has been different from reading my mother's. If she surprised me constantly, I recognized my dad, just the way I remember him in his long life. I recognized his humor, his repetitious and preachy style, his passionate and obsessive nature, his unequivocal opinions. It is as if at twenty-three years of age he was already the man he would become. We know that he had been sent to study at the Jesuit Seminary after his father died. His Uncle Miguel was his guardian who provided for him financially. When my dad realized that he did not have a calling for the priesthood and left the seminary, he had acquired an extensive education, particularly in the classics. He enrolled at the University of Valencia in what was called "free enrollment," which meant that he studied on his own, without attending classes, and took exams to pass the courses. As soon as the war ended, he was able to finish the few courses he had left and went on to receive his Ph.D. with a major in History. He started his academic career teaching Latin in private schools. I remember hearing about the Academia Martí in Valencia, one of his first jobs. University positions at that time were announced officially and anyone with the right credentials could apply, take the exams and the candidate with the best grades would attain the position. Soon my father had an appointment at the University of Valencia teaching World History and his first publications were in that field. (See Bibliography).

Aside from his literary knowledge, from his book lists in the letters we saw that he was interested in philosophy, psychology, and the sciences. In one of his last letters he wrote that he was translating a French novel (March 21, 1939). At one point we find out that he was also learning English, a language he never mastered: " . . . laying under the olive trees, we study the grammar. When I learn some more English and change my station a couple more times, I will be the perfect tourist" (September 28–29, 1937). I wonder if he was already thinking about a possible future life in the American Midwest as per his idol, Martin Arrowsmith. He also taught algebra to a comrade who was teaching him to swim in exchange, another one of his weak points (September 26, 1938).

Despite the relevance of my father's academic works, I always suspected that one of the frustrations of his life was that he did not write fiction. It is worth noting that he told my mother about his plans of doing so when she complained that her brother, Pepe, had tricked her into believing that my dad was coming home for a visit that very afternoon:

> We will give your brother his due when I get a hold of him. I promise you to give him the role of "traitor" in the first novel I write, he doesn't deserve less. Don't tell him, so that the punishment will surprise him. What you should tell him is that "he who laughs last laughs best" and it will be me with you. (September 8, 1937)

Notice the popular saying and that he considered his future possible writing as revenge. I wrote about my father as a Don Juan character in several of my works of fiction, and he did not seem to mind. On the contrary, after my mother died, he told me of some adventures I had not heard yet, urging me to take notes and write about them and, as I have already mentioned, his only request was that I use his real name, Juan Luis, and not José Luis, as I had done in my books. Perhaps my dad never told me about these hidden letters because he feared, without reason, that I would follow suit and commit revenge in my writing.

One of my father's passions was food. In that sense my parents were a perfect match; she was a great cook and he was her best dinner guest. Not surprisingly my father often mentioned food or the lack of it in his letters. He raved, for example, about the melons and grapes, typical of Valdepeñas, where he could eat right from the abandoned vineyards and fields (August 21, 1937). This is one of the instances where I recognize my father. I remember very well that he could choose the best melons, while my mother often brought home melons that, according to him, tasted more like cucumbers. I guess all those summers that my father spent in Salem, the small town in the countryside, with his paternal family, paid off. My mother was a city girl who loved the cinema and the beach, no melons there. In my home growing up, part of the ritual of eating a melon was to cut it perfectly. My father had beautiful, large hands and he could cut a melon, holding it upright with his left hand, no matter its size, and slice it with his right hand, without dropping a single slice. He could also peel apples and oranges all in one perfect round piece, without breaking it. As a little girl I thought he was magical!

To a certain degree the soldiers on the Southern Front suffered fewer food shortages than the civilian population in cities like Valencia. They were allowed to stay with local families and in some instances, as in my father's case, they could supplement the rations being served in the barracks. A meal outside the barracks cost three pesetas, including the wine and melon or watermelon. It is worth noting the kindness of strangers in times of war. Nevertheless, my dad complained regularly about the food:

> Food is like a white blackbird; everyone talks about it but no one sees it. We continue with the 'integral rations' because it is impossible to purchase anything in the market. Our host has offered several times to cook something for us, at least as a complement to the food in the barracks, but we haven't accepted because we don't want to take advantage of her. (September 30, 1937)

As in Valencia, where my mother had not eaten an egg in months, my dad beamed with joy when he accepted two fried eggs: "The rations are more tiresome than a courtesy call and they go all the way down to your feet at express velocity" (January 5, 1938). At one point my dad said that they were eating donkey meat, but no one worried about that anymore, since the lady of the house could disguise it perfectly. His humor came through as usual: "Here the famous saying 'even if the girl monkey dresses up in silk, she is still a monkey,' fails because from the kitchen the donkey comes out like a bull and even a bull with horns if one wishes to" (January 26, 1938).

When my father was not feeling well, the lady of the house made him a soup with some kind of bird he thought could be a thrush and even brought him coffee with milk to bed — one more instance of his country upbringing that he could tell what kind of bird he was eating. Some of his analogies were funny and food related: "The owner is a discreet and serious woman, she is as different from Carmen [a prior host] as a turnip from a chestnut" (January 10, 1938). Local men cooked for the soldiers, making them "migas" a typical dish of the Murcia region made from leftover bread cooked with garlic, something my dad had never tasted before and learned to appreciate during the war (January 11, 1938).

In addition to my father's intellectual ability, he was also physically fit and took pride in being strong and agile. He liked playing soccer, bike riding and excelled at Spanish "jai alai," a hardball game similar to racquet ball. During the war, he asked his family to send him his ball and glove, although he had promised my mother that he would not play, she found out and admonished him: "Your iron will is weakening, you told me that you wouldn't play for my peace of mind but 'no way'" (February 22, 1938). Interestingly enough, when I mentioned this to Jane, my youngest daughter, she asked me to add that my grandson is a terrific baseball player and that he does not go anywhere without his ball and glove. Interesting indeed, usually my daughters are mortified by my memoir writing! True to form, on the front my father also enjoyed cutting wood, which was necessary for cooking and heating in the towns where he was stationed: "With the woodcutter exercise I keep the cold at bay, my appetite grows and I take advantage of down time as I deserve. Besides, I acquire strength and health: I have turned myself into a colossus, cutie. You will see when I get to hug you" (January 27, 1938). How could my mother not fall in love with such a Titan of a man?

It seems that my father was already a smoker during the war, something he did for the rest of his life, even though he was diagnosed with emphysema when we emigrated to the United States. For some years, he switched to pipes and settled on cigars that defined the tell-tale odor of his home in Bloomington, Indiana. I could smell him on my clothes for days after each visit. During the war, while he was in Arjonilla, he made fast friends with the local school teacher who "has a glass of wine easy to drink" and the pharmacist "who has tobacco when no one else does" (January 5, 1938).

Surprisingly, my mother, who was so easily bothered by strong odors all her life, did not seem to mind my father smoking and on at least one occasion sent him cigarettes. Of course, her practical and healthy side was evident when she sent him a toothbrush, bicarbonate of soda and some hazelnuts (January 17, 1938)

It is remarkable that there was so little information about the war and nothing about politics in my father's letters. Undoubtedly, he was concerned about censorship and although he was at the front, he might not have been aware of the specific advancements of the Nationalist forces. My mother listened to the evening reports on the radio, and there was mention that my father could do that too. Gamel Woolsey in her book *Málaga Burning*, stated that: "Radio in time of war becomes absolutely fascinating. The Pronouncements, denials, alarms, rumors, propaganda, speeches of national leaders make it enthralling to the listener who is at all emotionally involved" (50). We know that in July of 1937, my dad started his deployment to Valdepeñas, close to Jaén, on the Southern Front, and from there he moved north to Andújar, Arjona and Arjonilla. He was very lucky that the big battles of the war, like Teruel or the ones by the Ebro River, were not fought near there. By the end of the war in March of 1939, he was in Utiel, close to Valencia. Although speaking Valencian after the war was definitely an act of defiance, during the war he seemed to be almost apolitical. His letters were essentially love letters to my mother with existential analyses of the futility of war, and no specific information about the battles fought.

Growing up I remember him talking about the war after our meals, at "sobremesa," the time when people in Spain sit leisurely at the table after a meal, while the adults drink their coffee, particularly on Sundays. But his stories were mostly humorous and had to do with food or the lack of it. The only time I remember him mentioning Franco was when he used to imitate the high-pitched dictator's voice and would repeat his first words on National Radio on April 1, 1939, making us laugh: "La Guerra ha terminado" (The War has ended) and then my father would add something like: "Don't let him fool you, the war has not ended yet." Of course, this was literally true of people like my mother's two siblings, Pepe and Vicente, who had to reenlist again during Franco's regime.

Diana, my oldest daughter, remembers that on one of our trips to Spain, my father, Abuelito as she called him, acquiesced to take

her to El Valle de los Caídos (The Valley of the Fallen), the spectac-
ular mausoleum on the outskirts of El Escorial where Franco was
buried, but gave her a big lecture as to the monstrosity of the place.
Noël Valis agrees with my dad when she states: "Franco's obsession
with past imperial greatness led him to emulate Philip II in the
building of his own mausoleum as a second Escorial" ("Civil War
Ghosts Entombed: Lessons of the Valley of the Fallen," 432). My
father would be glad to hear that now the current Socialist government in Spain is trying to finally exhume Franco's body and move
it somewhere else, even if it has been over forty years since the
dictator's death. As my father would say: "Nunca es tarde si la dicha
es buena" (It's never too late if it's good news).

On the surface I seem to be more like my father. I have his
coloring, his energy and his curiosity. I am tall and slim like he was;
I stayed permanently in the United States, as he did, and followed
in his footsteps career-wise. But I am a feminist and I took every
chance possible to remind him of that and to point out that he did
not include many women writers in his books about Spanish literature. I stopped short of calling him a misogynist, but I was aware
of his paternalistic attitude toward my mother and me, and women
in general. After my mother died, I conscientiously stayed in touch
with my dad, despite the fact that I found out about his affair with
my Aunt Conchita, Uncle Vicente's wife, the day of my mother's
funeral in Madrid.

Valencia 11 Septiembre 1938.

Queridísimo feo:

Son las seis y
media de la tarde. No he tenido carta.
No he salido ni a la puerta de la esca-
lera. No tengo ganas de salir tampoco.
No quisiera otra cosa que te estuvieras
aquí a mi lado. Te escribo en la ha-
bitación de mi hermano Pepe. Mis
tíos mis primos y mis hermanas Mari
y Amparo todos están en la galería
jugando al "parchís". Mi mamá en
teléfonos, mi papá en el trinquete (como
si lo viera) y Doro está bajo, con unos
amigos, jugando, lo oigo desde aquí. Fin
no sé. Hasta pues, la cuenta que estás

Family Matters

With regard to my parents' family background, they could not have been more different. My mother had a large family and was very close to her six siblings. Her letters are full of information about them, showing her love and concern, almost as if she were a second mother to them. My father, on the other hand, having lost his mother as an infant and his father at fifteen years of age, always felt like an orphan, despite the fact that he had several relatives who cared about him very much, such as his two aunts, Isabel and Vicenta. He was only close to his sister Teresa, born from my paternal grandfather's second marriage. We already know that my dad did not get along with his stepmother, also named Teresa, although there is considerable evidence in my mother's letters that she cared for him deeply, something that my father never felt.

Learning about my mother's side of the family has been one of the most rewarding aspects of reading these letters for me. Since we moved to Madrid when I was seven years old, I did not get to know my maternal relatives very well, with the exception of Pepe and his wife Elena, who followed us to Madrid in the fifties. My mother's frequent use of endearing diminutives — "Finita, Salvadorín and Tonín" — showed my mother's fondness for her siblings, although taking care of them alone proved to be a lot for her when she was in Llombay and my dad had to bring Salvador back to Valencia after one of his visits. Surprisingly, my dad wrote some nice comments about his future brother-in-law: "Your brother Salvador acted like a grown man the entire trip: he made a thousand touristic comments about the road and as many about the beauty of the chalets we went by; undoubtedly, he would love to own one" (June 22, 1937). Amazing that the "grown man" was all of nine years old.

My parents' first letters dated from those few weeks of separation in the summer of 1937 showed clearly the closeness of my mother's family. Taking advantage of the fact that my grandmother worked for Telefónica, they spoke every day while my mother was in Llombay. It seems that my grandmother was the disciplinarian in the family and, on a few occasions, my mother mentioned that she was arguing with her, which is surprising to me. Even so, when my mother was in trouble, it was usually because she was defending her sisters: "I wanted to get in the middle, so she wouldn't scold them, especially Amparín, and there it was Troy. The outcome was that the scolding that should have been for the young girls went to the 'big one'" (October, 20, 1937).

My mother had a special relationship with each of her siblings. Amparo, for example, is the one who cut the jasmine flowers for my mother to enclose in her letters, showing that way her sister's fondness for my dad. My mother and Amparo slept in the same bed, but there was not a single complaint in all the letters about this situation. I am not sure why there was a short time when Amparo was sent away with some relatives, possibly to make things easier at home in Valencia. In any case, my mother seemed very relieved when Amparo came back and immediately made plans to go with her to the beach: "My sister Amparín is with us, I believe indefinitely. She and Fina will come to be mermaids (and not of the strident kind)" (July 19, 1937). I also found out that Amparo broke her nose accidentally and never properly healed, which gave her face a strange look, particularly in comparison to the other good-looking siblings; this is the way I remember my aunt as well. This misfortune would explain my mother's defense of this sister in particular. Tonín was also sent away to stay with relatives for the summer months before he was to start school (October 31, 1937). My grandparents were concerned with their children's safety and most likely their financial situation. Certainly, lack of food was also a factor for sending the children to be with relatives temporarily during the war.

There was a brief mention that some relatives left for France and my mother went to see them off at the train station (October 12, 1937), but my Aunt Amparo was the only sibling who emigrated to France after the war. The immense number of Spaniards who left during the war or were exiled immediately after was one of the direst consequences of the Spanish Civil War. Omar Encarnación estimates that half a million people "were forced into exile" (3) and Enrique Moradiellos states that the largest number was exiled in France, with Toulouse being the unofficial "capital" of the

Spanish exile (456). Amparo is the only surviving sibling of the Carles family; she still lives in Carcassonne, near Toulouse in Southern France. Unfortunately, I have not been able to communicate with her because she is in very frail health at ninety-six years of age.

I think my Uncle Pepe was always my mother's favorite. They were the two oldest, close in age, and had very similar personalities; they were both caring, sage beyond their years, and somewhat reserved. It showed that the feeling was mutual when my uncle called my mother "unforgettable" in one of his letters and she planned to answer him immediately: " . . . otherwise I wouldn't hear from him until the next visit and I don't want that to happen, I love him so much . . . " (April 12, 1938). Pepe was my godfather, although I felt closer to my Aunt Elena, his wife, than to him and she was the person who took my mother's role when she died, sharing recipes and family secrets with me during my customary visits to Madrid. My mother was always very fond of her sister-in-law: "I love my future sister-in-law as if she were already [my relative]. I don't tell you that I love my brother because it is obvious, and it is very natural, no?" (February 20, 1938). In her letters my mother always mentioned Pepe, giving the latest news about his deployment. He was stationed close to Valencia and was able to visit frequently, which made my mother envious since my dad was not as lucky. There is a touching family scene during one of his visits:

> My brother and his girlfriend were lost for a couple of hours (at least) from the sight of their companions. Yesterday and today everyone is commenting about the happy mortals. Our friend Dionisio made the rice, my brother Vicente was the helper, Amparín was the sous-chef. As you can see the "couple" was well served. When the meal was ready, it coincided with the reappearance of the lovers (what a coincidence!). (October 12, 1937)

Pepe and Elena would go on to have the longest marriage of all the siblings; they were really an exemplary couple, loving and faithful to the very end, truly enviable, indeed.

Vicente, the next oldest, was the one who brought ink, envelopes and paper from his office for my mother to write her letters. When he was also drafted, as part of the "baby bottle brigade," my mother was devastated:

Believe me that this brother of mine is the one who worries me the most now, because neither you nor my Pepín are in such danger as him. When I think that something could happen to him I get sick. My mother doesn't know that there are some soldiers wounded in my Vicente's brigade, as I told you. If she were to find out . . . (June 6, 1938)

Vicente went on to marry my Aunt Conchita, the woman who had the affair with my father, breaking up the relationship between the Alborg and Carles families forever, after my mother's death. Why would my dad get involved with a sister-in-law, knowing how close the siblings were and what a turmoil it would cause, and with another Conchita no less? I'll never know. Not meaning to assume the role of the psychologist as my mother would have done, we could at least ask, as she did on another occasion: "What would Freud say?" (October 2, 1937). Fortunately, after many years of estrangement, I have become close with my cousin Inma, Aunt Conchita and Vicente's daughter, and we have laughed and cried together about our parents' story, but that is fodder for another memoir. I owe her thanks for some of the photographs included in this book.

My mother bragged to my dad about her sisters, Fina and Amparo, saying that they were becoming so beautiful and what a good appetite they had: "They wolf down such horse steaks that I fear they will start kicking any day" (December 20, 1937). Since getting enough to eat was such a concern, in this particular letter my mother mentioned what each sister weighed and how Finita was growing so tall; supposedly, I resemble my Aunt Fina. Salvador seemed to be the most rebellious one. He stayed out late one evening, past 10 p.m., and my grandfather gave him a spanking: "To make matters worse, there was also an air raid alarm. Outcome: between the airplanes and Doro, my mother got sick again and I am scared to death" (August, 24, 1937). This is the only time that such disciplining was mentioned. I always suspected that my mother was uncomfortable with my father's ruthless and physical way of disciplining my brother and me when we were young. It is obvious in the letters that this did not happen in my mother's family. It is noteworthy that my grandparents were looking for a better school for Doro who was nine at the time (October 31, 1937). There was only a brief mention that the two younger sisters were also attending school during those war years (February 17, 1939).

I believe that my dad felt envious of my mother's siblings and all the attention she bestowed on them. My uncles were all very handsome, with full heads of wavy hair until their old age. I remember my father admitting that they were handsome, but making fun of them and saying that they had such large heads. My mother defended them saying that they did not have large heads, that their heads seemed large because they had lots of hair, unlike my dad who became bald at an early age. Hair was an important element of the Carles mystique. It was always puzzling to me that I inherited my "pelo agradecido" (grateful hair) from my mother.

It doesn't matter how many years I have lived in the United States and how well I can understand English, but grateful hair is untranslatable. It is not that my hair is curly, but it definitely is not straight. It is sort of wavy, although that is not it either, since we have a perfect word for wavy in Spanish, "ondulado." Grateful hair lets you do whatever you want with it. The more humid the weather, the curlier it gets. That is how it looks when I visit Valencia, going back to its natural habitat, so to speak. Interestingly, my hair is only straight if I am in Madrid given the high altitude, I guess. My oldest daughter has curly hair and the youngest has the grateful kind; of course, they both wish their hair was straight. My twin granddaughters, who do not look like anyone on my side of the family, are almost identical, blonde and quite tall. But in a friendly wink to genetics, they have my mother's beautiful, grateful hair. They can wear it short or long; they can wear it in a pony-tail or any other up-do such as a French braid or a bun for their dance classes. My mother would have been smitten with them, as I am. When I look at them, I finally understand that having grateful hair is something to be thankful for.

My mother's relationship with her dad, who also had the trademark Carles hairline, was always a loving one. He protected her and did not allow her to visit my father on the front, telling her that my dad should be thankful that he was saving "su encantador pellejo" (her lovely skin) by not allowing her to go in such precarious circumstances (December 8, 1937). My grandfather also read the books that my mother was purchasing for my dad and, on some occasions, she brought books from my dad's room for him to read as well. I have a picture-postcard of my grandfather dated

December 7, 1922, written in Madrid, for my six-year-old mother on her Saint's Day. On the front it simply says: "To my very dear daughter Conchín on her Saint's Day," but on the back he went on to give her "a thousand kisses," asking her Aunt Pilar to write for her, closing with some words that I never heard from my father: "Your dad who loves you so much, content, happy, and thankful." I see that my grandfather had the same small, thin nose as my mother. The photo was taken in a photographer's studio in the iconic Puerta del Sol in Madrid. Perhaps his young family stayed back in Valencia when he was working in Madrid for a short time, although I have described a picture of my mother at about the same age with Pepe and Vicente possibly in front of El Retiro Park in Madrid, but they could have been visiting their dad and not living there.

My mother's family was boisterous and liked to play jokes on each other; she described it as being: "Chungona por excelencia" (Jokesters par excellence, September 23, 1937). This was something that my dad, despite his keen sense of humor, did not appreciate. I love my mother's descriptions of the times her family gathered together. On a summer day, after having been at the beach, they brought ice cream home and then they all sang and danced, except my mother who was too sad and would rather write to my dad (July 25, 1937). On another occasion, she was waiting for everyone to go to bed so she could write in peace. She wrote: "My aunt has taken out the Parcheesi board and is going to play with my sisters. My mother is reading the newspaper (one has to be educated) and my father is talking about the war with Vicente . . . it's the same theme almost every evening" (April 11, 1938). On a winter Sunday evening, my mother had made dinner while her father, an aunt who also lived with them, and Salvador were playing Parcheesi. Toni was sleeping and the two girls, Fina and Amparo, were out taking a walk. My mother was in her aunt's room writing to my dad because her own room was too far away: "It is so comfortable in this room, it invites me to talk with you" (December 20, 1937).

My mother's room was very cold because it faced the north side of the street. I remember my grandparents' house and I know that they did not have central heat. In winter, usually there was a "brasero" (a coal room heater) in the dining room, but the rest of the house was cold and damp. No wonder they all liked to sit together in the same room! Manuel Azcárate says in his memoir of the Spanish Civil War that the winter of 1938 was the coldest on record and "the cold was the biggest enemy" of the people (143). It even snowed in Valencia, something unheard of (January 5, 1938). My mother complained of the cold in her entire letter of December 26, 1938: "It is brutally cold; I'm going to bed as soon as I write you a few words . . . Well, I can't write anymore because I can't feel my hands, I'm frozen from head to toe."

Regardless of the weather, it was obvious that my mother's family got along well and loved doing things together. Despite the fact that my mother complained about how loud they were and how she needed peace and quiet to write, writing that they were making "una algarabía" (a racket, July 20, 1937), she loved being surrounded by her family and wished that my father could be there and be part of her family as well. It is surprising how much company they often had, and this was during wartime. Most days there were at least eleven people at the table, three times a day. Imagine what it must have been like to feed them all as scarce as food was, doing all those dishes in cold water and without a dishwasher. When I was growing up in Madrid, my parents had lots of friends and writers over in the evenings for literary discussions. It makes me happy to think that my mother must have been instrumental in creating an open-door policy similar to the way she grew up in Valencia.

I had to smile when my mother described family routines that I practice to this day in my home; "airear la casa" (to air the house), particularly when someone was sick, is one of them. Towards the end of the war my mother became sick again and had to stay home from work, she wrote: "This morning I got up while they were changing my bed and I was on the back porch sitting in the sun. If it wasn't because my doctor is as dramatic as you, I wouldn't have gotten back in bed. I obeyed him even though I was better off in the sun" (February 17, 1939). When my mother's family had to heed the air raid alarms, they did it as a well-organized unit. On a peaceful afternoon, when my mother was writing and my grand-mother was fidgeting in the dining room, the alarm sounded and my mother described what everyone did: Amparín was the most fearful and remained close to Fina, Doro and her father stayed home together, my mother put all kinds of warm clothing on top of her nightgown and went down to the shelter, something she did not do at the beginning of the war (February 17, 1939). This letter was remarkable, as were many others, in that my mother managed to mention every member of the family in it.

My father's superior attitude toward family matters contrasted sharply with my mother's dedication to her family:

> One should always look at things from above, since the measure of every one depends on the things on which they occupy themselves. An elephant walking at night in the jungle is not bothered by the nettles that would hurt some small and delicate feet. I always looked from up to down, with certain Olympic disdain for the family hogwash that preoccupies others who don't have anything else to think about. That's why I have seemed unpleasant perhaps to some people and the truth is that I'm proud of it. (January 27, 1938)

I grew up hearing about recurring conflicts between my dad and his relatives and I commiserated with him about his feelings of rejection and abandonment, which were very real to him. My father did not have an easy childhood studying away at school most of the year, away from his family. He spent summers in Salem, the isolated, ancestral Alborch town that I have already described, with his paternal uncles and aunts. He did not live in Valencia with his half-sister and stepmother until he left the seminary and started his studies at the university. In my father's letter of August 2, 1937, there are some explanations of his on-going frustration with his relatives. According to him, his aunts did not allow him to make his own decisions from the time he was a young boy and that bothered him greatly: "and it would have bothered me even more if it had not been for my hard and decisive character, to send people to hell when it was necessary and many times before then." He also resented his Uncle Miguel's complete authority: "Not to notify my uncle ahead of time [of anything] was like a crime."

My mother was mortified by my father's conflicted attitude with his family and took the role of peacemaker; I witnessed how she tried to implement peace all her life. In her war letters she begged my dad to be nice, to write to his family, telling him that his stepmother loved him, to no avail (July 24, 1937; September 10, 1937; February 20, 1938 . . .). When he was angry with his sister, the one relative he supposedly cared for, my mother told him: "Teresita loves you very much . . . don't have such a hard heart" (January 21, 1938). She told my father that his stepmother cried when he wrote to the family without sending his regards to her or mentioning her name: "This is not dignified of a professor of your stature" (July 28, 1937). My dad was not teaching yet; perhaps he had started to tutor some private students. In any case, even if my mother was projecting onto his future career, it was clear that she did not approve of his critical stance.

My mother was very close to her future sister-in-law Teresa who was four years her junior. They used to see each other every day, whether it was to mail their letters at the Central Post Office, to stand in line for food or to go to an occasional movie, although Teresa had said that she would not go until my father returned, a promise she did not keep. My mother always celebrated Teresa's sunny disposition; they used to "pelar," (gossip) together: "Teresín is very funny when she gossips about her friends . . . (I think that her gossiping is contagious)" (January 24, 1938). I can attest to my Aunt Teresa's good humor. She was my godmother and I stayed at her house during my yearly visits for Las Fallas, the traditional Valencian holidays, when we moved to Madrid. She accompanied me to have my portrait done wearing the regional dress and I faithfully visited her on all my trips from the United States until she died in 2013.

Once my mother had met my dad's stepmother, she started to stop by her house after work and often stayed there for a couple of hours knitting and chatting with her and Teresa. My mother commented to my father how nice they were to her as he was very curious about their blossoming relationship: "I was at your house at least two hours and of course Tere as much as your mom are very loving with me. Is your curiosity satisfied, my love?" (July 15, 1938). In the same letter, my mother wrote that Teresa acted like my dad, talking non-stop, and how she "sang her praises about him."

My mother also stopped by to see my dad's aunts, Isabel and Vicenta, regularly. They had moved to Valencia by that time. They used to live in Salem when my father spent summers with them. They fulfilled the maternal role somewhat, and called my dad "Juanito" since they had taken care of him as a child. They never married and were very funny together, finishing each other's sentences and repeating phrases as in a duet. I remember that they never spoke Spanish, and their Valencian was peculiar and full of expressions that I did not understand. They always lived together with their elderly father, my great-grandfather, who lived to be 103;

his genes must have been the source of my father's longevity. The three of them moved to the house where we lived in Valencia after my family moved to Madrid and I loved visiting them as a young girl and seeing what they had done with our first home, which was not much, since some of our furniture stayed behind because it would not fit in the smaller flat in Madrid. My mother only mentioned the great-grandfather once in her letters: "Your aunt as much as your 'abuelito' gave me their regards" (March 20, 1938). On the same day, Aunt Isabel had finally received a letter from my dad and she was very happy.

Aunt Isabel told my mother that the first thing she did each morning was to think about my dad, wishing that he would be safe: "Your aunt was telling me that when she wakes up at night, the first thing in her imagination is you; you can see that you are present in her mind. You can be proud, so write a few lines to her, 'miquito'" (January 30, 1938). This shows that my father was loved by his family indeed — how he felt is another story, of course. I believe to this day that my father resented his stepmother so much because the person he really missed was his mother, Agustina Escartí. I was supposed to have been named after her and I have a silver baby cup with my name as Conchín Agustina, but that name does not appear on my birth certificate or anywhere else. I like to think that I resemble her, she was taller than my grandfather in her wedding picture and I am still the tallest of my generation in my family.

In my desire to keep my family's history alive, I restored and framed a beautiful formal photograph of my father as an infant with his parents, in his mother's arms (and we know how important that is in terms of Donald Winnicott). This is the only existing picture of the three of them; my Godmother Teresa must have given it to me. Thinking that I was going to give my father a wonderful surprise, I had a copy made for him beautifully framed. I will never forget that when he saw this photograph he broke down and was inconsolable, the one and only time I have ever seen my father cry. Interestingly enough, only a few months ago, when I was finalizing the selection of the family photographs for this book, I paid attention to a photo of my dad playing dominoes with my daughter Diana during one of her last trips to Bloomington. With the magnifying glass I can clearly see that the photograph of my dad as an infant with his parents is in the center of my dad's writing table. I was right to think that my father would have loved it.

Uncle Miguel was my grandfather's brother and he kept the family cheese import business when my grandfather died. He stayed a bachelor and lived with my dad's sister and stepmother — with whom he was supposedly in love. In his role as the patriarch of the family, he managed the purse strings and provided for my father financially. In a family where kissing was not the norm, Uncle Miguel was the most distant of them all. My mother wrote about him in an elegant style, reminiscent of my dad:

> Since your Uncle Rabasa was there, naturally, they were talking about food as it's their custom. I laughed more than once because your Uncle Miguel threw some well-aimed darts to your other uncle, who was lamenting in a sea of complaints and sighs the gastronomical pleasures of yesteryear. I had never seen your Uncle Miguel in that vein and I liked it. (December 11, 1938)

Uncle Miguel had tried for months to get permission to have my father sent back to Valencia from the front lines. As we know, according to the existing Spanish law at that time, the only son of a widow would have a dispensation not to serve and, technically, that was the case with my father. Unfortunately, my Uncle Miguel's efforts were never successful and my dad, did not appreciate it. In fact, he said that it had made his adjustment as a soldier worse:

> I continue awaiting still my dispensation from Valencia. I confess to you that I'm quite disgusted and bored already. If I had the certainty that I'm going to stay here, I would be getting used to it and I would be adapting myself to this life, but the uncertainty of the continuous wait makes my nerves tense at all times. (August 17, 1937)

As the war dragged on, there was also some mention that Uncle Miguel could be called to serve; he must have been well into his forties by then. Luckily, that did not happen as it would have been financially devastating for the family (January 13, 1939). It is interesting to mention that Uncle Miguel reminded my mother of my dad when he said that he would rather be fighting than being stuck in a small town dying of boredom (February 16, 1939). Uncle Miguel would continue to help my father financially and he made it possible for my parents to move to Madrid and purchase a lovely new home right in front of El Retiro Park. One of my father's first books, *Hora actual de la novela española*, 1958 (Present Hour of the Spanish Novel) is dedicated to him with these words: "For Miguel Alborg Vilaplana, for the many reasons that, since he knows them, it is not necessary to name them."

Although my parents' families lived in the same neighborhood in Valencia, the Alborg family was better off financially due mainly to the cheese import business. My Aunt Teresa, for instance, never had to work as my mother did. There were only three or four people to be fed at their home when my father moved in. In fact, the Alborgs owned two flats in the same building, one where they lived and another, on a lower floor, for the business office. My mother mentioned that my Aunt Teresa played the piano and described an endearing scene in their household; no Parcheesi was being played there:

> Your sister played the piano for a while. I danced two waltzes with Carmencita and we 'la-la-la' a bit of what Tere was playing. How I wished I had wings in that moment and be able to fly there and be with you or that you had been able to come, but it wasn't like that. (February 20, 1939)

Supposedly, my father's stepmother was crazy over my brother, her first grandchild — and a boy — and she knitted all kinds of clothing for him. We know that lots of pictures were taken with the borrowed camera of the adorable baby boy with my radiant mother. Before I was born, for a reason I have never been able to discover, my father broke up with his stepmother for several years and thus no pictures of the new baby Conchín exist. In any case, there was a dramatic deathbed scene, which is part of the family lore, when my father was allowed to stop by his stepmother's house to make up with her. But by then I was four or five years old, it was too late to borrow the camera and I was never able to meet my Grandmother Alborg. I have no recollection or memories of her whatsoever other than what is contained in my mother's letters and the stories I have heard from my family. Luckily, I have been able to maintain contact with my father's side of the family through trips from Madrid and also from the United States. Almost all of my cousins have come to Philadelphia to visit their long-lost American expatriate relative. They seem to be eagerly awaiting this memoir. My cousin Juan Miguel Alborg texted me recently with dates I needed to finish this chapter.

tontamente por ahi mejor se está en
la cama.–

    I basta por hoy, queridísima mía.
¡ Qué largo y qué pesado se me hace
el tiempo aguardando el momento feliz
de poder verte para siempre ya ...!

    No me olvides por nada del mundo,
chatírísima.–

    Un fortísimo abrazo de tu

                            Juan

                                    he 55

28 Marzo 1929

Exemplary Letters

In some ways this has been the most difficult chapter to write. After I finished writing the rest of the manuscript, I decided to read the complete letters one more time. It is a daunting task to commit to read over 800 letters again; if I read forty a day, it takes twenty days. I have lost track of how many times I have read them already. My intention has been to choose a few exemplary letters to give the reader as complete a narrative arc as possible, creating a similar feeling to reading the entire treasure-trove — an impossible goal, perhaps. The fact is that I dread the day when I will have to part with these letters and take them to the University of Málaga to join the rest of my father's documents. There, digitized copies will be made available to my brother and me as well as the rest of the family, which is a good thing, but it will not be the same as having this pivotal and evocative part of my parents' life with me, sharing the intimacy that the original letters have brought into my life.

The letters I have chosen are included in chronological order to show the fundamental change of my mother from an insecure young woman, writing in a school-girl calligraphy, to a mature woman ready to enter into marriage with my father. Likewise, he transformed himself from an adventurous student into a committed partner, ready to share his life and have children with her, despite the long separation and the indirect influence of Martin Arrowsmith. Hopefully, these letters will show how my parents mood evolved from frustration at the situation to the deep existential, pessimistic tone of the last months when they feared more than their own survival that they had wasted their youth, not knowing that the end of the war was around the corner.

Surprisingly, I enjoyed reading the letters even more this last time. It was as if I were saying good-bye to my parents, thanking them for saving these letters, aware of the immense gift I was fortuitously granted. I laughed and I cried again, sometimes at different

115

situations than I had before. I laughed when my dad described that his legs were open like a compass after riding a mule for four hours (February 14, 1938) and I cried with him when he opened the hazelnuts my mother had sent him (January 27, 1938). I should add that on the final count, my mother won the marathon; she wrote 418 letters to my father's 404, for whatever it is worth. I hope to write a Spanish edition of these letters and will revisit them anew. In the meantime, I have translated twelve letters included here in their complete form, without adding or substituting a single word and adhering to the original punctuation. I have left her "feísimos" (very ugly one) and his "chatísimas" (very pug-nose one). This is as close as the Anglophone reader can get to my parents' story.

August 2, 1937
Written by my mother a mere two weeks after my father left for the front lines. Her life seemed to continue somewhat carefree and with little change, although she was already making plans for their future together as my father's wife. The thought that my dad would come back soon was still a possibility that did not materialize. Her letter-count had just begun.

Valencia, August 2, 1937

Dearest:

Last night I received the letter from the 30th, this morning the one from the 31st and now the one from yesterday (with my "beautiful" picture).

I assume you know about yesterday's outing, but not the details.

We left at nine on the bus that goes directly to Serra (we didn't take the one to Porta Coeli). The country-side on this road is more beautiful and varied than the other one. From Serra to the Berro Fountain it took us two hours with "stops" in honor of some fig groves and vineyards.

We only stayed at the Fountain about four hours, eating and resting.

116

The return trip, after staying in line (same thing as we did in the morning) was at seven in the evening. As I feared, we returned to Valencia at eight-fifteen. If I had left writing your letter for my return, I would have written to you in my thoughts because I still had to accompany Elena to her house. After that, since there was no one home, more waiting and I got home after nine.

The people who came on the outing were, in addition to Elena, my brother, Blanco and Garcés.

I plan to do this outing with you soon and even later on when we can stay there a week all alone. You can suppose that I mean when we are a forever couple, that is when I am Alborg's wife.

There are no homes around there at all, but we can take a tent as my brothers did two summers ago with their friends.

It will be the most ideal vacation, you'll see.

If Ferreres thinks that I am sad due to your absence, how can it be possible that I'm thinking about an official transfer?

I know that you get the irony, although you tell me that it's not clear.

So, is my child happy now or is it necessary that I tell him that I love him much, much and much until I run out of paper? I don't think it is, because even if I don't tell you, you know it full well. Besides, aren't my letters eloquent enough? If they are not, I give you permission to add the rest, assured that you won't be mistaken.

Since I don't really feel like going out today, Amparín will go to the mailbox. I think that Teresita *will accompany her since I'm calling her first.*

Yesterday I went purposely to see her at seven and she wasn't home. Your sister had already told me on Saturday that she probably wouldn't be home.

I will go visit your aunts tomorrow. Give me the big happiness that you are coming right away.

I love you and don't forget you, your,
Chatita

September 5, 1937

My father's details in this long letter — one of the few about military life — and his new surroundings are striking along with his gift for description and imagination. I was constantly surprised at how well he adjusted to his environment and how much he appreciated whatever luck and beauty came his way, including women of all ages.

Andújar, September 5, 1937
   Conchita of my soul,
I don't need to ask your forgiveness for my silence these days because you could easily put yourself in my place and it would be unnecessary. Yesterday I wrote to my sister and I told her how grateful she should be. Because I wrote to her, I left you without a letter. The lifestyle of the barracks leaves us little time for episto-lary tasks. We have instruction from seven-thirty to eleven in the morning, and then until twelve we have technical instruction. Since they give out the food between twelve and one-thirty it is not worth it to go back home, from where I write you, because the barracks are on the outskirts and somewhat far away. In the after-noon we go back for our instruction at five and we finish at seven-thirty (at the same time we used to start so many of our strolls). After that, half an hour is wasted until eight, time for dinner.

   I give you so many details about my current military life to demonstrate how it is almost impossible to write to you. It's true that after lunch I have free time until five o'clock, a couple of hours, but these past few days I had to spend them taking a nap for sure. Given the lack of practice, the long and heavy morning instruction leaves us exhausted. Yesterday we went back and forth on a field left fallow, very hard to walk on and, in the evening, we had a repeat performance. When I get used to it, very soon I hope, I will dedicate the warm nap hours (here it's still so) to write to you every day. I remember you all the time and love you every second, even when I sleep, because then I dream about you and I imagine that I hug you.

Today, since it's Sunday, we have the entire day free and I'm taking advantage of the morning to write to you peacefully in "my" house. I will call it thus for short. It is on a very ugly street and the outside is not beautiful, but inside it's neat, spacious, airy and cool. It has four patios full of flowerpots, with jasmine and evening gladiolus that smell wonderful.

The lady of the house, a widow with four or five children, seems to have lost her joie de vivre, but she treats us well. This unhappiness on the part of our hostess is more obvious because women here are as I have never seen. They answer our compliments with such grace and impudence that makes it easy to talk to them all evening. The truth is that the poor women have been left alone; at mail time there is a crowd of young girls who are waiting for news from the front. There isn't a single man left who is not a soldier.

Precisely because of the absence of men the excess of women is more evident, aggravated by the many evacuees who are here from the towns close to the front lines. A few days ago, I chatted for a while with a "girl" from Marmolejo, the famous birthplace of the Sister San Sulpicio [the protagonist of the novel by Armando Palacio Valdés].

I trust that you won't be worried by these "interviews" as I always act the literary role and, since I'm far from you, my old cerebral self has reappeared.

I have promised myself to come back to this land that has really surprised me, despite the fact that the war must have taken away lots of its attractiveness. I love the famous Andalusian patios. At night, even though the street lights are off, the patios are lit and, over the dark exterior, they show poetically the lines of the wrought iron gates. In peace time it must be marvelous.

The day we arrived I got close to one of these patios to check it out; when she heard me, the owner came out and cordially asked me to come in. She excused herself because a bomb had damaged the patio. She showed me her bedroom where she was sleeping moments before the explosion and how it was left completely destroyed. In "my" neighborhood there are entire streets ruined and the market is demolished. As you can see these are things to take one's joy away but nevertheless there is still some left.

We have finally gotten our wish to take a dip. The Guadalquivir River, although greater when it goes through Córdoba and Sevilla, flows abundantly through here. Its course is a few minutes from the town and, if we stay here long enough, perhaps I'll finally learn to swim.

By the place where we went swimming the last day, there are some ruins of an old Arabic mill that are screaming for a photograph. While we were in the water, a herd of about two hundred bulls were grazing on the opposite riverbank. We were in the middle, wearing our Adam suits, in a note of local color.

All my friends are taking a swim now. I have stayed to write to you; perhaps I'll go in the afternoon.

A pause now and let's change the subject too.

Regarding my return trip, I am completely confused right now. As I told you in my previous letter, I wrote to my uncle telling him about my assignment to the "89 Brigade" and my first impressions. I await his answer in a couple of days. I trust that he will tell me if my dispensation is possible now and when it will arrive more or less. If you want to find out more about it, you should ask my sister who should have the latest news.

In the meantime, I'm waiting anxiously for the moment when we will see each other again. When I thought that luck was going to strike, it has gotten away again. I suppose that now I have to recommend patience.

Last evening, we spoke with a soldier from our brigade who was in town and had a day off. He told us some details about life in the trenches; he assured us that it was fine there and he left us wishing to try it out. We parted saying "see you later." He was from Granada, one of the fighters on its streets against the uprising; he signed up afterward with the militants who later formed the "89." He has been on the front lines for three months: a hero.

I have a new group of friends now, the first was dissolved in the Valencian region. There are five of us, one of them knows you well, he is the clerk in "Eustadio's Store" in Ruzafa's Market.

The new group is very different from the one before in tastes and personalities, but they are good chaps and good companions.

I don't know if I told you that I have received one of your stray letters from ten or twelve days ago. I read that the doctor has forbidden you to go in the water and has prescribed I don't know what. Give me (without delay, you hear me?) news about your health. And I repeat to you to take good care of yourself. You see how I was right.

I'm becoming a true athlete; the sun and the countryside are good for me. Perhaps I'm a bit thinner but like steel.

Nothing more, cutie. Tell me that you love me, if it's true, and repeat it without fear that I will get tired of it. So far away sound gets weak and it's necessary to reinforce it as much as possible. With this new distance I fear again that you will forget me little by little if you haven't forgotten me already.

Until tomorrow, dearest. A very strong hug and all my love forever. Yours, Juan

Give my greetings to your mom, tell me how she is feeling.

October 5, 1937

Oftentimes my mother's letters were full of news about family and friends and the chores she was doing for my dad. Although she did not like to, she wrote about the bombings in Valencia. Her health was already a concern.

Valencia, October 5, 1937

Dear Juan:

Yesterday I received your letter from the 2nd – 3rd and I didn't answer it the same day because when they brought it, I wasn't home. I went with my mom to purchase a dress, a skirt and a blouse.

Since this week I work mornings, I'll write to you in the afternoons.

I don't have any news from my brothers and "Dionis" yet.

The first day you had guard duty coincided with the day you left (three months later, of course). Here it has also been rainy and quite cool, too.

Yesterday I spoke with Tere and told her what you told me. She tells me that they won't send the package since they are awaiting good news (about his imminent return). I'll tell you then when I can send the vest; in the meantime, keep as warm as possible, what can we do!

When I saw Ferri I told him what you told me to tell him, so you are late on your warning.

I'm sure you have already written me giving instructions about your registration at the University.

It isn't as if I have lost my appetite again; I lost it three months ago and it doesn't feel like coming back.

I'm taking some small pills the size of an O (this exact size) that they are giving me for my bones and I don't know what else. Do not worry, although I'm a tad thinner, I continue to be strong and that's the most important thing. In fact, I don't do crazy stunts as you suggest.

Ferreres is here, I saw him the other day crossing the street (I will take care of that next time I see him).

I saw Berenger today on my way to work. He was going to the barracks to see if he found out today where he is being sent. He says hi.

I'm also seeing Tere this afternoon.

I phoned your aunts. They send their regards and I add kisses. Tomorrow I'll go visit them.

Feísimo, I have a guilty conscience because of the letter that I wrote to you on Sunday, do you forgive me?

Since your vest is already finished now, I'm going to knit another one with a different yarn I like better for myself. Besides, I don't need a color that is not appropriate.

I'll knit you another vest (if the one I made fits you well) but with a better yarn and a lighter color. Tell me how it fits you (it would be even better if I could see it, no?).

Conchita's sister cannot make you the trench jacket (for now). If it's urgent tell me and Amparín can make it (she made the plaid coat for me). Conchita's sister, Josefina (the one without a boyfriend) is dealing with some issues with her ears and is going out of town to see if she gets better. Since she is the one who knows how to sew, all work is on hold until she gets back (the other sister cuts the cloth and works in the Veneciana store). Since I mention them, they also send their greetings and from Joaquín as well.

Since I'm sending you so many regards, I don't want to leave my family out of this, they all send their greetings every day, but I'm not going to tell you each day. You understand me, right?

Sunday's bombing was the most horrible we have seen here. All the prior bombings together were a "joke" compared to this one. There are more than sixty houses destroyed, among them the office where my father works. If it had been a weekday, I have no idea what would have happened. Nevertheless, there have been many dead and wounded.

My father's office has been moved now to Paz Street, I believe.

They also hit two movie theaters. I don't need to tell you that if it had been in the afternoon, it would have been terrible.

As you can see, it isn't very safe here either. But luck is on our side for now.

Tell me if you are advancing in your English studies. How is Morse learning going? If you are a telephone operator it will be easy to speak sometime. Since I am in the Ministry, I sometimes talk (well, I put people through) with the front lines. If by chance you are on duty at the same time as I work and I call long distance there . . . too many coincidences. Let us be happy writing to each other whenever we can.

I wanted to work on my handwriting, but I can see it isn't possible. I have to write slowly for that and my nerves are shot.

Until tomorrow or the day after, it depends.

You know that I don't forget you and I love you very much. Your, Conchita

November 8, 1937

The reality of war had set in and there was no further mention that my father would return to Valencia. There were more health concerns from my mother. In general, her tone was more resigned and philosophical with a more assured sense of humor.

Valencia, November 8, 1937

Dearest:

I'm back to the poor letter paper because I don't have a better one.

Four hours ago, I finished writing my letter to you today. I imagine that what I told you about the wound in my mouth has not made a good impression on you.

Since as evening came the hemorrhage was increasing, when my mother came home, she called your friend and told him what was going on. I went to his house and he plugged the cavity where the tooth used to be. It hurt a bit, but now the pain is almost gone. Tomorrow I have to go back to take the dressing out.

I have eaten some because this morning I didn't eat. This evening I had a cup of coffee with milk and I'll drink another one when I go to bed. I tell you all this so that you can be sure that I'm not fibbing to you.

You can see how well I am since it's midnight and I'm not sleepy and I don't feel bad at all.

When I arrived home from the dentist's office I lay down on the rocker and took Veramon. Within one hour I was almost as well as I feel now.

In today's second letter you tell me that you could be with my uncle and my brother. I don't like this business that one bomb could kill you three at all. Are you hinting at something? I can take a lot, but if you lie to me, I'll suffer more than if you tell me the truth. Why in the world do you think that a bomb could kill you? The endings of novels are dramatic and I like them a lot, but from this to the ending of "my novel" there is a big difference. I don't admit, even in a dream, that my child is going to die and even less in that way.

Since it is so late, I don't want to mention any more military subjects in case I dream something barbaric. If even in my dreams I don't have the peace I desire I will go crazy one of these days. (If this were to happen, I'll let you know beforehand so you can be the nurse in the mental hospital).

*"Cavalleria Rusticana" is on the radio this evening.
Really, I don't know how listening to this music I
could come up with such silly thoughts. But this is how
I feel and since I wrote it, I leave it.*

*Until tomorrow then, feísimo. Does not forget you,
your, Conchita*

December 19, 1937

Burdened by family responsibilities and wartime routine, my
mother would rather write to my dad than do anything else. She
was supposed to be knitting an outfit for the new baby in the household where my father was staying. Her style was clearly more
descriptive and mature.

Valencia, November 19, 1937
Beloved:
*It's been barely an hour and a half that I closed my
last letter to you.*

*I made dinner. Well, dinner is cooking on the stove.
My dad, my aunt and Salvador are playing
Parcheesi; Antonio is sleeping, my sisters are out for a
walk because my parents didn't want them to go to the
movies since the alarms have sounded twice. The truth
is they could go off again and being in the theater and
on Sunday is somewhat problematic. Since I don't
play games, I think that the best thing I can do is
write to you and, as you can see, I'm doing it. I could
be knitting the sweater for the "little boy" (that's what
they think I'm doing), but it's so comfortable in this
room that it invites talking to you.*

*I'm in my Aunt Carmen's bedroom since she has an
"up and down" light, it's here where I usually sew,
read or knit because in the dining room, where they
are playing now, it's not as peaceful as I like to be.*

126

I'm not in my bedroom because it's the farthest away and the coldest since, as you know, it faces the street. As I was telling you, I am here all tucked in and comfortable, thinking of "my child" in that Arjona of my sins. Well, maybe not . . . perhaps I'm mistaken. The mistake may be due to how cold you told me the other day you were (your introduction to the wool socks).

On my knees I have a pretty strong cardboard box where I keep the paper and envelopes that I use to write to you. I employ it as a table, so you can visualize my present position as I write to you.

My mother, as you have probably figured out is at work. She gets out at nine. I pester her once in a while, asking her what is wrong with Jaén that I haven't had a call. I don't think she will be able to speak with you. Since it's eight o'clock, there is still an hour left.

This morning I was going to the Viveros Gardens with Tere, but we didn't go because there was an air raid alarm.

I don't know if I told you that I had a permanent done again. I went at morning time, so I left with daylight. My hair looks like when you left. I have put on a little weight since I got back from Barcelona. Before I left, I weighed 49 kilos and now I weigh 51. I was losing weight when I was working at the Ministry. Then I had no appetite, now it seems to have woken up. I should tell you that this is due to the fact that I'm obeying you about sleeping more and working less. I sleep about the same, but I'm sharing the housework with my sisters. I told them that, according to mom and dad, they are getting so "beautiful." The two of them eat by the mouthful, to say it plainly. Their heads are as empty as a pumpkin. They are oblivious, the two of them. They don't have a boyfriend; their only concern is their "diet." They eat everything and as much as truckdrivers, I say. They wolf down such steaks of horse meat that I fear they are going to start kicking any day. Since I am picking on them, I'll tell you that they tease me duet-like when I'm sad or I don't want to go out with them because I'm writing to you or waiting for your letters. They have to go out to the movies with my aunt many times. Finita is very tall and she seems to be filling out a bit. Amparin already weighs more than 60 kilos, nothing to laugh at, she is only fifteen. What will she be like at twenty? Now that I have mentioned everyone's weight, tell me what is yours, feisimo. Do you also eat horse meat? I do not.

It's getting time to eat. The "children" have discovered me and they are having fun teasing me. I'm going to put the finishing touches to the dinner and serve it to them. Would you like some? I would love to serve you more than anyone else.

The light reflectors are going full blast and if by any chance it's my turn this evening, I want you to know that I will think about you until there remains a breath of life in me. The ink stains are unbearable sometimes, it's because it's getting late and they are complaining in the kitchen (I'm getting nervous, you know?).

Until tomorrow, my love, love me lots,
Conchita

Juan Luis Alborg Escartí as an infant with his parents, Agustina Escartí and Juan Alborg. Valencia, 1914.

Conchita Carles Abello with two of her siblings, Pepe and Vicente, around 1923.

"Juanito" around five years old. This is the photograph that Conchita described as "My niño, my child."

Conchita during the Spanish Civil War. Valencia, 1938. This is
the photograph that Juan had with him of his future bride.

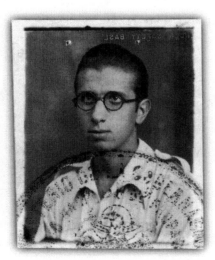

Juan Luis Alborg in his student ID from the University of
Valencia. This is one of the photographs that Conchita had
of him during the war.

Conchita and Juan's wedding day. Valencia, December 26, 1942.

Newlywed Conchita in the couple's first home in Valencia, Calle Turia 39.

The Alborg family on a Sunday stroll. Valencia around 1950.

Juan Luis Alborg in his study. Valencia, around 1950.

Conchita Carles with her children, Juan Luis Alborg Carles and
Conchín Alborg Carles. Valencia, 1952. "A punto de caramelo,
eye candy."

Conchita Carles wearing the Valencian regional dress. Valencia, around 1953.

The Alborg family in Madrid, by El Retiro Park, 1954.

Conchita Carles pretending to drive the Iruña scooter.

Rita Hayworth look-alike. Conchita Carles in Madrid, in the late fifties.

Mother and daughter Conchita Carles and the author in Madrid, in front of their home, Plaza del Niño Jesús 2, 1960.

The Alborg family driving across the United States, 1963, with the cat, a U-Haul trailer and the Plymouth Fury.

Conchita Carles, the professor's wife. West Lafayette, Indiana, 1968.

The grandfather with Diana Day and Jane Day. West Lafayette, 1972.

The author wearing the Valencian regional dress. Valencia, 1980. Like mother, like daughter.

April 2, 1938

The lack of food, including bread, became an issue, accordingly, my mother continued mentioning how much she weighed. She was surer of herself as shown by her flirty ways. My parents had not seen each other in nine months, but news that the soldiers may visit with a permit began to circulate.

Valencia, April 2, 1938

Dearest:

Last evening, I went to the movies and since I arrived late, I didn't write to you; this morning I wasn't able to, so I missed one mail.

In your letter of yesterday, in other words the one from the 29th, you tell me to send you two books, but we are not allowed now, you know? I already told you about this in my prior letter and it's the same today as the past days.

Today I received your letter from the 30th and I see that you write a lot, barely one small page. You say that you are upset because you haven't been receiving my letters. This is wrong because I write to you every day and if I miss one it's never two days in a row. I think you have to be more trusting with me. I don't want to say anything else because I know that when you get this letter you won't be upset anymore and besides, I think that this is enough, no?

I was bored at the movies. It has been a long time that I don't see any "good" films. This coming week, I'll go again to the Tyris and I think that it will be a better program. I saw the trailer and I liked it.

When I left the office, I went to see your aunts, my sister Amparín came with me.

It has been a long time that I wanted to walk by

Alameda at night and today I had a chance to cross it, it was completely dark, as I had never seen it. If I had been there alone, I would have been afraid. You can imagine that walking on this avenue I thought of you, since it was part of our strolls. When will we be able to go again?

I weighted myself again, I weigh 53 kilos, not bad, huh?

I spoke with Tere this evening and she has a cold, but it's not serious. She is somewhat vain and she was wearing too light clothing, and of course. She gave me some bread that has been as welcome as manna from heaven. It has been several days that they only give us five cents worth of bread per person. I don't need to tell you that at home the adults have forgotten what it tastes like, we leave it all for the little ones. However, there is fish, frozen meat, vegetables, oranges, so it isn't so bad, we've had more difficult times but with some bread. It would compensate if we had potatoes, but not even a token one can be seen.

I've told you all this rigmarole because I know how much you love bread and you told me on one occasion that you would get sick without bread and, since I don't want that to happen to you, I warn you in case you get a permit (let's hope it's soon), to bring your own rations. I don't want you to lose the kilos you have gained.

Despite having received today your "long" letter, you can see that I don't skimp on writing to you, huh? I'm behaving like a good "girl," since you tell me that if it's my fault that you didn't get a letter from me, I would have to pay, and not precisely with kisses. The truth, I'm afraid and that is why I write. Would you take off your glasses to make me pay?

I think that tomorrow I'll go to Pinedo all day. If I do, I'll tell you how it was in the evening. I don't want to make castles in the air. It seems that "it always rains when there is no school," (written in Valencian). Now there are times when it rains and . . . we don't get wet.

Feisimo, do you love me? Since I don't love you at all, I'm asking you, you know that we ladies are curious.

I forgot to tell you that if you are coming tomorrow to see my bathing suit, be at the corner by your house at nine-thirty sharp. Don't make me wait because I won't wait for you . . . and it has been nine months already!

It's two in the morning, so it's Sunday already and the 3rd. Even though it's so early, I'm going to bed.

Now you know, if you want to see "your" bathing suit (it's the one you gave me), at nine-thirty on the corner. I'll be stood up if I wait for you tomorrow, so I won't wait for you. I wait for you forever and always,

your,
Conchita

September 4, 1938
My father was in Valencia on leave from August 10 to September 1, but in some ways, it was even more difficult to live apart after that when they realized how long the war could be. My father was even more in love and obsessed than before. His letters had been censored and he could not put the name of the town where he was located, he used "On the Field" from then on.

On the Field, September 4, 1938
Dearest:
Now that it seems that I'm going to have a few moments of peace, I write to you, although I think that I will spend more time absorbed looking at the paper than moving the pen. I'm feeling such homesickness and nervous despondency that I feel completely paralyzed and I only feel relatively well letting my thoughts go toward you in a vague and imprecise way. I wish I could shake off this mood and occupy myself in some activity that could raise my spirits, but right now I lack enough will power to do it. I could go to the river to swim and take a walk under the fruit trees and breathe in the open air and the sun, but I'd rather dedicate this time entirely to your remembrance. As you can see, since I got back, I've been wishing to go out and now that I can, I don't do it.

It's two-thirty in the afternoon; it has been over an hour that we ate, since the dinner has to be during daylight, we also eat lunch early. I imagine you are eating now as well and I don't know what you'll do afterwards. On weekdays and during office hours I know almost exactly your rhythm because the last few days I was with you at every moment. It seems that I feel the separation less because, to a point, I'm accompanying you. But since it's Sunday, not knowing where you are or what you are doing, I make an effort with my imagination to guess your destination and accompany you from here with all my soul. And with the realization that I won't be able to do it I feel upset and uneasy because it seems that we are farther apart. And until when, chatita of my soul? If you could know how sad evenings are when those happy, unique, moments are so recent. And how the days would end, after seeing you and hearing you continuously, hugging you and kissing each other voraciously. You will never imagine, feísima, to what extent your presence is necessary for me to live. I for one, who is so sure about this, need to be away from you to realize the magnitude of this need.

Now is when I measure exactly to what degree you are all of my life because all my thoughts and my acts are directed exclusively to you. Since my constant bad mood is evident, my friends tell me that I am an incurable romantic. So that you will be convinced,

144

since you were doubting and when you admitted it, it was with reservations, saying that I was "a romantic in disguise." Maybe I am that way for other things, but about you I am an authentic romantic, with trademark. I don't think that there exists a boyfriend who loves his girlfriend as much as I do. I say it because everyone is surprised when they see any of the traits by which I define it.

I brought with me some novels from "Literary Review" and among them one by Tolstoy that is all a passionate statement against marriage. Three or four of my friends are reading it at the same time and often we discuss one of its ideas. Well, what is strange is that I agree with almost all of them and after realizing it, I have to admit the paradox that I love you even more. I think that it's more a matter of contradiction between my life and my ideas; what happens is that I am in love with you "above and despite it all."

Enough already, cutie, because if the entire letter is about my love for you, you are going to get conceited.

I have interrupted the letter, dearest, because we have started the construction of our hut and I took advantage to get some exercise. When I was tired, I went down to the river with Eliseo and we swam in a place he discovered. It's not too deep, but there is enough length to swim and everything. We have tried to swim against the current, something rather difficult, but I succeeded twice, by the way. Eliseo was surprised because I always say that I swim like a brick and now it's no longer exact. I think that when we go swimming together again, you will no longer win, cutie. What I haven't been able to do is float belly up, I'll try tomorrow and will let you know if I succeed.

On the way back, we have picked up blackberries, corn, figs, walnuts and a big basket of apples so ripe that our hands were saturated with an intense aroma. Of course, we have eaten like starved men, although it was close to dinner time, which was being served when we got back. No matter, I ate anyway, for me fruit is like an appetizer.

Now after finishing and smoking a cigarette, I take your letter to continue it as long as there is daylight. It is eight o'clock and, even though I'm close to our "refuge," it's getting dark.

I asked Vicente to check with his family if there is a way to send packages of "printed matter" in order to have reading material and not lose the habit of using our head that is becoming stagnant with this purely vegetative life.

I think that Vicente has an uncle in the post office. I remember that you or Elenita know him. One way or another let's see if there is a way to send me the books that I'll mention to you and will return them to you later, of course. Otherwise they could get lost or I would have to carry them after each move.

Let me know how your father's reading is coming along and if you need any help.

That's enough, cutie, inside where my table is, I almost can't see.

Since there is one side of this sheet left, I may add a few words tomorrow, although I'll write later then as well.

Good night, dearest. Now it's eight-fifteen. At this time, we hadn't started dinner [during the days they were together] and we still had the dessert left! Patience is a lot to ask, chatísima, when it is necessary not to be with you. If it were for anything else, whatever it was, I wouldn't mind, but this . . . !

A million kisses, your,

Juan

December 23, 1938

This was a typical letter, full of sadness and frustration. They were writing to each other in very small handwriting to save paper. My mother's handwriting even looked like my dad's.

Valencia, December 23, 1938

Dearest:

I didn't have a letter today either. When will it be the very happy day that this would not be a worry? Will this separation ever end?

Yesterday I didn't write to you because I was feeling low and I would rather not write. Today I do it because I don't want you to have another day without a letter. The truth is, feísimo, that I am sad and

146

perhaps I will make you sad too. If I had written yesterday, I would not write today either.

Everyone is sleeping and the radio is playing "The Dollar Princess." It's happy music but, on the contrary, it makes me sad. I'm thinking of the dates we are in; tomorrow is Christmas Eve and twenty-three months of our engagement, day after tomorrow, Christmas. Pepin will probably come but you and my Vicente will not. Why will these days come without the two of you not being here?

My co-workers say that they won't be celebrating but it's not true and even if they don't celebrate Christmas, their personality is different from mine and one can't tell their bad mood or at least I can't tell. If I were that way, perhaps I would be better off . . . this way I wish I could go to bed and wakeup when you are here on leave. Each day that passes seems longer to me and there are so many hours in a day!

Today has been and it's colder than ever; I don't know how come we don't freeze walking on the street. It's been two days of extreme cold and today is even colder than yesterday. I can imagine, feísimo, that you would not be any better there, right? Next year we'll see if we are luckier and we are not as cold as this year and if we are cold, we can console each other.

When will this damned war end?

Since I am such a pessimist, when I go to bed, I can't think of happy moments and, since I always think sad thoughts, I have strange and ugly dreams. Almost always I can't remember my dreams in the morning, but nowadays I do. So, I spend the day obsessed by what I dreamt, which is all about the war and puts me in a foul mood.

I think I'm becoming afraid instead of being strong and brave, I'm making huge progress going backwards. See if you can come to give me an optimist's shot or I will become ugly and old. Last night I dreamt that I was an old lady, but I wasn't ugly, you know? I saw you for a moment and you were young as you really are. But I don't think you were my boyfriend because you gave me a kiss on the forehead and left. Being your grandmother, I was sad because I didn't see you anymore. Thank goodness that I was your grandma, you know? Had I been your girlfriend I would have been upset. Is it fair that even in my dreams you don't come for a long visit?

I just heard the war report. Now the fascists have attacked Catalonia, Levante is peaceful for now. Let's hope that it lasts to calm somewhat my constant worry.

You can't complain about me, right, feísimo? I'm writing lots and in a small handwriting. We'll see if you write me lots as well, feísimo.

The reason I haven't received a letter today, must be because of the mail. If it's your fault, get ready to pay for it all. I don't like to get mad at you in the letters.

And now, my eternal song: don't forget me, love me lots, lots and more lots, because no matter how much you love me, you won't love me more than I love you.

Always, always, your,
Conchita

December 23, 1938
This letter was from my dad on the same day as the one above from my mother. It is uncanny how much alike they were in their thoughts and worries.

148

December 23, 1938
    Dearest chatita:

One more day in the long chain of arid and gray days, thinking all day about you and waiting for the happy moment to arrive when I'll be marching by your side indefinitely. I don't think that last year during the Christmas holidays we thought that this year we would be separated still. However, that's how it is and, worse yet, without knowing remotely if next year we will be in the same situation. I don't think so because in that case I won't be able to endure such an awful prospect. I hope that luck will reunite us much before then, completely and forever, dearest.

You refuse to believe in the relative proximity, of course, of that moment. The eagerness with which I desire it makes me see it far away too but, except when my nerves and my overflowing impatience darken me, I do not share your pessimism, chatita. I have thought that when the war ends, if Destiny grants us life and health, we have to get married as soon as possible. As long as we have some sure means to earn a living, at once. Without waiting to acquire many of the traditional things; those will arrive later little by little. This will undoubtedly be inconvenient, but we will be happy in exchange and it will be a dream to make our home in concert with our happiness. It's necessary to recover the time that fate has made us lose now and not dally because we lack some detail here and there. Tell me what you think of this project, chatísima. I told you once before that I would only tolerate that you work at any job if it was to accelerate our union as it may happen when the war ends. Of course, you would stay at home as soon as I can provide for you on my own because I plan to give you enough work, although not of the kind that you are undoubtedly thinking about now. Let's hope that you change your mind by then.

Believe me, when I think that Conchita Guillén who used to come with us as the "chaperone," without anything close to a boyfriend has already gotten married, it makes me really mad and envious. It is a consolation for me to think that it's like a suit, when theirs is old, ours will be brand-new. Now we must maintain this love "suit" new as long as we live. Of course, we will live for a long time (start by doing all you can and take care of yourself). Besides, we are young still; I certainly am. You too ,even though I tell you sometimes to

149

tease you that you have the face of a little old lady. It isn't true, although these difficult times have left some traces on all of us, but this misfortune will end and take the traces away.

Last night there was no mail; I don't know if I'll have a letter from you today. If the mail were as diligent as it should be, I would have one, but it probably wants to try my patience some more; you don't know how I await your news telling me all about your musings.

Until tomorrow, unforgettable. Take good care of yourself and always tell me the truth about how you are feeling. Love me until I tell you enough.

   I adore you with all my soul, your,
   Juan

January 3, 1939

The last three months of the war seemed to be the most difficult for my parents. Not knowing when the war would be over was taking a toll. My mother defended herself from my dad's accusations about her letter from Christmas Eve. Her affinity for keeping an exact count of the letters was evident. She seemed to imitate my father's style.

Valencia, January 3, 1939
   Dearest:
   I finally heard from you; I received four letters and I'm missing one, that is the one from the 26. I have the ones from the 27, 28, 29 and 30. The two first ones are the kind I like, but the two last ones are not the same, particularly the one from the 29. In it you scold me for the way I wrote to you on Christmas Eve.
   I wrote to you that way, curtly as you call it, not because I felt distant from you as you suppose. On the contrary, that night nothing was right; my sadness and upset were so large, I think I even felt sick. My little siblings and cousins ate early, as usual, and my

Aunt Adela kept them company (eating early as well). Then Amparin and Fina did the same thing. The only reason my mom didn't was because she was waiting for my dad. I didn't eat that night. When the children finished eating, they kissed everyone and went to bed, without being noisy as other times. Once we were alone, my mother and Aunt Adela started to cry. When Fina and Amparo saw the situation, they went to bed too. My father arrived and he and my mom ate right away. They turned themselves in before nine o'clock Aunt Adela had also gone to bed when the children did. Finding myself alone at an hour so out of the ordinary for me, I felt so sad that I couldn't bear it. My mom heard me from her bed and told me to go to bed, that it would make the night more bearable. I thought that the best thing I could do was writing to you a few lines and that way I finished the night. When you come back, I will read the letter I wrote to you and we can discuss it and I will make it up to you if you like. If this year I don't have the infinite pleasure of being with you on a night like that, I won't write to you. I don't want you to tell me that the letter seemed like a distancing . . . if you had been in my place, you would understand well.

And this is enough, no? Now something else. Since I didn't get the letter from the 26th, I don't know how it happened that you washed your clothes at home. You mentioned it on the 27th and the day before. Maybe your letter will arrive tomorrow and I'll find out.

I spoke with Tere this evening and she told me that Mariana called, but she didn't speak with him because she wasn't home. Vicente has come on leave and you will too, it can't be any other way! Listen, don't start with you heard this and that, you have to come on leave and everything else is nonsense. I want to see my chatito feo so much!

Feo, I think that when we don't have to resort to letter-writing in order to communicate our impressions, we are going to be very happy; seeing you every day at first and afterwards together for ever . . . it seems too much happiness. I don't want to hope too much, but that hope will be my life later and it's my life now. There are times, that guided by my pessimism I don't see things that way and then . . . Why aren't you here now? When will be the end of this hateful separation?

I'm anguished when I think about this and I don't know if I can suffer much longer. I'm not afraid to suffer for you, but suffering for our separation is frightening, feísimo. I love you so much that everything bothers me and bores me when you are not here. I only live waiting for your letters and with the eternal hope that I'll see you soon and not to be apart anymore.

They have bombed us again close to your aunts' house. They are fine, but somewhat afraid, naturally.

I'm fine, a tad heavier but if I lose my peace, I know that I won't be. Tonight, we've had an alarm. Let's see if that's all. We were getting used to life in the city without air raids. We'll have to drop that supposition. I for one have dropped it already and this evening I was pretty afraid, darn! This morning I could see the bombs dropping and . . . good night, I'm getting upset and I don't want to write anymore.

Kisses, many kisses from your, Conchita

March 21, 1939

This was my mother's last letter, ten days before the end of the war. She must have written a few more that my father never received and, therefore, were not saved. The fact that her girlfriend was expecting a baby accentuates how much my parents were delaying their life together.

Valencia, March 21, 1939

Dearest:

Only a few lines, I'm tired and I'm going to bed right away.

Last night I went to bed at two; I was doing some sewing and it got late. Then I almost didn't sleep because it was very cold, my feet were frozen and that's why I couldn't sleep. I fell asleep when it was getting light. You'll understand that I need to go to bed and it's already getting late, it's eleven-thirty.

From the time I left the office I have been crocheting and since everyone was hanging around here, I couldn't write. I'm next to the radio and I write to you on my knees.

I received your letters 45 and 46. I see that you are sad and worried. You will see that I'll always be good, so that you won't remember these bitter hours. We have to be very happy.

I spoke with Tere, she told me that Mariana was there eating with them today.

Conchita Guillén is already expecting her "baby." I congratulated her, I suppose the baby boy (that's what she wants) will be born in peace time, no? At least that is what I hope. I don't know how long this infernal war is going to last, when I am dying for it to end! The truth is that I can't imagine what it'll be

*like to have you next to me forever. So much happi-
ness will seem unreal and I don't want to dream
anymore...I am anguished and afraid.*

*I'm waiting for you to tell me that you are tired of
doing the jumping exercises.*

*Until tomorrow, feo. Write to me a lot. And don't
forget me ever. You know that I love you with all my
soul.*

Always, always, your,
Conchita

March 28, 1939

When my father wrote his last letter, he was near Utiel, about fifty miles from Valencia, not knowing that the war would end in three days. Madrid had fallen to Franco's forces the day before. The officers seemed to have relinquished command and mail delivery had stopped. We know the rest of the story: by hiding during the day and walking to the city at night, he saved himself from prison time or much worse.

March 28, 1939
Dearest:

I will only write a short note today because I got up late and in a little while I'm going to eat and, as soon as I finish, I'm going to Utiel to bring the supplies. Since the Quartermaster has not arrived yet, it's up to us to take this daily trip; today I will go because I don't mind taking a stroll.

Since no one is coming over here I continue not to receive your letters. You can't imagine how upset I am about this. Today I will try to find out if it's going to take much longer and, in that case, I will give you the address of a house in town, so you can write there. It has been five days already and this silence is very hard.

You have no idea how frustrating it is to see all this time that I'm spending here so stupidly wasted. If I had known that it was going to take so long, I would have gone to see you right away. But, since we arrived, we have been waiting for the troops to join us at any moment and that is why I haven't been able to leave. Now, as more time passes, it's even worse because if they are going to come, it can't be much longer.

In the meantime, days are becoming very tedious and unending. To make matters worse, it's so cold that we can't go anywhere. Yesterday I tried to take a walk in the outskirts and I had to come back. This is such a large and awkward space that I don't know where to go.

Since the firewood in this town is so far away and, obviously, we don't have the mule here, there is no chance to bring it. Yesterday afternoon I asked a neighboring woman, so we were able to spend the evening half-way decently. Otherwise, the only solution is to go to bed. That's why I wasn't in a hurry to get up today, to be freezing around here senselessly; I'm better off in bed.

Enough for today, my dearest. How long and how difficult time has become, waiting for the happy moment when I can see you forever!

Do not forget me for anything in the world, chatísima.

A very strong hug from your,

Juan

Valencia 29 Agosto 1946

Queridísima Chelita e Hijitas:

De nuevo, como en épocas ya remotas, volvemos a coger la pluma para comunicarnos. Pero esta vez, por fortuna, por motivos menos dolorosos y con dos destinatarias más. Claro que en compensación está el tintero menos lleno de romanticismo y más rayada la cabeza de preocupaciones "peseteras".-

He recibido tus dos cartas. Ya veo que el viejo fue feliz y me alegra muchísimo que vayáis resolviendo las dificultades y acomodándoos gustosamente. Imagino la alegría de Juan Luis al verse suelto por esos campos y me duele muy de veras tener que contentarme con tus descripciones.

No ciertamente por lo malas que son sino por lo agradable que debe ser lo otro. (Ya-

Life in Spain

One of my earliest memories is of the house in Valencia where I was born, sitting in the bright Levantine sun on the back terrace that faced the Botanical Gardens, watching the tall, graceful pine trees swaying in the breeze. If I close my eyes, I can almost smell the dry needles that piled up on the dirt paths of the gardens. I used to sit on the terrace next to the washing machine while our maid hung clothes out to dry. I did not like milk, probably because it was not pasteurized and tasted awful, but I drank condensed milk, which I loved for its sweetness. I had a special way of sipping it without stirring it so I could eat the thick mixture by the spoonful. I always had a sweet tooth. In fact, my mother's siblings called me "La Melengues" (Miss Meringue) pronounced with an "l" not an "r," the way I used to mispronounce it.

We were not a well-to-do family by any means but after the Spanish Civil War, scores of young women had flocked to cities in search of work and even modest households like ours could afford them. We had one live-in helper who took care of my brother and me and another woman who came in to do heavy cleaning and the laundry. María Carmen García Nieto says in her essay about Franco's dictatorship that women and girls as young as twelve started working as servants in the cities: "This work was a strategy that women used to escape from the country and bring their families to the city" (667). As a child I heard that my mother caught a maid eating my porridge and fired her — that is how hungry people must have been. Benjamín Prado says in his novel about the children who were stolen from Republican mothers, that the decade of the 1940s in Spain were the hunger years (181).

My mother always took care of the daily grocery shopping and cooked all of our meals. I can only imagine how difficult it must have been to find fresh food during the postwar years. There were shortages of everything; families had a "cartilla de racionamiento," (rationing card) with coupons to get staples like milk, sugar, rice and beans. García Nieto says in her essay that 1945, the year of my birth, was characterized by "the black market, the rationing cards and the long lines" (666). Just like we saw in her letters, my mother liked walking all over Valencia; I remember going with her to the Ruzafa Market, close to her old home, and stopping by my grandparents' house to say hello or to have lunch with them.

Our home was on Turia Street, next to the movie theater, in the neighborhood of Torres de Quart, the medieval Christian gate to the city. Being next to the Botanical Gardens was my mother's consolation prize for leaving the old part of the city where she grew up. Our flat was large and full of light. My father's study was the first room located off a spacious foyer, furnished with heavy, traditional Valencian furniture, which stayed behind when we moved to Madrid, where homes were much smaller. The study faced Turia Street and had bookshelves lining every wall — my mother's book purchases during the war were not all for naught. My father's furniture was also very large, but it did follow us to Madrid where it barely fit. Eventually, my dad taught World History at the University of Valencia and tutored private students at home in the evenings until 10:00 or 11:00 p.m., a practice that he continued in Madrid until we moved to the United States. Since he hated public transportation, he rode his bicycle to the university. As a child, I was fascinated by the metal bands he tied around his ankles to protect his pants from the bike spokes. Few people owned cars in those years; only Uncle Miguel had a Renault 4L, where miraculously a family of three adults and three children all fit.

The living room was next to my dad's study, also facing the street. It was the most elaborate room in the house and had a fake fireplace in one corner. I do not remember using this room much, other than to look out from the balcony if we were expecting company. A long hallway, with three doors to the bedrooms, went all the way to the back of the house, which faced the Botanical Gardens. I slept in the small bedroom with the maid, next to my parents' room. I understand that my crib turned into a youth bed where I slept until we moved when I was almost eight years old. My favorite room was the dining room adjacent to the back terrace, also with a view of the tall pines. In addition to the large table, there was a "mesa camilla" (a round table with a floor-length tablecloth) where my

158

brother and I did everything: ate our meals, colored, played Parcheesi and read. Hidden by the long tablecloth was the "brasero" (the coal heater) because there was no central heating back then. Valencia is known for its temperate winters, but it surely got cold if one ventured from the "mesa camilla" to any other part of the house in the evenings.

My parents ate by themselves at the long dining room table, sometimes even after the maid had gone to bed. We never went out to eat; the only time I remember being in a restaurant was the afternoon of my First Communion, when we went to Barrachina, an establishment that is still in business, famous for its "horchata," the truffle drink typical of Valencia. We had a "merienda" (a small meal similar to the British high tea). I am sure that one of the reasons my brother and I celebrated our First Communion together was to save money. My mother also loved the idea that, between my beautiful floor-length, white dress and my brother's navy-blue sailor suit, we looked like the "parejita," the boy and girl little couple desired by Spanish families back then. Too bad that in the evening I swallowed my brand-new gold ring and had to use a potty until it was rescued. I have to give my mother credit because she did not write about this shameful incident in my First Communion album. She wrote instead:

> May 22, 1952, Thursday, Ascension Day. It wasn't sunny, it even rained a little, but not everything goes according to plan. Conchín soiled her dress coming out of the photographer's. Juan Luis didn't get out of his suit until dinner time. La nena was able to get out of bed three days ago, but she endured it very well. It has been a "Unique" day.

I was a small, sickly child born with perforated eardrums. I have crystal-clear recollections of visiting Dr. Selfa's office getting my ears drained. I remember the elevator in his building had huge mirrors and a red velvet seat — how could anyone forget that! And my mother would buy chocolates or a meringue for me afterward. One of her biggest worries when we moved to Madrid was how to replace Dr. Selfa. I started school in Valencia, at the Sagrado Corazón, but I do not remember it well. I learned to read with my loving grandfather, who also prepared me for my First Communion when I was sick in bed. I wonder if I reminded him of my mother.

We saw our cousins and other relatives often, but we had few friends who were our age.

I actually remember being a quiet little girl in Valencia, playing mostly alone or with my brother. My favorite toy was my kitchen. It was kept in a large hall closet, near the real-life kitchen. It had a sink with "running water" that dripped from a tin deposit in the back. Half the fun was carrying the water, without spilling it, down the hall and filling it up every day. My kitchen had wooden cabinets full of tiny pots and pans. It had a make-believe cook top and the oven door snapped shut like a real oven, another source of fun and danger. In the years after the Civil War, using the real gas oven at home was considered a luxury. Everyday meals, such as rice dishes or casseroles cooked in earthenware pans were taken to the corner bakery where they were chalk-marked with our address, Turia 39, and placed in the big, communal oven to bake. I also had wicker baskets-full of porcelain dishes. My favorite was a tea set similar to the one my mother kept on the dining room buffet. She used it to serve coffee, hot chocolate or tea if someone came to visit at "merienda" time. The fancy tea set also made an appearance on her Saint's Day.

Everything was done at home in those days. A seamstress used to come regularly to sew bed linens — even the towels were homemade. I know, because the clothes for my doll, Manolín, were made with the remnants. My mother had a noisy Singer sewing machine; I could hear her energetic pedaling from anywhere in the house. She embroidered the initials "A" and "C" on each sheet, pillowcase and towel for Alborg and Carles, since women in Spain do not change their last name when they marry. Everything got recycled then. My mother's black dress could become a uniform for the maid; a summer dress would turn into an apron. My First Communion dress became my Sunday best, shortened and adorned around the waist with a big, red velvet ribbon. When I got older, I started inheriting my mother's clothes, but that did not happen until we lived in Madrid. Her clothing and my dad's suits were the only clothes not made at home; she purchased the fabrics for her dresses in her old neighborhood, where she knew the merchants, and went to a dressmaker to choose the patterns and to be fitted. I remember going with her and sitting on the floor, in front of a large mirror, picking up the pins as they fell to the floor.

We only had what was called then "quita y pon" (one to put on and one to take off) and that included pajamas and underwear. Both my brother and I shared an armoire with my parents. Sometimes I wonder if the reason I have so many clothes now is because I am still trying to make up for having grown up with so little. Our only possessions were our toys and books, which were stored in the hall closet. Since we did not have many things, we had to take very good care of them. I remember my dad coming home from the university and the first thing he did was change into another pair of pants, take off his suit jacket and put on a plaid house jacket, leaving his shirt and tie on. In the summer, he would roll up his shirt sleeves and skip the tie and jacket. My mother changed into a housedress when she came home too, unless company was expected.

When we did venture outside, we walked fast without staring at the many crippled men who were missing a limb or walking on crutches, begging on every corner — vestiges of the Civil War, I realized later. Strolling was reserved for Sunday mornings. We did not go to church regularly, but got dressed up and went to the Botanical Gardens. My brother and I loved to run around the fragrant pines and along the meandering walkways, despite the warnings to be careful, that we could ruin our Sunday clothes. We did not have bicycles or skates; our fast legs were our only fun. My brother had a bike when we lived in Madrid, but I did not learn to ride until many years later when my daughters shamed me into learning, threatening me with training wheels if I did not learn.

I have a picture of my family on what must have been one of those Sunday strolls. My beautiful mother was dressed all in black, probably in mourning for my grandmother who passed away in 1950. My father wore a black tie and a black band sewn around his jacket sleeve. My brother is standing between my parents under their smiling gazes. I am holding my father's right hand, wearing an impeccable fall-looking dress. It was brown plaid with red trimming embroidered around the yoke and the hem. Since we did not have a camera, our pictures were usually taken at the photographer's studio and they were all in black and white, but I remember the precise color of each of my outfits. In this photograph, my parents and my brother have little Red Cross flags on their lapels. I look forlorn without a Red Cross flag. My consolation prize could be that, as a five-year-old I was already taller than my brother, although he was two years older and was upfront in the picture while I stood more in the background. After those walks, we would stop at the flower shop at the Gardens' exit and my father would buy a bouquet for my mother. I do not need to close my eyes to smell those flowers; Valencia is not called the city of flowers for nothing. The flower shop still exists and I stopped there to get a bouquet for my Godmother Teresa on my last trip there when she was still alive.

One of my favorite memories of Valencia is going to El Saler Beach with my mother and brother. My dad did not come with us; he was probably teaching or writing at home. We would take the trolley right after breakfast, all the way to El Grao, the harbor where my grandfather used to work, and change trolleys there to reach the beach. Sometimes, we stopped by my grandparents' home on our way back and my grandmother would have a snack of bread and chocolate ready for us. We always took something to eat at the beach, such as tasty sandwiches made with "sobrasada" from Mallorca, a chorizo-like spread that melted in the heat, my favorite! My mother was a good swimmer and always did a few laps parallel to the shoreline without taking her eyes off my brother and me who were supposed to sit still and play on the sand for a while. To this day, it is impossible for me to look at one of Joaquín Sorolla's paintings without remembering the golden light of the Mediterranean Sea and the short, twisted pines of El Saler Beach. I remember getting my sweaty legs stuck on the faux leather trolley seats on our way home, falling asleep and resting my head on my mother's lap and going straight home to bed for our afternoon nap. I can almost hear my mother's voice in the distance saying how much better we slept if we had been to the beach.

In the same box where I found my parents' wartime letters, there were many other personal letters that I also brought back to Philadelphia. In my self-appointed job as the family sleuth, I read with great interest nine letters that my father had written to my mother during two weeks at the end of the summer of 1946; they illustrate how life in Valencia must have been like for my family. It is too bad that I do not have my mother's letters because she might have written something about me to make up for the missing baby pictures. I was ten months old at the time and my brother was almost three. We were spending a few days in Jávea, a quaint beach town on the coast of Alicante, south of Valencia, where my mother used to go before she was married. It seemed that she was recuperating from an illness or she needed to rest and get stronger, because my dad asked her several times about her health and if she had been able to find her medicine. My father stayed behind teaching at the Academia Martí and tutoring at home; he was not working at the University of Valencia yet.

This was the first time that my parents were separated again since the end of the Spanish Civil War, seven years earlier. My dad made references to his "two new addressees." Starting with his: "Queridísima chatita e hijitos" (My very dear 'chatita' and little children), it is obvious that they were still very much in love and were a doting couple with their two small children. My father missed my mother more than he thought possible and he made a point of saying that he loved her as much as during their courtship. He also missed my brother and asked my mother to mention him often so he would not forget his dad. There is an endearing episode my father described when he heard a truck on Turia Street and knew that my brother would have loved seeing it. There is practically no mention of me, other than he sent cans of condensed milk for "la nena" (Valencian for the little girl).

The most striking part of these letters are the details about the food my father could and could not find in Valencia to send to my mother who needed such basic things as milk, sugar, rice and olive oil. My father had coupons to get rations for us while other family members shared whatever else they had for him to send to his young family. There is such a difference from reading about this situation in history books to seeing the lists of items my dad had found and was sending to her: "17 bread rolls, 2 and a half kilograms of rice, half kilo of sausages, 6 chocolate buns, a can of milk and a little bit of sugar" (September 4, 1946). The package was sent inside a basket by bus. I can certainly appreciate how lack of nutrition impacted my mother's health, my brother's growth and my own physical development. There was a direct reference, for example, that after a child was nine months old, only two cans of milk per week were allowed and I was about to turn ten months old (August 29, 1946). It was also shocking to read that my dad had to go from house to house to get paid; even Academia Martí would not pay his August wages until October. I had heard these stories before but for me these evocative letters full of emotion and suffering more than redeem my parents' role as providers. As in any family, their love may not have lasted forever, but there was love indeed. We were a happy family then.

True to form, there were some funny elements in my dad's letters as well. When my mother wrote without proper punctuation, he said: "I beg you to at least use some commas and indispensable periods . . . your paragraphs are so long that they seem like a roll of toilet paper" (August 29, 1946). While my mother was away, my dad ate his mid-day meal with my Aunt Elena and Uncle Pepe who lived close by. My dad was on his own for his evening meals, but after a few days and when the cleaning woman did not come, he did not know what to do with the dishes. He had to ask one of his aunts to send her maid to clean up the kitchen. For once, I am speechless and I can see why my mother needed to hire help during the years that my brother and I were little.

On another occasion my father told my mother to stop complaining and to come back if she was having such a hard time: "You don't eat, you don't sleep, 'la nena' doesn't take to the breast, 'el nene' has an upset stomach and I don't know how many more calamities . . . When you get this letter, pack up the knapsack and without any more explanations come back" (September 4, 1946). The truth was that he did not like being alone and he was helpless on the domestic front. He was so upset that he used the "f" word and underlined it, something he never had done in his four hundred plus war letters: "I have never had such a '_jodida_' week as the last one" (September 3, 1946). He hated writing letters about food and pesetas; I am sure he would rather write about his forlorn love or his career. At the end of our stay he found out that my mother still needed to pay the rent and another lecture ensued. He told her that she was not practical or decisive because he had to borrow some money then (September 6, 1946). All is well that ends well in this roller-coaster of a summer vacation, because he ended his last letter with these loving words: "Take good care of the 'nenes' and your-self. Hope you three are very strong and very beautiful. I have never loved you and desired you as much as now . . . I adore you, Juan" (September 10, 1946).

A not-so-loving find among the family letters was a note written by my Aunt Teresa, inviting my father to her wedding during the time that my dad was estranged from his stepmother. She wrote that she had been forbidden to visit him by Uncle Miguel but, neverthe-less, wanted to invite him to her wedding. I wish my father had not

164

left a copy of his answer for posterity as this letter was painful to read: "I'm sorry that I can't change at all my personal stance. Three months ago, Uncle Miguel and I promised that we would never see each other again . . . on my part it's true that I have kept my word with pleasure . . . " (November 11, 1946). I will spare the reader the rest of two-page letter. At least my dad came by his propensity for vendettas and family drama honestly. Now I know that the infamous breakup lasted five years, from the year I was born until the deathbed scene of my dad's stepmother in April 1951, but I never found out the reason for the estrangement.

One of the last recollections I have of my life in Valencia is of our furniture, tied up with giant ropes, coming out from the living room balcony to the street and the moving truck below. I had never seen anything like it before and I remember that I stayed very close to my mother's skirt that day so as to not be left behind; I did not care where we were going.

The house my parents had purchased in Madrid was not ready at the time promised, so my mother, my brother and I stayed behind in Valencia and joined my dad a few months later at the beginning of the school year. When we arrived to Madrid, we lived in two rooms at a "pensión" on Menéndez y Pelayo Boulevard, waiting for the building in Plaza del Niño Jesús to be finished. I can only imagine how difficult it must have been for my mother to leave Valencia and her beloved family. I know that she insisted and got her way about living next to the beautiful El Retiro Park, which made up for leaving the Botanical Gardens behind.

In the same box in the attic I also found eighteen letters from my dad that he wrote to my mother during those months that they were apart in 1952–1953. In some ways these letters are the most moving yet. My dad went to Madrid without a secure job and took whatever classes he could find in high schools, religious schools or private students. Fourteen years after the end of the Spanish Civil War, there seemed to be plenty of food, no more rationing or coupons. In fact, my father wrote in great detail what he had to eat and it seemed plentiful. His biggest concern, aside from his customary obsession over my mother's absence, was getting a salary to support his family. Both he and my mother made detailed expense accounts from a pair of socks (12 pesetas) to the mattress man (20 pesetas). I remember that mattresses were made of raw wool and a man would come and whip the wool spread out on the building's sunny terrace until it was fluffy again. People were late paying my dad's wages and he had to go, practically begging, from place to place. I admire how brave it was of my parents to leave the relative security of Valencia, moving to what they hoped would be a better life in Madrid. When my father received his first payment for an article in *El Alcázar*, a Madrid newspaper, he said: "Literature doesn't pay for our food, but it at least gives enough to have breakfast" (July 29, 1953).

In these letters it is evident how much my father loved us and how concerned he was for our wellbeing. He typed letters for my brother and me so we could read them, telling us to have fun, to go to the beach and to eat a lot. Here is his answer to a little note I had written to him that was replete with spelling mistakes:

> Very dear Conchín: It is necessary that I start this letter dedicating it to you because you have been the best with your daddy . . . you wrote me a very cute and nice little letter, with stupendous hand-writing. I thank you very much. I hope that you have a good time, that you eat more each day, that you get a bit fat because then you will be very beautiful and stronger . . . In the meantime receive the most loving kisses and many hugs with all the love of your dad that never forgets you. (August 3, 1953)

It was worth the wait, reading hundreds of letters to find these loving words from my father to me alone. Notice the emphasis on eating a lot and getting fat, always making up for the time when we did not have enough to eat. In addition to the letter above, there was one letter that I found particularly endearing. My dad had been desperately looking for more teaching jobs and a suitable place for my mother, my brother and me to stay temporarily and he was feeling "alicaído" (down in the dumps) when he wrote to my mother: "The truth is that perhaps I am but a grown child and I need your contact even to breathe" and at the end of the same letter he added this note: "I have the children nailed to my soul. Give them lots of kisses" (October 6, 1952). I cannot think of my dad as a family man at a more vulnerable and loving moment.

There was also a mention of my father being sick with what I remember him calling "el pinchazo," a very sharp pain in his chest that plagued him during the years we lived in Madrid. Dr Jáñez, was already our family doctor in those early days; he made house calls for 100 pesetas. Both of my father's parents had died young of tuberculosis, something that my family never spoke of, as if it were something to be embarrassed about, although it was a known fact. My father finally revealed this family's pseudo-secret to me many years later during one of my frequent visits to Bloomington when he taught at Indiana University. I wonder if my father was afraid that he had tuberculosis as his parents did. The only letter from my mother in this batch told about my brother getting all the end-of-the-year school prizes and how my brother looked so formal in his sailor suit and gold medals. The same day, I premiered a new hairdo, wore the First Communion dress — shortened, of course — insisting on wearing my white gloves too. According to my mother, the three of us were "a punto de caramelo," something similar to eye-candy (October 12, 1953).

Once we joined my dad in Madrid, my brother and I were the only children in the "pensión." I slept in the same bedroom with him and, although we fought like siblings are known to do, we could talk sotto voce until we fell asleep and felt more grownup. We lived directly across from the zoo in El Retiro Park, since this was before it was moved to La Casa de Campo in 1995. We could hear the lions roaring at their meal time and could smell the elephants. The best day ever was when it snowed. We had never seen snow before, being children from the Mediterranean provinces as we were. We had the day off from school and my brother and I made a giant snowball that we rolled home and tried to keep in the bathtub. I would not be surprised if my mother was part of this adventure, since we were not allowed to cross the boulevard alone yet.

I was almost disappointed when our new house was finally ready. It was — and still is — right in front the Puerta del Niño Jesús entrance to El Retiro Park. Although it was situated on the outskirts of the city then, it is considered centrally located nowadays. My toy kitchen did not make it to Madrid. This house was not as big and there were no hall closets. I still did not have my own bedroom; I slept on a Murphy bed in the family room. To console me, a family friend who owned a toy store, brought me a Murphy bed that looked just like mine for Manolín, my boy doll. My mother kept her promise and crocheted an entire outfit in periwinkle blue wool for him. He is wearing it to this day: his short pants held up with suspenders, a long-sleeve jacket, booties, and a dapper looking beret. Manolín is the only doll that made it to this side of the Atlantic when my family emigrated. He is no longer on my bed; he is not suitable for prime time, but he still sits in my closet. His blue eyes no longer open and he does not cry when I tap him gently on his back as he used to. But he still smells like my mother, a mixture of lavender cologne and soap.

I did not mind having to sleep in a Murphy bed; I got used to sleeping with everyone sitting around the old "mesa camilla," although we did not need the "brasero" because our home had central heating. There was a shelf behind the door, on top of the radiator, where I kept my books. I loved this room, especially because it faced an interior garden with an ornamental pool full of goldfish. The enclosed walls of the garden had an echo effect when the street vendors passed by screaming their wares: "Afiladooor" (the knife sharpener) or "Trapeeero" (the rag man). My favorite spot in the house was sitting on the family room balcony to read in the summer since I was finally too old to take a nap.

I was still a mousey little girl, thin and small to the point that my schoolmates in Nuestra Señora de Loreto, the uppity school my parents sent me to in Madrid, nick-named me "canija," the runt. Where were the Christian values of the French Ursuline nuns? I had my period late, at fourteen, and when it finally arrived — in gym class, of course — I still did not know what was happening to me and thought that I was bleeding to death. My mother and I had arguments about this for years afterward. She claimed that I was such a "sabelotodo," a know-it-all, that she thought I knew about "those" things. How I went from being mousey to becoming a know-it-all, I have no idea.

The University of Madrid, where my dad taught Latin and Classical Greek, was too far and too dangerous to reach by bicycle. My father bought a brand-new Vespa-like scooter — an Iruña, a Spanish make he was very proud of. He took me to school every morning. At first, I had to stand on the scooter in front of him, protected by the windshield. Later, I could sit behind him, holding on tightly to his waist, as my mother did. She picked me up after school and we walked home the two kilometers down the boulevard, next to El Retiro's wrought iron fence, passing our old "pensión," stopping for errands along the way. Since we were saving money not taking the bus, we often shared a gelato from Ilsa-Frigo on Alcalá Street. University professors received free tuition for their children at the best schools in the city and my parents chose the most academically prestigious. My brother went to the Jesuit School and excelled in his studies. I was a late bloomer; I would not really come into my own until we moved to the United States. I cannot brag about my grades, since I also found my report cards from Nuestra Señora de Loreto School — another vicissitude of being the family sleuth!

My brother and I knew that our classmates came from wealthy families, but I do not think we minded. Having a uniform helped to hide the class differences, although I did not even have "quita y pon," one uniform to put on and another to take off. I only had one regulation gray jumper with a red polka dot blouse, a gray sweater, a gray coat and a gray beret. A red striped gingham duster, which we wore at school, helped keep the uniform clean. My mother's philosophy was that being clean was more important than being rich. I had a special dispensation to arrive at school after the daily Mass. Fortuitously, my father knew the Mother Superior from Valencia, Sister María Margarita, and she was happy to oblige. I was more embarrassed to skip Mass than by the economic differences. It was suspected that, being from Valencia, my dad had been "un rojo," "a Red," because he had fought against Franco, although those things were not spoken about, at least not among the children.

Although my grades did not show it, I received a solid academic education with the Ursuline nuns, particularly in French and the Arts. I hate to admit it, but my favorite class was sewing, in part because Madre María Matilde was so kind, unlike the other nuns. We had to make a complete baby layette, first in tissue paper and, when that project was approved, in mousseline. Mine was perfect for Manolín, my boy doll, in celeste blue. We also learned traditional embroidery stiches and some lace making. It was an all-girls school and I was not aware that we were being indoctrinated in the ideals of the Sección Femenina, founded by Pilar Primo de Rivera, the sister of the Falangist leader. Under the Franco regime, girls were brought up to be mothers of as many children as possible to perpetuate the Spanish race that had been decimated during the Spanish Civil War. Mary Nash explains it this way:

The Francoist discourse about women was elaborated from the traditional gender discourse in its configuration of women as wife and mother. Its purpose was the limitation of women to their domestic chores at home, and the recuperation of the patriarchal family and the social subordination of women in an androcentric patriarchal order. (621)

As I got older, I became aware of my family's liberal tendencies and wanted to leave the religious school. My father said that if I passed all the subjects of the 4th year State Exam (la Reválida) he would allow me to transfer. I am sure he thought I would fail math, as I had done other years, but I surprised everyone, including myself, and passed all the subjects with a "notable" (a solid B). My father kept his word. The last year of my life in Spain I went to the progressive San Estanislao de Kostka School on Atocha Street. By then I could walk to school alone through El Retiro Park, coming out by the bookstalls on Moyano Street and I felt like what Carmen Martín Gaite called a "chica topolino," a modern girl American movie style (87-89). How prophetic was that? However, when I travel with my daughters to Madrid, we always stop by Nuestra Señora del Loreto School; it looks just as formidable as it did back then behind its tall brick walls. The only difference is that it is no longer on General Mola Boulevard, now it is on Príncipe de Vergara, because the names of the streets in Madrid have been renamed to their original names before Franco.

There were other vestiges of the Spanish postwar years that I remember very well. For example, the many widows who had lost their husbands during the war on the Nationalist side, were given government jobs by Tabacalera, the Spanish tobacco monopoly (widows of Republican soldiers did not receive such benefits). Every block, including ours, had at least one of those stores that also sold stamps and candy. We used to meet our friends there to go for our evening strolls. There were electricity and water restrictions. In the mornings we had to fill up the tub, just in case we needed water before it came back on. Children were not allowed to ride the elevator to save energy; thank goodness that we lived only on the third floor. It was also the time of the polio epidemic. We knew children who were sick for months and walked with crutches. We had to wash our hands the minute we got home and if my father saw us touch our eyes or mouths, we were sure to get a good smack. (I realize that we cannot blame Franco for the polio epidemic).

A very worrisome time was when the Turia River in Valencia flooded and my parents could not reach family members to make sure they were safe. I remember that my dad took the Auto Res and left in a hurry to check on his old aunts who lived at our former house on Turia Street. For years after that, one could see watermarks on the sides of the buildings. Now, I do need to give Franco credit for something. Rivers like the one in Valencia that flooded regularly were diverted out of the cities. An outstanding part of Valencia nowadays is the old river bed where gardens and postmodern projects have sprouted up, including Santiago Calatrava's futuristic Ciutat de les Arts i les Ciènces (The City of Arts and Sciences) and El Palau de les Arts Reina Sofía (The Art Palace Queen Sofía). Also, during Franco's regime an extensive irrigation and water maintenance system was constructed that provided electricity and water. Huge dams appeared all over Spain, where there was not a drop of water before. During the summer, we used to go to the San Juan Reservoir in the province of Toledo near Madrid. It was not the beach in Valencia, but we knew how to swim by then and could dive to see submerged under water the small villages that had existed before.

Another emergency trip to Valencia was when my maternal grandfather passed away in 1961. He used to visit us regularly, taking turns staying with us and Uncle Pepe. It was my first experience missing someone and seeing my mother cry. She left for Valencia alone, dressed completely in black as I had not seen her since we were little. I wore a black bow with my uniform as was the custom then to show that we were a family in mourning. I do not know why my parents did not go back to Valencia unless it was for an emergency. I wonder if my dad was still feuding with his family. I went back with my cousins every year for Las Fallas holidays in March, something that I still love to do whenever I can.

A highlight for my mother while we lived in Madrid was when Uncle Pepe and Aunt Elena also moved to the capital and bought a flat around the corner from ours. It was traditional for families then to live close to each other, particularly if they moved to the same city as was the case with my mother's brother. We did everything together. They had a TV before we did and my brother and I were allowed to run to their place after dinner to watch *Sea Hunt* with Lloyd Bridges — *Investigador submarino* as it was called in Spanish — my brother's favorite show; I was still running behind my brother

171

to do everything. Since the opening of diplomatic relations between Spain and the United States, President Eisenhower's visit to Madrid in 1959 and the opening of American military bases in Spain, including the one near Madrid, Torrejón de Ardoz, American culture began to permeate Spanish culture, especially in film and television. We loved everything American: Elvis Presley, Rock and Roll, Coca-Cola. Several American families moved to our neighborhood, but the children attended their own schools and did not play with us. They used their typical yellow school buses; little did I know that I would have American children of my own in due time!

In addition to his academic duties at the University and tutoring at home, my father had started to publish literary reviews in magazines and newspapers. His first full-length book on contemporary writers from Spain, *Hora actual de la novela española* (Present Hour of the Spanish Novel), was awarded the National Prize for Criticism in 1958 and his reputation catapulted from then on. Writers from all over Spain would come to our home for lively discussions, some coffee or wine and heavy smoking, I could smell the tobacco from the family room, even though my father's study's door was always closed. My mother continued being as fervent a reader as we saw in her letters as a young woman. She participated in these literary salons and was an essential part of my dad's intellectual life. For example, she attended all my dad's lectures at the Madrid Athenaeum and Public Radio, which my brother and I were not allowed to do because we had homework. Although she did not have a job outside of the home as she did in her youth — we saw that my dad would not consider that option — she was more than a traditional wife according to Francoist ideals. My father was the family patriarch and an intellectual, but she was his first supporter and helper if not a collaborator and muse.

Under my father's tutelage I became a good reader too. Occasionally I would make an appearance in his study and he introduced me to some of the writers. Surprisingly, in due time, I would write myself about some of our visitors: Josefina Aldecoa, José Luis Castillo-Puche and Jesús Fernández Santos, the theme of my future Ph.D. dissertation. My dad often wrote about contemporary American writers as well: Faulkner, Dos Passos, Steinbeck, Hemingway, Sinclair Lewis. These articles would become the door that opened the opportunity for my father to emigrate to the United States under the auspices of the Fulbright Program.

Life in Spain

My parents seemed very happy then; they did many things together, including traveling throughout Spain on the scooter. My mother had a special "falda-pantalón," a "skort" to ride comfortably. She would come back from her trips tanned and beautiful with her chestnut hair almost strawberry blonde. My father was so dark that we teased him, saying that he looked like President Nasser of Egypt — "with less hair," my mother would whisper. My brother and I also took turns going with my father on shorter trips around Madrid Province. A memorable one for me was going to Segovia and Ávila and hearing my father's explanations of the historical buildings and the artistic details that could be found in the most insignificant towns. I remember thinking on those trips that I understood why my mother loved my dad so much, even though he could be so strict with us. My parents also made their first trip to France and Italy with another couple who had a car, the Salineros. That was a big event in those days, the first European trip! I must have been paying attention because I have my dad's adventurous character and I love to travel too.

Although my mother suffered frequent liver colic flareups that kept her in bed for days at a time and she had to watch what she ate, I do not remember her being sick in the hospital or having medical emergencies yet; those would come later when we lived in the United States. Her dentist, Don Tirso, was more frequent in her life than Dr. Jáñez. She would go see him even if she had to wait for summer trips when she was back in Spain.

By 1960, our life had changed considerably for the better. We belonged to the trendy Apóstol Santiago Club that opened on the Avenida de América on the road to Barajas Airport. My brother and I went swimming every day in the summers and I started playing tennis there on the red clay courts, perfectly equipped with white short tennis dresses. We did not have a car yet, but we were on the waiting list to buy one. There were still lines for some things. When we finally bought a SEAT 600, the Spanish version of the Italian Fiat 500, my father had not been able to pass his driver's test and this made for some funny situations for the rest of the family. The tests were given inside El Retiro Park, around the Fallen Angel Fountain — perhaps that should have been a warning. After the second try my dad was so nervous that he could not eat or talk about anything else. By then, the car was parked in front of the door of our building and my dad and brother would start it every day so the battery would not die; they would sit inside for a while with the motor running and nowhere to go. They would try the windshield wipers, the horn and the lights, studying the gearshift. My brother was not old enough to get his permit yet, but he seemed to know more about the car than my dad, which did not sit well within the family hierarchy. Finally, my dad passed his driver's test on the third try and the Alborg family had arrived, so to speak. We took one trip to Valencia to say goodbye to our family, because my parents were leaving for the United States for a year as my dad was going to teach in Seattle at the University of Washington.

My brother and I were ecstatic with the news. The thought that we were going to be alone in Madrid for a year without our parents was the talk of the neighborhood. Aunt Amparín would stay with us, but we had stayed with her before and we knew we could get away with everything. We were going to have a "guateque," a party with music and dancing, every weekend. I had secret desires to steal Jorge, my brother's best friend. I was tired of doing everything with my brother and I wanted to act on my first boy crush. My parents were going by ocean liner from Barcelona to New York City and then by airplane to the West Coast. My mother started making bed and kitchen linens, with the customary initials, that were going to be sent ahead in a big trunk. The seamstress and the Singer sewing machine were working non-stop.

One day that summer, my father came to pick up my brother and me at the Santiago Club, which was very unusual. When we got in the car, he gave us an envelope. My brother opened it, but neither one of us understood what was happening. We had never seen an airplane ticket before and our names were the same as our parents . . . they had changed their mind and we were all flying to America! A whirlwind of activity ensued. We had to get passports, visas and shots at the American Embassy, all the things that our parents had been doing, but in a hurry.

My mother equipped us with heavy winter clothing and snow boots, since she had seen on the map that Seattle was very close to Canada. We purchased some clothing at El Corte Inglés, the famous department store, which we did not use to do, but we were running out of time. My mother's fur coat was shortened and remade for me to wear in the Canada-like winter. That must have appeased me somewhat. But it is strange that I do not remember how I felt those short weeks before our departure; probably I could not anticipate how our lives were going to dramatically change. I only recall the trip to Valencia. My mother and I sat in the back seat; if you had seen a SEAT 600, you would know that the back windows did not open and my brother decided that the car ran better with the heat on. Never mind that it was the month of August in the Castilian sun. He sat in the front passenger seat, of course, because he was smart enough to announce that he got carsick in the back. How he knew that is a miracle, since this was our first trip, —and our last together in Spain.

The SEAT 600 was sold; the Antonio Mingote family, the famous cartoonist from the *ABC* newspaper, who was still waiting for a car, bought it. All four of us purchased white, airplane-weight suitcases from the Taurus store, no less. My mother and I also bought matching beauty cases, outdated pieces of luggage the size and shape of a large tool box, that clogged up my closets for years afterward. On the day of our departure we were all dressed up for the flight. My mother wore a cream-colored linen suit, newly made for the occasion. I wore a pleated navy-blue skirt that had been hers, my red suede jacket over a white blouse and white gloves, as a young lady should.

Red, white and blue. How appropriate for our upcoming American experience.

Queridas nietas:

Tengo mu-
chísimas ganas de veros.

Me pongo triste que no poda
mos reunirnos estas fiestas.

Tenéis una prima española
muy salada y parece que se
parece a a los Alborg. ¿? que se

Espero de veras que nos po-
dos reunir para que os podáis
ver.

Dios querrá que ese día yo lo
pueda ver.

Besos, Besos y Besos de la abue
lita y "yayo".

concha

Navidad 20 de Dic. 1974.

Life in the United States

We arrived in New York City on Labor Day weekend 1961 and, just as we expected, were immediately in awe of all things American. On our first morning in the new country we saw a colorful parade marching down Fifth Avenue: high school bands, one after another in bright uniforms, the boys wearing long pants and the girls shorter ones over flesh-colored stockings; majorettes, even more scantily dressed, with tasseled boots, twirling their batons in unison behind a drum player. We had seen extravaganzas like this in American movies, but nothing matched experiencing it live. We ate in Horn & Hardart automated cafeterias, not for the food, which my parents did not like, but because we had never seen anything like it. All of those strange dishes revolving behind doors under bright lights were amazing. The most memorable event of those first few days was when my dad insisted on taking us to the Museum of Modern Art to see Pablo Picasso's *Guernica*.

During the Spanish Civil War, the Republican Government commissioned Picasso to paint a mural representing Spain at the Paris International Exposition, that was celebrated in July 1937. Despite its large measurements of 11½ by 25½ feet, Picasso painted it in merely three weeks, what Carsten-Peter Warncke calls " . . . surely the best-known 20th century work of art (145). Appalled by the brutal bombing of the Basque town of Guernica on April 26, 1937, by German aircraft that supported Franco's forces during the war, Picasso created his masterpiece that became an allegory of the Spanish Civil War. Although the accounts as to the total number of casualties have been surrounded by controversy, many hundreds of townspeople were killed during three hours of the horrific attack, perpetrated to scare the Basque region into surrendering. Xabier Irujo argues in his book, *Gernika: Genealogy of a Lie*, that: "There were more than 2,000 deaths among a population of the approximately 10,000 to 12,000 civilians who were in the urban area" (xvii).

Painted in shades of black, gray and white, it is clearly structured as a tryptic: two rectangles of screaming victims on the sides and a triangle of destruction and confusion in the middle. According to Warncke, even the animals represent Spain: "The bull and horse, through their association with bullfighting, stand for Spain: the horse is the people suffering, the bull the people triumphant, but both are victims of aggression and destructive violence. All the figures in *Guernica* are victims" (153). Picasso lent his famous painting to MoMA with the stipulation that it would be returned to Spain only after Franco's death and the implementation of a democratic government.

I remember climbing the steps with my family to the landing where the mural was displayed. It was absolutely mesmerizing! We heard my father's explanation and knew how much it meant to him to show it to us. It seemed that our trip to the United States had a purpose, yet we had no idea that our stay would be much longer than a year, especially for me. *Guernica* finally arrived in Spain in 1981, six years after the dictator's death, and the implementation of the new democratic Constitution in 1978. I saw it the following year in el Casón del Buen Retiro, an annex of the Prado Museum, where it was first housed. It was moving to see long lines of Spaniards who had never seen the masterpiece before, many of them who had probably fought in the Spanish Civil War, standing on Alfonso XII Street. It was showcased in a huge room, with the color studies and related paintings in two side galleries. There was room for hundreds of people, who were all standing in complete silence, something very unusual with a Spanish group.

I have taken my two daughters several times to see this painting in the Museo Nacional Centro de Arte Reina Sofía where it is now housed. It does not show as well in this new venue, where it shares space with other contemporary works, as it did in MoMA or when it was first shown in Madrid. But I repeat my dad's teachings faithfully and I am pleased that Diana and Jane are moved, listening and watching — a lesson learned from my dad for the younger generation. As Margaret Van Epp Salazar has said: "These personal narratives form a bridge in time between the present and the civil war. Just as our parents' and grandparents' stories connect us to an earlier era, eclipse the distance between decades and centuries, so these voices with their own particular vision and focus offer an unprecedented look at the Spanish Civil War" (372).

Memory is a strange process, as I have no other recollections of those first days in New York City with my family. I am sure we went to many tourist sites; we must have gone to the top of the Empire State Building, visited the Statue of Liberty and Rockefeller Center, but I do not recall. In this case my memory works similarly to a computer that saves the last version of a document; subsequent visits have erased the memories of the original one, which should have been unforgettable. The next American experience found us on the long flight to Seattle in a propeller airplane that made several stops and took all day. My father kept repeating that the distance we were flying was similar to going from Madrid to Moscow, as if we had ever been on such a trip. I looked it up and he was right, it is about 2,500 miles or 4,000 kilometers.

The reception we received by my father's university colleagues in Seattle could not have been more cordial, nothing like the Americans we had seen in Madrid. A modestly furnished faculty house in Union Bay, close to the campus, was all set for the immigrant family with the trunk my mother had so lovingly prepared waiting for us. This was the first time that I had my own room; no wonder I loved the new country! The faculty wives took my mother and me to a thrift shop. I guess that such places did not exist in Spain because there was nothing to be given away there. We bought kitchen utensils, curtains and small lamps to tide us over for a year. We collected coupons for free dishes at the A & P supermarket, another American phenomenon. My mother helped me decorate my room with a lively print of big red apples; she made me a bedspread with the leftover material. It was probably meant for a kitchen, but I did not notice it then.

In those very first days my father and brother went to buy a car. In the States people did not need to wait to get government permission and, better yet, my dad did not need to take the driver's test again. My brother passed his on the first try, so we then had two drivers in the family. Our car was a huge, yellow 1952 Mercury Monterey with black trim in near-perfect condition. I can only imagine what it must have meant to them to go to a used car lot and just drive away with the car to our new home.

Despite being so close to Canada, Seattle turned out to have milder weather than Madrid. A misty rain permeated the air almost every day, but it made for a lush, green beautiful city full of gardens and woods with the Puget Sound always in the background. My father said it was similar to Galicia, in Spain, another place we had never been. There were many other immigrant families in our neighborhood and some from Latin American countries with whom we could speak in Spanish. As luck would have it, an Argentinian family with a toddler lived nearby and I started babysitting for them. Young people in Spain never had jobs and there I was working and earning dollars. When they moved, I got their television set as part of my salary. I wonder how my brother felt about his little sister having a TV in her own room.

I had a year of high school left, but it was decided that I could not go to a traditional school because I needed to learn English first. For some odd reason, girls in Spain studied French while most boys studied English. My brother was able to start his university studies and he and my dad commuted together. My mother and I studied English at Thomas Edison Technical School. My dad dropped us off in the morning. My mother and I started in the same class, but I was soon moved up. I read an article that said "Learn English With Only Ten Verbs" and I really believed it. Compared to the Latin and Classical Greek I studied in Madrid, English was easy. It was like a game, filling out notebooks with simple sentences, answering in unison as if we were children.

But learning English became a bone of contention for my family. In no time I became the family interpreter, even though it was a new language for me. My dad could speak English somewhat, but he used to say that he could not understand anyone without a Ph.D. That left him at my mercy from the moment he was away from campus. There were times of high frustration for him. My mother could not speak English at all. She would say "squish me" instead of "excuse me," but for some reason she could understand better than my dad. When we were out together, people would start talking to my mother, asking her to tell him something or other. My father would intervene saying that he could speak and she could not. People thought differently and kept addressing my mother instead of him, which infuriated him.

Most of the students at Edison Technical School were Asian and I began speaking English with a Japanese accent. After a Chinese student I exchanged stamps with asked me out, my father gave me a lecture in good old Castilian Spanish. I had never dated; young people went out in groups in Spain and I always tagged along with my brother. My dad suggested that I stick to stamp collecting. The tension mounted when I finished all the English courses and one of my teachers suggested that I work as an interpreter at the Seattle World's Fair that was opening in April of 1962. I was hired immediately and started working at the Spanish Pavilion a few weeks before the fair opened. It was unbelievable to me that I was working and making serious money just a few months after our arrival. I loved working there and showing off in front of the newly arrived Spaniards that worked at the Pavilion, pretending that I knew about Flamenco or bullfighting, things that we never did in my family and I knew nothing about. I had a lunchbreak in the afternoons and could roam the fair like a tourist. I went up in the Space Needle with its beautiful view of Mount Rainier blanketed with pink snow. I discovered Belgian waffles with strawberries and cream; the only problem was that, on one occasion, I rode the roller coaster after gorging and got sick all over the attendant at the end of the ride. I have never ridden a roller coaster since, although I still like Belgian waffles.

Immigration is not easy for families and not everyone adjusts at the same speed. My mother was not happy in Seattle and was not sleeping well. She was not able to go out on her own and had to rely on my dad for everything. "One could not walk anywhere in an American city and she could not drive," I heard her complaining. My dad lectured her about missing Madrid and El Retiro Park then, while she used to miss Valencia and the Botanical Gardens before. She was prescribed phenobarbital for her insomnia, which we found out later was harmful for her liver. On the only snowy day we had that first winter in Seattle, my dad lost control of the Mercury on a steep hill and my mother broke her left ankle. With a cast up to her knee, on crutches and in pain, she never went back to Edison Technical School. A 1958 white and red Plymouth Fury with huge fins replaced the Mercury Monterey that had been totaled in the accident.

There were some good moments too. We went to a fish market where the merchants were Sephardic Jews whose ancestors had left Spain centuries ago. Some still had a symbolic key of their ancestral homes. Some spoke Ladino, their original medieval language, and my father could converse with them — how ironic that he could understand Ladino but not English. My mother and I enjoyed shopping in F. W. Woolworth's. They had everything there, from clothing to sewing notions, and, since it was self-serve, we did not need to talk with the employees. I bought some of my first bras there; the late-bloomer was growing at a fast pace.

We still did things as a family. I remember going together to our first American film, it was *West Side Story* with Natalie Wood and Rita Moreno. In one evening, I went from adoring Sissi, the Austrian Empress played by Romy Schneider — I had seen her in three films in Madrid — and wanting to be like European royalty to Maria, my new American idol, in love with a rabble-rouser. From Viennese waltzes to American swing jazz, I learned the lyrics for all the songs. My Spanish accent came in handy for something; I could belt out "I Feel Pretty" and "America" with gusto, oblivious to how the rest of my family was feeling. But nothing compared to our first American Thanksgiving. Some university colleagues invited us to their lovely home with a view of the Puget Sound, so typical in Seattle. Turkey was still a rarity in Spain, and all the other dishes were truly exotic: that mixture of the sweet cranberries with the savory corn stuffing, the yams with marshmallows and pumpkin pie. I was proud of my parents who tasted everything and did not complain. Well, only when we were in the car, I heard my dad say that "these Americans had everything but a good wine."

My father must have started to think that he would never go back to live in Spain. His teaching load consisted of two or three classes a week which, compared to his schedule in Madrid, gave him a lot more time for his writing. He was one of the stars on campus; his students, mostly female, adored him. Other universities came courting and that summer he planned to teach at Purdue University, in Indiana, where he had the best offer. I wonder if he remembered his old idol, the Midwesterner Martin Arrowsmith, and if the upcoming move was part of his American dream.

We left Seattle on June 1 because Glacier National Park did not open until that day and we could not miss it. The Plymouth Fury was more comfortable than the old SEAT 600; my mother and I still shared the back seat. My brother and dad shared the driving. We ran into a snow storm as we arrived in Helena, Montana. According to family lore, I was screaming hysterically, afraid we would have another accident, but I do not share that memory. We drove through the Dakotas and the Great Lakes to Chicago where in the Art Institute Cafeteria my uncomprehending dad threw a temper tantrum because he was served a gravy-covered hamburger when he had asked for a Salisbury steak! We continued all the way north to Niagara Falls, one of our favorite spots. It was a rainy day, but we did not care since we had to wear the bright yellow raincoats for the tour. By then, we knew that my father's one-year Fulbright contract had been extended, but we wanted to see as much of the United States as possible.

On the way back to Seattle we drove through interminable Kansas south to Albuquerque, New Mexico, where my father had been invited by another famous expatriate writer from Spain, Ramón Sender. It was so kind of him and his young wife to host a family of four, although my mother was critical of the May–December couple. We loved the American West best, stopping at every place that said "The World's Largest . . . " whether it was a serpent farm, a gold mine or a stalactite cave. Needless to say, the Grand Canyon and Sequoia National Park did not disappoint us. By the time we arrived in San Francisco, we were exhausted, sick of pizza and other American road food; we had not discovered Chinese food yet. We were ecstatic on our last leg of the trip that summer. My dad and brother had become excellent drivers no matter how long the distances — 800 miles to Seattle from San Francisco — and they never complained. My mother and I loved our backseat, often riding with the windows open and the wind twirling our hair. Air conditioning in cars was unheard of then, but at least we did not need to have the heat on. We took U S Highway 101 all the way north through Portland, Oregon. I still think that this is one of the most beautiful drives in the United States. When we arrived in Washington State, we felt at home in its luscious cool-ness. Seattle had never looked so gorgeous to us. I did not know yet that one the best experiences of my life awaited me, my senior year in an American high school!

My English had become a little rusty after speaking only Spanish with my family during the summer, but from the first day at Lincoln High School I was a happy senior. There were three other foreign students in exchange programs who were living with American families: Jerker from Sweden, Jorg from Germany and Joyce from France and we became fast friends. We were placed in some of the same classes, which was a great idea because then we did not feel self-conscious. In order to graduate with the rest of my class, I had to take American History, Health, Social Studies, and English. I also took French, which was the easiest class for me; the Ursuline nuns would have been very proud of me. But my favorite part of that year was the after-school activities. We did not have anything like that in Spain and I joined every group I could. I was the Vice President of the International Club. Although I could not sing, we performed at convocations, wearing appropriate clothing for each season. There is a picture of the group in the *Totem*, our yearbook, and we are all wearing ski sweaters, scarves and mittens (*Totem*, 1963, p. 37).

The French Club was also fun, I was a star there because of my excellent accent. We organized theme parties and it was not easy explaining to my parents what a Hawaiian Luau was and what it had to do with French culture. When I told them that a party was a sleepover, they insisted on calling other parents, which embarrassed me to death. They could not understand anything about American high school such as the senior cruise through the Puget Sound or the prom, although I did not attend it because I was not allowed to date yet. The one time I went to a Valentine's Day party with Jorg Rustige, the German exchange student, he made up with an ex-girlfriend and I had to call my brother to get a ride home — talk about being embarrassed!

Nothing compared to the Drama Club, though. In the fall I auditioned for Sabina, the maid in Thornton Wilder's *The Skin of Our Teeth*. How I dared to recite the opening and closing monologues with my thick accent, is a miracle. Since I got the part, it meant that I could direct in the One-Act Play Tournament in the spring. That was my shining moment. I directed *The Apollo of Bellac*, the Theater of the Absurd play by Jean Giraudoux. Mr. Rideout, the drama coach wrote in my yearbook: "Conchita, forgive me for doubting that you could play Sabina, or that you or anyone could present *Apollo* for a high school. I do hope this year has been happy for you. Sincerely, HB Rideout." On the final evening of the competition, my parents came to the performance and, surprisingly, I won the Best Director award. I ran up to the stage when I heard my name called and made a short acceptance speech thanking my cast and my parents, as if I were in Hollywood. I was wearing high-heels and a yellow angora wool dress with a bolero jacket that my mother had sewn. I believe it was the last homemade outfit that she made for me. I wonder if she told me that she used to love the theater as a young woman in Valencia before the war as I discovered in her letters. If she did, I was too absorbed in the moment, and only rediscovered this passion in her letters. By the end of the school year I knew that we were moving back to Indiana, and I would be attending Purdue University.

Unbeknownst to me, as I was all caught up with my senior year, the family dynamic kept changing. My brother had broken a leg playing soccer and had dropped out of the university. My mother grew unhappier as her health deteriorated; in addition to her liver flareups, she had developed an ulcer. She was not looking forward to the move to the Midwest to such a provincial town as West Lafayette, Indiana. In Seattle there were many faculty families like us and she would miss them. The battle lines were drawn: my father and I loved life in the USA and my mother and brother did not.

As soon as I graduated high school and the university semester was finished, we took another epic drive from the Pacific Northwest to the Midwest, this time pulling a small U-Haul with the Plymouth Fury and Kitty, our tabby cat who hated the car. We were becoming Americanized fast, hauling our possessions cross-country. I have photographs from that trip and we look happy. But, as soon as we moved into a large, furnished, ranch house in a subdivision in West Lafayette, my brother announced that he was going back to Spain. Within days he was boarding a Greyhound bus to New York City for his solo flight to Madrid. I really do not know what precipitated my brother's departure. Maybe it was something like Alison Bechdel says in her memoir, that in her family: " . . . there wasn't enough room under one roof for several geniuses" (71). We would never live together as a family again.

My mother was devastated by my brother's departure. In those days it was unheard of for young men to live alone, at least in Spanish culture. She was constantly worried about him. Was he getting enough to eat, was he depressed living alone, did he need more money? She waited faithfully for the mailman to see if there was a letter from him. He was a good correspondent because there were about a hundred letters between 1966 and 1973 from him to my parents in my collection of found treasures. These letters were carefully saved in their air mail envelopes, numbered and with little notes from my mother as to when they were answered. These would make another story altogether. Suffice it to say that my mother probably missed her son as much as she had missed my dad during the war years. She was counting the days when we would return to Spain permanently. How could anyone live in a country where one could not even find olive oil? It may seem crazy now, but we had to buy olive oil on our day trips to Chicago; it was not like nowadays when the whole country has turned gourmet.

In the meantime, I could not have been happier as a coed. During a trip to Chicago I outfitted myself with some mini-skirts and high, black Capezio boots from Peck & Peck, a long way from F. W. Woolworth's. I lived at home with my parents, but commuted to the university with a neighbor and spent most of my time on campus. I was given university credit for French, Spanish and Latin and began as a sophomore in my first year at Purdue with a concentration in Spanish literature, a minor in French and with the plan that I, too, would be a college professor someday. How could I not love it? I had started dating and met someone who I thought at the time, was the American man of my dreams. He was in his senior year and would be joining the Marine Corps Officers Training School in Quantico, Virginia, in the fall, but I did not think that far ahead — the present was too wonderful!

However, my parents were not happy with the person I was becoming. Despite how well I was doing academically and that I was following in my father's footsteps, I had some serious arguments with him. He waited up for me in the evenings. On one awful night, when my boyfriend's Jeep stalled in the snow, I came home after my curfew. My dad started to hit me, but I held his arm, screaming and told him that if he ever struck me again, I would call the police, that he would never get a green card and he would never be able to stay in this country; American parents were not allowed to abuse their children. I have no idea how I came up with that threat and how I dared to stand up to my all-powerful dad. When had little Conchín, "la nena," stopped existing? Where was my mother in those days? Why did she not stand up for me? She had changed too, from the young Conchita to Concha, from a happy woman to a sad, nostalgic shadow of herself. I was the new Conchita fast after her footsteps, although I did not know it yet.

Before my father could attain a permanent position at Purdue, he had to finish his contract with the Fulbright Program and return to Madrid for two years. My parents were leaving at the end of the school year and I flatly refused to go back with them. During those years, studies were not validated as they are today. I had not finished high school in Spain and would lose my university credits. In addition to that, I would need to serve six months doing the Servicio Social which was required of all young women under the auspices of Franco's Sección Femenina. Camen Martín Gaite wrote in her essay about life in postwar Spain, that the Social Service was a requirement for all women between seventeen and thirty-five years of age in order to obtain a job, whether they were single or widowed without children: "From January 1, 1945, the certificate will be required to obtain passports, driver's licenses, permits to hunt or fish, as well as to belong to artistic organizations, sport clubs, cultural or similar organizations" (59–60). My father's laws were equally strict in that they could not afford to pay for the upkeep of an American coed. Since I was so independent, I would need to pay my own expenses.

During the summer I became a facilitator with the Modern Languages Association. All I had to do was speak in Spanish with the high school teachers while they attended the program. Probably to pacify my parents, I became engaged on the Fourth of July (how American was that?) before my future husband left for the Marine Corps. His father was also a professor at the university and his mother made sure that an announcement was printed in the local newspaper with all the proper family pedigrees — my father-in-law had been hired at Purdue from Harvard. Nevertheless, I'm sure they were as mortified as my parents were, for different reasons; I was so young and an immigrant. In the fall, I moved into Purdue's first high-rise dormitory. I had two jobs: salesgirl at the University Book Store and Spanish tutor for the Boilermakers, Purdue's football team, including Bob Griese of future Miami Dolphins fame. It was fun, but it was not easy and I felt lonely. I really did not miss my parents as we had practically stopped talking to each other, under what became my father's sig-nature reprisal tactic: the silent treatment.

I do not have any letters from those months. I guess I was not as good a correspondent as my brother had been, but I am sure my mother suffered from being separated from me too. My fiancé and I decided to get married in Madrid as soon as he finished Officer Candidate School. The date was set for December 26, my parents' 22nd wedding anniversary. The department chairman's wife orga-nized a linen bridal shower for me and my roommate arranged another. I bought my own wedding gown on sale in the only bridal boutique in Lafayette for $99. I used one of the white suitcases my family had purchased a little over three years earlier for our trip to the States to carry the wedding dress to Madrid. I returned to finish the semester and took the exams after a short honeymoon in Madrid, before moving to Quantico, Virginia, to be a Marine Corps wife. It all seems absolutely crazy to me now, but it made sense at the time; I just wanted to start my own family and leave my "Spanishness" behind. Later on, when I had my own family, I used to tell my daughters that if they ever did anything like this, I would disown them. They both married late, interestingly enough in a joint wedding celebration, and had their children much later than I did.

I went to the Marine Corps officers' graduation with my future in-laws, who were so proud of their son since his father had also been a Marine officer during World War II. It all seemed surreal to me; all these tall and trim young men, with shaved heads in dress uniforms, carrying swords and looking alike. I could not recognize my future husband, since I had not seen him in five months. The days in Madrid before the wedding were a whirlwind of activities. My mother chose my veil and headpiece to go with the bargain wedding gown. She took me to the same photographer, Lagos, who had taken some gorgeous pictures of her. I looked, and was, so young, and I resembled her somewhat. Spanish weddings did not used to have attendants or bridesmaids and only my parents' friends, relatives and neighbors were invited. Traditionally, my father was the godfather and the groom's mother the godmother, dressed in black as per Spanish custom. It must have seemed just as surreal to her as the Marine Corps ceremony had been to me.

The honeymoon consisted of a few nights at the Ritz Hotel, one of the fanciest hotels in Madrid, on Plaza de Neptuno off El Paseo del Prado in the heart of the city. My husband loved Spain on his first trip, and he always would. He had studied Spanish at Purdue and was smitten with the culture from Hemingway to bullfighting. I could not wait to get back to the States. I felt that I did not belong in my own country anymore. There I was, a new bride, when a little over three years before I had left Spain with my parents and I was playing with dolls. Surprisingly, I had grown taller than anyone in my family, including my dad and my brother. It all had happened so fast. My family could not believe how tall the ugly duckling had become and they said that it must have been all the Coca-Cola I drank. In time, I had two daughters, never a boy to name Manolín; the thought of having a brother with that name used to send the two of them into hysterics.

In two short years, I was expecting my first daughter and my parents were returning to the States permanently. I think the following years were the most difficult ones for my mother. She must have been experiencing empty nest syndrome, although it was not a known term then. A trip to the Mayo Clinic confirmed what the Spanish doctors had been saying all along; she suffered from chronic liver disease and there was very little that could be done, other than rest and a special diet. The diagnosis had an official name, dietary cirrhosis, and the outcomes were daunting; biopsies, procedures and hospital visits followed with greater frequency. Her abdomen was swollen and she was jaundiced. In all of the photographs from those years, she looks dark, as if she had a suntan. There was talk about a liver transplant, but the first successful one was not performed until 1967 and the surgeries were experimental until the 1980s.

Despite my past rebelliousness, I was still very much my parents' daughter. When my husband served in Vietnam, I moved back to Lafayette and lived in the same apartment complex as they did. Both of them enjoyed their new roles as grandparents. During those sixteen months we were a family of sorts, although the arrangement was far from perfect for me. I took care of my baby — her father had left for the war when she was a mere six weeks old — but I lived practically in hiding, since I had dropped out of school without finishing my degree, something that my parents objected to, my mother in particular. I was in the awkward position of being a young married woman with a baby and a husband in the Marine Corps fighting in Vietnam in the midst of the anti-war demonstrations held on campus by my former classmates.

My parents were both loving grandparents to their first grandchild, a relationship that nurtured my daughter in her father's absence. My father used to sit on the floor with Diana and play silly games with her with complete joyfulness. I did not see that there were problems in their marriage then. I had enough to deal with in terms of raising my daughter and worrying about my husband flying over North Vietnam, dropping bombs from an F-4 Phantom. When the Marine returned and we moved to California, the fragile relationship I had reestablished with my parents floundered. They did not miss an opportunity to tell me that I had married too young, that I had not finished my degree, that they were not fond of my soldier husband. During those three years as a Marine Corps wife, I had moved four times.

I remember when my mother visited us in California as a particularly difficult time. She missed her granddaughter who had just turned two years old. I was happy to have a chance to share with her my life as a Marine Corps wife. We lived in a modest apartment in San Clemente that was full of light with a view of the Santa Margarita Ranch, where Nixon established his California White House. We had decided not to live in base housing because it felt too isolated, although I was proud to show my mother the Officers' Club where we went swimming. The waves in the Pacific were too rough for a toddler and the water was too cold compared with the warmer Mediterranean my mother was used to. I remember going to the San Juan Capistrano Mission with her on a bright, sunny day and strolling on the grounds, much of it in ruins then. She probably commented on the dry weather and how much it felt like the climate in Spain. No wonder the Spaniards settled there over two hundred before. Unfortunately, my mother's visit to California so many years ago did not end up well. I heard her say to my dad on the phone that she did not like the tacos I made for dinner, something that I thought was so trendy back then. I wanted to share with her my culinary expertise and my newfound interest in Latin American culture, which is something that my parents with their old-world prejudices, never embraced. I remember that we argued when she asked me what was I doing so far away in California, as if Seattle had not been just as far. She told me once too many times that I had to finish my degree, as if I could leave my husband and go back to my parents in Indiana, as she suggested. I ended up shouting at her that I had married so young to get away from them and their old-fashioned immigrant expectations.

On the surface my parents seemed to have adjusted well to their permanent life in the United States, although they spent long summers and sabbaticals in Spain and my mother traveled there alone on a few occasions to spend more time with my brother. But, once more, the letters revealed their true feelings. During one of her extended visits to Madrid my father wrote an awful, angry letter to her because he thought that she had organized a dinner party and had invited her brother Pepe and his wife Elena — as if that was the wrong thing to do. My Uncle Pepe, despite his lack of a formal education, had risen to a top position in Madrid's Banco Central and I believe my father was envious of his success. He had always resented my mother's closeness to her siblings. Given his feelings as the eternal orphan, he could not understand how my mother felt. I am including my mother's complete answer because it exemplifies her emotional intelligence and the depth of her love:

Madrid, June 3, 1970
    Dear Juan:
Your letter of the 28 just arrived. Very crumpled, perhaps it didn't want to arrive.

    I'm truly sorry that my "made in Carles hypocrisy" has made a man who is my husband insult me in such way. I regret that you are not right, your true feelings have shown as many times before. It's not necessary for me to comment anymore, a talented man like you does not need lessons from his wife, although she is the person who loves him most in this darn world. I will tell you that there were seven for dinner, not six, since I didn't count myself. They were friends of Juan Luis, a son from my bloodline (if you allow me).

    It was a mistake, undoubtedly, that I didn't make this clear; but I thought I was writing to an intelligent and good man whom I met on the same day as Unamuno died.

    A hug, Concha

How ironic that she was then the one declaring her love and making the literary reference to Unamuno. It is as if she could surpass him on his own turf.

At my urging, we lived close to my parents again when my husband left the Marine Corps and went back to Purdue University while he studied for his Master in Business Administration. Then, I became the family provider, working at the campus library with the added benefit that I could take one class per semester tuition free. After two years, I was still short of finishing my degree and we were expecting our second child. My mother's health was worsening considerably. I took her to doctor's visits and was her advocate. My father was never comfortable in the caregiver role; he might have been afraid that he was going to be left alone. My mother still looked beautiful at my brother's wedding in the summer of 1973, wearing a long, print dress that hid her enlarged abdomen. It is the last picture I have of her where I can still recognize her beauty and grace.

Despite her declining health, my mother tried to make a life for herself at the university campus. She took classes to make silver jewelry and ceramic classes where she made some lovely pieces, including a striking vase and two black on black plates that I still display proudly in my home. I have her class notes about the art books she had read and a list of 39 pieces she crafted. Interestingly, in the same notebook she wrote a three-stanza poem about the wind, the sea and the trees in which she used a clever play on words, reminiscent of her style in the letters that my parents exchanged during the war. I am still discovering my mother. It seems that she liked writing poetry because I found nine more poems on loose pages. One entitled "Guerra" (War), is very moving and seems to have been written with me and my daughter in mind:

> Y si entonces yo sufrí
> más estoy sufriendo ahora
> que es mi hija la que sufre
> y mi nieta la que llora
>
> Y si mi vida valiera . . .
> si toda mi sangre se fuera
> para acabar esa guerra
> toda mi sangre yo diera
> que ella sola no es nada
> comparada la riada de sangre cada hora

If I suffered then / I'm suffering more now / since my daughter is the one suffering / and my granddaughter the one who cries. If my life were worth it / if all my blood could be / to end that war / I would give all my blood / since that alone is nothing / compared to the flood of hourly blood.

In addition to her recipe and menu notebook, my mother kept up her correspondence with family, friends and my brother in particular as corroborated by the many letters I also found. She continued reading as well, probably still under my dad's tutelage, until the end of her life. I have her agenda for 1972, for example, and the list of books is impressive. In three months, she had read ten books, including some Latin American authors: Borges, García Márquez, Uslar Pietri and Mariano Azuela, which were unusual for my father's repertoire. It is worth noting that my mother got along well with my mother-in-law — much better than I did, that is for sure. Also annotated in the 1972 agenda is a visit to Spain during the summer by my in-laws. My mother believed in family above all and used to say that there was not an English word for "consuegros" (the parents of both spouses) because the relationship did not exist in American culture. My mother-in-law reciprocated in kind and was wonderful to my mother, taking her to doctors' appointments and filling in for my father and me when I lived away.

In this seemingly endless trove of letters, there are only sixteen letters and cards from me to my parents between 1966 and 1972. It amuses me now to see how innocent I was in my twenties and how much I was trying to hide about my married life at such a young age. Most of the letters have to do with my two pregnancies, getting the nurseries ready both times and the babies' milestones, such as the first time Diana took swimming lessons or when Jane got her first tooth. I also wrote about taking driving lessons when I was seven months pregnant with my first child and having to take the test in a girlfriend's car because I had not mastered the clutch in our old 1960s Rambler. I urged my mother to learn how to drive too since I loved being more independent once I had my license, something she would never do.

The most surprising aspect of my letters for me now is what I wrote about Marine Corps life; although I was masking the truth, it is amazing what I revealed. While we lived at the base in Cherry Point, North Carolina, in particular, the Marines were often deployed for training at other bases, in preparation for their tour of duty in Vietnam, leaving their wives to fend for themselves. Despite the fact that the base commander had told the wives at an Officer's Club luncheon how lucky we were because our husbands would not come back wounded as infantrymen did, my next-door neighbor indeed returned with a serious injury. Adding insult to injury, literally, the same neighbor was found out to be a Peeping Tom and had to resign his commission and move with his family in disgrace. I told my parents how thankful I was that "I had not caught him outside my window or I would have to testify" (October 20, 1966). What we were not told was that many flyers came back with their dog tags (military identification) between their teeth — which meant dead — or they were MIAs — missing in action — as happened to several of our friends.

My mother was at her best as a grandmother. She visited us as often as she could and as soon as she was back from her summer sojourns in Spain. The only objection from my daughters was her haircuts. When I was a little girl, my mother used to cut my hair, I suppose to save money, but she always made it too short and I did not like it. We might have had the same kind of grateful hair but we had different tastes when it came to haircuts. I wanted to have a "melena," a mane like hers, long, shoulder-length hair and to wear it down. She continued her hobby when my two daughters were born with the same results; neither one liked their hair so short. I remember Diana's long ringlets, Little Lulu-style and Jane's pageboy cut like Toni Tennille, the pop singer, and that was how they liked it. But she could play for hours with my daughters making Playdough figures for them while I was doing my homework. She made clothes for their dolls as she had done when I was little. She cooked everyone's favorite dishes: Diana's macaroni with chorizo, Jane's potato omelet and Valencian "arroz al horno" (baked rice) for me. In a short note after one of our trips to Indiana she wrote: "my granddaughters are precious" (September 23, 1972).

I made several visits to Lafayette accompanied by my daughters as my mother's medical emergencies became more frequent. She told me once, when she was in a hospital in Indianapolis, that she could hear my energetic footsteps coming down the corridor and she knew her daughter had arrived to take care of her. A compliment from my mother meant the world to me. When we moved to Atlanta, I went back to school, determined that I would finally finish my undergraduate degree at Georgia State University. But Atlanta was too far to drive back and forth to Indiana and, in the summer of 1974, when she was critically ill, I brought my mother to the hospital at Emory University, where I would finish my Master's degree three years later. By then she wanted nothing to do with my father and would not allow him in her room. I took it as a sign of her illness, but now I think that she had found out about his affair with my aunt and was hurt beyond words, although she never mentioned it to me. The doctors at Emory confirmed that she should go back to Spain if that was what she wanted, because there was nothing else they could do for her there. My parents flew back to Spain together one last time directly from Atlanta.

I have only a few letters from my mother written lovingly during those months before her death when she lived in Madrid with my brother who took exceptional care of her. My mother wrote about her dear brother Pepe and Elena, who stopped by to see her daily; she had the same dentist and the same family doctor who had taken care of us since we arrived in Madrid. In her letter of November 7, 1974, she sent "Kisses, kisses and kisses," specially on my 29th birthday. Her last correspondence to me was a Christmas card on December 20, 1974; in shaky, almost unrecognizable handwriting, she addressed my two daughters, expressing her sadness that we could not be together for the holidays. By then my brother's first daughter, Lorena, had been born and my mother was equally smitten with the new granddaughter. Her only wish was that she could see her three granddaughters together. Unfortunately, she would not live to see that, but her last wish was granted when Lorena spent one summer with her American cousins in Philadelphia and, years later, Lorena's daughter, Nerea, would do the same with my twin granddaughters. We have not lost touch despite the miles and the years that separate us. This is also part of my mother's legacy.

The biggest regret I have with regard to my mother is that I did not go to see her during those five months she was dying in Madrid. I knew how sick she was, but I could not imagine that it was the end of her life. Maybe I could not admit it. Without family connections or reliable babysitters, I had to wait for my mother-in-law to arrive to stay with my daughters. When we finally got a call saying that we should go to Spain immediately, I met my father at John F. Kennedy Airport in New York and we flew together to Madrid. We went directly to the hospital from Barajas Airport. When we arrived at her room, I could smell her characteristic lavender scent, but she was not there. She had died less than two hours before.

I had never been to a funeral in Spain. In the basement of the hospital, the deceased were prepared and the viewings were held there that evening. The formal funeral took place the following morning. Traditionally, burials were held within twenty-four hours, probably a leftover from Muslim law, unless for some unusual reason the deceased was embalmed. My father and I were allowed to see my mother for a few minutes. She was smaller than I had ever seen her. Her beautiful hair had turned straw-like in color and texture. Her skin was dark and dry. Only her hands were still smooth and familiar. I do not remember ever feeling sadder or more overcome. I cried until I could not see her through my tears anymore. Then, I found myself in the waiting area separated from her forever by a glass partition.

I was distraught when that evening and the next morning in the cemetery, I did not see my Uncle Vicente or my Aunt Conchita. I could not fathom why they had not come to my mother's funeral since they had always been so close. I feared that one of them was sick too. I was told to be quiet, "please." It is strange what details can be upsetting at such sad moments. The burial was as expeditious as the viewing. The gray January morning felt frozen and sad. As soon as we got home, my sister-in-law took me aside in the living room and told me that my father and my Aunt Conchita had been engaged in a long affair and the Carles family was having a very hard time dealing with this. I was the last one to find out. To say that I was devastated would be an understatement; I was in shock. When I finally went to bed that evening I was terribly confused, grieving the loss of my innocence as well as my mother's death.

My mother was 58 years old and had been married to my dad for 32 years. Franco died on November 20 of the same year at 82.

Para Concha,

mi hija,

con lo cual queda dicho todo.

Con el cariño de

Papá

HISTORIA DE LA LITERATURA ESPAÑOLA

TOMO VIII

Determining the Truth

My mother did not get to witness the demise of my first marriage. I was the first to divorce in my family and she would not have liked that, despite the fact that she did not care for my husband and she thought I married so young. But she would have understood that military life and then corporate life, which was exactly the same but in civilian clothes, was not for me. When I moved to Philadelphia, where I now live, I had been married thirteen years and had moved eleven times, with two little girls in tow. We were divorced after seventeen years of marriage, fodder for my novel *American in Translation: A Novel in Three Novellas* (2011). My mother would have loved that, not only had I finished my undergraduate degree as she wanted, but I went straight for my Master's and had started my Ph.D. Before I knew it, I was married again. She would have approved of Peter, an endearing man, although he turned out to be a Don Juan like my dad. He used to say that he missed my mother and he wished he had met her. The twenty-plus years with him passed in a whirlwind of academic careers, musical his and literary mine. With a Ph.D. from Temple University in hand, I was able to start an academic life and raise my two daughters. I thought I had a happy marriage for almost twenty-five years. I found out differently after his death, as chronicled in my book, *Divorce After Death: A Widow's Memoir* (2014).

During all those years, I did not condone the pain that my father's affair had caused our family, but I also did not want to lose yet another parent, so I made the conscious effort, particularly for my daughters' sake, to keep in touch with him for the rest of his life, something that cost me dearly. Despite our differences and the geographical distance, it is a miracle that I have been able to reconcile with family members on both sides. My hope is that this memoir will bring us closer together rather than further apart.

My father remarried soon after my mother's death. People

thought that Oriana, a Latin American graduate student in her forties who resembled my mother, seemed like a perfect fit; they could not have been more wrong. I attended the small wedding in Lafayette with my daughters and husband and felt happy for my dad. I teased him, calling him Amadís de Gaula, the name of Oriana's knight in shining armor in the famous medieval chivalry novel, so perfect for a literature professor. But the marriage did not last and a painful divorce ensued. Taking advantage that my father was single, we arranged for him to take a summer trip to Spain with my daughter, who was twelve then. On the evening of their departure, he announced with his characteristic smirk, that someone else would be joining them. It was another one of his graduate students, Muriel, who was almost forty years his junior, closer in age to my daughter than to him. I had to hastily arrange for Diana to stay with my Aunt Teresa in Valencia rather than cancel her trip, not wanting to punish the granddaughter for her grandfather's dalliances.

Muriel and my father married in Bloomington, Indiana, in May of 1980. At Purdue, the retirement age was enforced at 65 and my dad did not want to get married and retire in the same year. A new start was a good move, particularly since my dad had also been involved with the department chairman's wife. Indiana University welcomed the renowned Spanish scholar and his young bride. I also attended that wedding, this time by myself, teasing my dad on this occasion by telling him that he looked younger at each of his weddings. Despite their age difference, Muriel and my dad were married for almost thirty years. She took loving care of him until his death in 2010 and for that I will be forever grateful to her. She has more than earned her place in the family, for whatever it is worth.

Not surprisingly, without my mother as the peacemaker, my father kept escalating arguments with my brother and eventually they broke all contact with each other, the one thing that would have hurt my mother the most. I cannot help but wonder if Martin Arrowsmith was showing his ugly head again, since he also abandoned his son. My father never met his only grandson, Junior, who shares the same name as him, and did not keep in touch with his two lovely Spanish granddaughters. I, too, saved some family letters, including one from my dad where he practically disowned me for not following his advice to break off realtions with my brother as he had done. He wrote:

I have given orders to have the lock of my house in El Escorial changed and that no keys be given to you. Since you share and support so decisively your brother's point of view — something that I will never accept — from now on you should stay where he lives . . . I don't think that I need to add any comments or explanations, since you don't want to listen to me. Have a good trip, Merry Christmas and all the best to you for the future 1988. (November 29, 1987)

How is this letter for a holiday greeting?

My father's reference to my not wanting to listen to him had to do with an earlier confrontation during a visit to Bloomington. I do not remember what the argument was about, probably his relationship with my brother. A few days later, I received a certified letter from my dad, but I refused to accept it, marking it "Return to Sender." I sent my dad my own letter explaining my refusal:

> If yours was a paternal and kind letter, perhaps about my book or encouraging me in my efforts somehow, then please forgive me. I do not want to think ill of you, but I know you and, as much as I can, I will not allow you to hurt me anymore. Whenever you want to talk — without insulting me or threatening me — if you are able to, I am always willing, on the phone or face to face as I tried to do in Indiana. (July 20, 1987)

As my mother had done in the past, it was like a one-upmanship with my dad and I beat him at his own game by taking away his most powerful tool: his pen. Subconsciously, I had emasculated him and I do not think he ever forgave me for this.

Despite the tensions, I called my father every week and visited him faithfully, usually in June to mark his birthday on the 18th and his Saint's Day on the 24th. He seemed to revel in telling me stories of his conquests as an aging Don Juan reminiscent of the Marquis of Bradomín in Valle Inclán's *Sonata de invierno* (Winter's Sonata). He also came to Philadelphia on occasions, for my wedding to Peter in 1985 and Jane's wedding in 1995. During one of those trips, on his way to Madrid, he became distraught at the Philadelphia Airport because of an unexpected delay, insisted on flying back to Indianapolis and never traveled again. When we took my three grandchildren to visit him in Bloomington, he seemed to be appropriately moved as a great-grandfather should be, especially with Jake, his first great-grandson, who bears his American namesake.

My father made copies for me of letters that he thought I would appreciate about literary friends and foes. But once when I showed up with a tape recorder to interview him in depth, he proceeded to tell one off-color joke after another, making Milagros, the lady of the moment, laugh uncontrollably. It is worth noting some of the concerns my father had as an octogenarian. For example, in a letter to Luis Estepa, a critic who had praised his work, my dad made an "autorretrato" (a self-portrait) stating that he was a "navegante solitario" (a lonely mariner). My mother would have laughed at that — my father a sailor who could not swim! Although, he went on to affirm that he did not travel anymore because "airplanes are like torture" and for that reason he had not been to Spain in six or seven years. Perhaps the most interesting aspect of this rambling letter is that my dad said he "resided in America, but didn't live in America," that he had built himself something like "a crystal globe where I live completely incommunicado of everything around me." He continued to explain himself by saying:

> . . . since I retired, several years ago, I don't relate to anyone . . . I spend weeks, I could say months, without talking to anyone but my wife and my dog, a beautiful female Doberman, whom I'm sure understands me, because she has more intelligence and sensibility than many people I know. (September 12, 1999)

Nora, the Doberman, got me in trouble more than once. I kept confusing her name with Nelda, the opera singer my father was infatuated with for several years.

In the same letter my father explained the reason for his coming to "reside" in the United States: "My coming here, which I didn't ask for, because I never thought it would be possible and it was offered to me, changed my life from top to bottom. From then on, I could unconcern myself about money . . . I had what I had always desired: time, time, time." My father never became a citizen and he "never even considered it" (September 12, 1999). Another letter my father copied for me is the one he wrote to Hipólito Escolar, his editor at Gredos Publishing Company in Madrid, who had written proposing to name a "successor" for his monumental *Historia de literatura española*. Of course, my father repudiated the idea of naming a successor in an intense, single-spaced, four-page letter, stating as his last Will that no one was to update or revise his books upon his death in any shape or form. He was hoping to live much longer as his grandfather had done, who lived to be 103 (January 7, 1983). This time, my father was absolutely correct, since he lived for twenty-seven more years and, in the meantime, he wrote three more volumes and thousands of pages of his History of Spanish Literature.

My dad was not as supportive of my career as I had hoped, despite the fact that I followed in his footsteps, more or less. He had his own agenda. By the time he asked me if I wanted to write the twentieth century volume of his History of Spanish Literature, I was more interested in pursuing creative writing and turned him down; furthermore, his extensive work cannot be compared to my modest output. On one of my last visits in Bloomington, my dad suggested that I be his successor, but by then it was too late. Although it flatters me that he even thought about it and reiterated it in his personal dedication of his fourth volume: "For Concha, who perhaps will write the ninth volume of this series. With a very strong hug from, Papá" (1980). In fact, I have to go to another of his book dedications to read the words that I always wanted to hear from him: "For Concha with invariable love from Papá" (Volume VI, 1996) and my favorite: "For Concha, my daughter, which implies everything. With love from, Papá" (Volume VIII, 1999).

Nevertheless, a few months before his death, my dad accused me of having taken, without his permission, one of my mother's ceramic pieces that he had given me years before. I found photos with earlier dates of that very piece at my home and sent them as proof, but to no avail. Determined to end his life alone, as the orphan he always considered himself, my father never spoke to me again. Muriel and I continued talking, but my father never got on the phone to speak to me. In late April of 2010, after writing all day, my father was struck with severe abdominal pain due to appendicitis. He had surgery the next morning, but died on May 10 from several complications. Since then, I have not really missed my father, but I have forgiven him and, certainly, I have not forgotten him. Muriel continues to be in touch with my daughters, my grandchildren and me.

As it is known to do, time flew by and I found myself downsizing from a large Philadelphia townhouse to a small high-rise condominium in the center of town. I have decorated it in earthy Spanish colors: burnt sienna, olive greens, with some indigo blue in my bedroom. This is the only time I have lived in an apartment in this country and it has been a déjà vu experience. From the first day after moving in, when I came out of the elevator, I thought I was back in Madrid. I could smell the neighbors' dinner just like my dad used to walk into our family home, with the announcement that he smelled cauliflower in the hallway. I have a small terrace where I grow red geraniums in the summer and my favorite herbs year-round: lavender, thyme, and oregano, which smell like the countryside in Spain and remind me of my mother's scent. I enjoy my urban view of colonial brick buildings all the way to the Walt Whitman Bridge. I have a small galley kitchen and it seems that I am still playing house with my childhood kitchen. I love my Talavera dishes; I cook mostly Spanish food and treasure it when my family comes to visit. I live alone now, but I am not lonely. I am resourceful just as my mother was and, as she would say, "Mejor sola que mal acompañada," better alone than in bad company. I am writing about her and discovering who she was all the years she was hiding from me. I think I have found her; she is in the four hundred-plus letters she wrote to my dad. What is more, she is inside me, deep in my heart.

As I reflect on the war letters and all the other correspondence on which this memoir is based, I have to confess that I have changed my mind. Because they were hidden under his class notes, I had assumed that my father had hidden all these letters to keep them from Oriana, his jealous second wife. Now I am convinced that it was my mother who saved them. We know that she was the one who decided to number the war letters and she numbered the correspondence from my brother the same way; all the annotations on those envelopes are also in her handwriting. On one occasion, when she had to send back to my father one of her letters, she asked him in no uncertain terms to return it to her "because it is mine and I want it for me alone" (November 2, 1937). I was struck how possessive she was with one single letter no less, imagine how she must have felt with her entire collection. She must have also saved the other family letters, including the ones from me. I cannot imagine my father keeping those. Who else but my mother would have saved the answer to my dad's mean letter of June 3, 1970? We know that my mother died in 1975 and there is not a single letter after 1973; she was too sick to go to the apartment in El Escorial on her last trip to Spain in 1974. If there had been even one letter after that date, we could deduce that my father hid them, but there were none.

If my father had been the one to hide the letters, he would have told me about them. He used to relate his stories to me, encouraging me to take notes. If I could not be his successor, he seemed to relish being a literary character in my fiction. He gave me copies of his letters to keep me abreast of his musings as we have seen in this epilogue. Most of all, if he hid them, he would have included the letters from his affair with Aunt Conchita and those, as hard as I tried, I have never found.

If, indeed, it was my mother who not only saved all the letters but was the one who hid them in that box in the attic as well, we need to establish a reason. I am certain she knew about my father's affair with her sister-in-law, even if she never told me about it. She must have confronted him and that is why she wanted nothing to do with him during the last months of her life. My father must have destroyed his letters of the affair with Aunt Conchita — since they have not been found. My mother, on the contrary, decided to save hers. These letters so carefully kept in secret were the beginning of her legacy. She could not have known that her daughter would want to tell the rest of her story, but I did. This is my dedication:

Mamá, these are your letters. This is your story and
your book and it is dedicated to you, with all my love.
Your daughter who does not forget you,
Conchín

Rollitos de Anís =

1 cup de Aceite refinado de Oliva
1 cup de Anís (fuerte)
1 cup de Azúcar
2 huevos
1 cucharadita, limón rallado
2 cucharaditas levadura en polvo
Harina la que admita, y un
poco de canela si gusta.
Modo de hacer la pasta →

Se pone en un recipiente, el aceite
el anís, los dos huevos y el azúcar:
se bate todo bien, se le pone el limón
y la canela, luego la levadura y
por último la harina; se bate bien
todo y se le pone la harina, hasta
formar una pasta manejable, se tra-
baja bien esta pasta y se forman los
rollitos que se pasan por azúcar an-
tes de hornear (Horno 325 F.)

Some of Conchita's Recipes

My mother was a wonderful cook. Before I found the war letters, I was planning to write a cookbook with her recipes and some anecdotes about her life. Most of her typical dishes came from her native Valencia, but she was adventurous in the kitchen and she adapted her recipes to the places where we lived, whether it was Madrid first and, later, the United States. No matter how much household help we had growing up, she always did the food shopping and cooking. I remember how upset she was when we lived in West Lafayette, Indiana, the small midwestern college town, where she could not find olive oil. We had to drive to Chicago to find it. She would be so glad to know that nowadays olive oil is as ubiquitous in the States as it is in Spain. I never cooked with her as a young girl, and since I married so young, I did not start until I had left my parents' home. Thankfully, she taught me some of her specialties when she visited me as a young mother; she loved seeing her two granddaughters and she visited us often. Sometimes she would include a recipe in a letter or I would call her with a question or a special request. In my role as a self-appointed sleuth, I even found a typically American, spiral notebook that she started in the States with her favorite recipes.

When my father was upset, which happened regularly, he would refuse to eat to show the gravity of the situation. In one of his first letters written during the war, even before he was on the front lines, he described a situation like this when my mother left with her young siblings for a few weeks: "I refused to eat. After much begging I ate "un simulacro de cena" (a sham of a dinner) and went to bed" (June 4, 1937). The funniest thing was that, days after one of his tantrums, he would remind my mother that he had missed this or that meal and wanted second helpings of whatever was being served. Now that I have read how many meals he missed during the war and how much hunger he experienced, I wonder if he was always so hungry because he was trying to make up for all that starving time.

After my mother died, despite being married to Muriel, who was a fine southern cook, my dad learned to make some dishes that his new wife did not make. For instance, he used to barbecue chicken legs, one of his specialties. He also made a tasty dried codfish dish with red peppers as a "mullaret," Valencian for a dipping sauce with bread. He baked his own bread from a supermarket mix, but nevertheless amazing for such a novice. I will not include his recipes here, since they were all only in his head. But I will give him credit for the way he fixed strawberries, sliced with lemon juice and sugar, which is delicious and I make to this day. My mother would have been amused to see him cooking, cleaning up the kitchen and going to the market until he had to stop driving because he had an accident on a snowy Thanksgiving morning and was fearful of driving again.

These recipes should be taken with a grain of salt, because there were many falsehoods about food around my mother's kitchen when I was young. For example, aioli could not be made if the cook was having her period. If that was true, how come I was not allowed to make it when I was young, since we have already established that I was a late bloomer? Or why did the men in the house, who did not lift a finger, make it? Were they menstruating too? Aioli could not be made if there was "una corriente de aire,"a breeze or the kitchen window was open. Living at sea level was also a requirement. If that was true, how come my mother continued making aioli when we moved to Madrid, the highest capital city in Europe? I figured out that it was all a big fib. When I confronted my mother with all this overwhelming evidence, she must have answered with her dismissive tone.

Eventually, I learned to cook and I love preparing Spanish dishes. I had to go on a scavenger hunt to find my mother's recipes in my Spanish relatives' kitchens. Included here are some of her signature dishes and some of my favorites. How I wish I had learned more recipes directly from her!

Cauliflower Béchamel for unexpected guests
Since I married so young, my mother worried that I could not cook and that I would starve or, worse yet, make my husband and daughters starve. Getting enough to eat was an obsession in my

home, probably caused by the lack of food during the Spanish Civil War. When I told my mother about the first meal I cooked for my husband as a new bride, she was shocked. I had received an electric frying pan as a wedding gift and it came with some recipes. I was intrigued by the pork chops with onions, apples and sauerkraut, something my mother would never have made, since traditional Spanish food did not mix sweet with savory. I purchased the ingredients at the Quantico Marine Corps Base PX, followed the recipe and, pronto, there was dinner. My husband loved the dish and I figured that as long as I could read, I could cook, and I have never looked back.

Nevertheless, I often called my mother to get one of her recipes or ask her a question about a thorny issue, such as how to flip the flan or make the aioli. We ended up talking about food during most of our phone calls, which was a lot safer than rehashing family issues. I remember that she told me the story of the day my father showed up for lunch with unexpected guests from the university. She served an antipasto of cold cuts with a salad for the first course and cauliflower in béchamel sauce for the second and it was a big hit. That was the reason a good cook should always have some frozen cauliflower in her freezer. Did I have a lot to learn or what? I had never purchased cauliflower, frozen or any other kind.

At least two courses are de rigueur at each meal in Spain. Spaniards would much rather have two small entrees than one large portion of anything as Americans do. No wonder they love tapas, the small dishes to share before a meal in the many bars in any Spanish city. My family did not go out for tapas but olives, almonds, cheeses and cold cuts were always on hand whether guests were expected or not. Those I had ready too, but cauliflower was another story.

Now I serve this dish as an accompaniment for any meat, particularly on holidays because it can be made ahead of time and it serves eight to ten people as a side dish.

INGREDIENTS
2 one-pound packages of frozen cauliflower or a fresh head of cauliflower
3 tablespoons olive oil
1 medium onion, chopped
3 tablespoons unsalted butter

5–6 tablespoons flour
Whole milk, about 2 cups
Nutmeg, salt and Parmesan cheese, to taste

METHOD
Cook cauliflower according to directions, minus a couple of minutes. With fresh cauliflower cook al dente. Drain and set aside.
Preheat oven to 400 degrees.
Sauté onion until translucent in large saucepan.
Add flour, 1 tablespoon butter, salt and nutmeg.
Add milk very slowly, stirring constantly until béchamel is of desired consistency, it should be creamy and free of lumps.
Melt 1 tablespoon of butter in a baking dish.
Arrange the cauliflower in baking dish.
Pour the béchamel over the top.
Dot with remaining butter and sprinkle with Parmesan cheese.
Bake at 400 degrees for 30 minutes, until bubbly and golden on top.
It can be kept warm in the oven, covered with foil.
Serve warm.

My mother's Valencian Paella
Originally, the paella was made outdoors, in the open air over a fire, with rice, fresh vegetables, meats (usually chicken) and some seafood. The dish takes its name from the pan it is cooked in, a round paella pan of approximately 16–18 inches with handles, also called "paellera." Eventually, paellas were cooked indoors; most families had a special stand used only to cook paellas hooked to a butane bottle in order to get a full flame. Paellas can also be cooked on a gas stovetop and even an electric stove will work, but do not tell a purist.

Traditionally, paellas were considered to be Valencian and Catalonian dishes served in typical restaurants only in those regions. When we moved to Madrid, my mother could not believe that paellas were served in the capital. She would remark: "What did they know about paellas?" Today, paella is almost the Spanish signature dish, it is ubiquitous all over the country. Of course, I think the best paellas were the ones my mother and aunts made. On the Valencian beaches there are many restaurants specializing in this dish and they are a suitable consolation prize. La Marcelina in El Cabañal Beach is my favorite.

Nowadays, there are all kinds of paellas: seafood, mixed with chicken, with rabbit, and with black rice (from the squid's ink). A new version is "Paella del Senyoret" (Gentleman's Paella) when every morsel is shelled and cut in small pieces and can be eaten without using a knife; it is served with aioli (the garlic mayonnaise) on the side. Another innovation is "A fideuá," substituting the rice with tiny noodles or "fideos." In fact, each restaurant has a "paella de la casa" a house specialty paella and heaven only knows what kind it is — I am aware that I sound like my mother.

My mother's paella was a traditional Valencian paella that she adjusted according to what vegetables were in season and to the fresh seafood in the market. When we lived in Madrid her paellas were cooked on the gas stove, but her biggest adjustment was cooking paella in the United States. She experimented with all kinds of rice, settling on Uncle Ben's Converted Rice that I use to this day.

The best paellas should have a bottom thin layer of "socarrat," some crispy rice that tastes divine, something like the crusty caramel part in a flan, although it is savory. It is hard to explain. Suffice to say that this part is often lost in translation and it is impossible to attain on a regular stove. Just do not tell your waiter that your paella is burnt if you are lucky enough to get some "socarrat" in a restaurant.

For some reason, paella was only served at the mid-day meal, usually on Sundays and holidays, never in the evening because it was bad for our digestion. I learned early on not to question my family's digestion pronouncements, just in case I have inherited a Spanish stomach. Another very important rule was that paella was never saved as a leftover. There was nothing worse than "split" rice, which could not be served, period. With the discovery of Uncle Ben, we found out that his rice never split and my family started enjoying the delicious leftovers. I have never mentioned this to my Spanish relatives.

My Godmother Teresa also made a delicious paella and she would oblige whenever I visited her at La Eliana, her family's summer place. I remember one summer that I was visiting with my daughters and she was preparing snails for the day's paella. Snails can be very sandy and she put them in a big bowl of water to rinse them. During the morning, the snails would crawl out of the bowl and slither on top of the kitchen counter all the way down to the floor. As people walked by and saw the escaping victims, they would pick them up nonchalantly and put them back in the bowl. My daughters were not amused; they do not like snails and felt guilty eating them after seeing them alive all morning. When the paella was served, Jane, who must have been around five or six years old, started to cry and emergency macaroni had to be hastily prepared to appease the squeamish little gringa.

When I lived in Toledo, Ohio, I belonged to a gourmet group and prepared a traditional Spanish meal of gazpacho, paella and flan for dessert. *The Blade,* the Toledo paper, published an article titled "Happiness Is Cooking Up a Gourmet Luncheon" with "Conchita Day's Spanish Paella." Conchita Day was my imperson-ation and name as a suburban wife. The Spanish Paella was a mixed paella recipe that must have been inspired by my mother. For some unknown reason, she made several copies of this article and saved them in her recipe notebook. I do not know if this meant that she approved of my recipe; perhaps she was pleased to see that I had finally learned how to cook something Spanish and my family was not starving. Conchita Day's recipe has become obsolete now, since I much prefer my mother's Valencian seafood version. It serves 8–10 people.

INGREDIENTS
6 tablespoons olive oil
1 large onion, chopped
1 large green pepper, chopped
1 large ripe tomato, chopped
3 garlic cloves, minced
¾ lb. Spanish chorizo or spicy Italian sausage cut in small pieces

¾ lb. shrimp
½ lb. squid, cleaned (no ink)
¾ lb. fish, cut in small pieces (cod, sea bass, monk or any other solid white fish)
1½ cups Uncle Ben's Converted Rice
1 four-ounce jar of red pimientos cut in thin strips
½ cup frozen peas

1 lb. mussels or small clams (more if serving as a first course)
1 cup white wine
1 lemon
Herbs

BROTH
3 cups chicken broth
½ teaspoon saffron
1 teaspoon parsley flakes
½ teaspoon Sunny Spain (Penzeys' spice)
Salt and pepper to taste

MUSSELS AND / OR CLAMS (OPTIONAL)
Steam mussels and / or small clams in white wine, lemon slices and your favorite herbs until they open. Discard top shell and set aside.

PAELLA
Prepare broth in a small sauce pan, simmering chicken broth with seasonings.
Heat oil in paella pan and sauté chorizo with fresh vegetables and garlic for about 5–10 minutes.
Add fish, squid and shrimp and sauté all together five more minutes.
Add rice, mix well and add broth to cover. Top with pimientos and peas.
Cook over low heat until most of the broth has evaporated, 15–20 minutes. Do not stir.
Finish cooking in a 350-degree oven fifteen to twenty minutes more.
Can be kept warm in oven (turned off), covered with aluminum foil.
Add mussels and / or clams on top right before serving or serve them as a first course as the paella finishes cooking in the oven.

Stuffed Flank Steak in a letter
Often my mother would include a recipe when she wrote to me. I am sure this was part of my indoctrination into her cooking world. I do not have the date of this letter because I only saved the page with the "carne mechada" (stuffed flank steak) and the rest

of the menu she fixed for my dad's birthday dinner. So, at least we know that it was sometime in June and when they were on one of their sojourns in Spain because she used thin, airmail paper. My dad complained that she had written so much and had only left space for him to send "a big hug and a million kisses for each little girl." He was always fond of his two granddaughters. I am glad that somehow, I did not involve them in the family drama and they were able to forge a loving relationship with their grandfather.

Every family in Spain has its own version of this dish. It can be stuffed with just about anything you have in the refrigerator or whatever is in season. My mother usually made it with colorful ingredients (carrots, eggs, celery, pickles) in order to have the meat slices look beautiful in addition to being flavorful. This was one of my favorite dishes growing up, especially when it was served with "patatas a cuadritos" (French fried potatoes cut in small squares). For this occasion, my mother served it with white, baked rice with a savory sauce over it and she wrote that she had prepared it the evening before. Notice how, in her diplomatic way, she was also letting me know the importance of planning ahead, something that I am a consummate expert in doing. She would be so proud of me!

Her instructions for this dish were very detailed, even if the ingredients may vary. She started her letter by reminding me that I had asked for this recipe, thus she had carte blanche to expand herself and promised me: "We will make it as it should be done and your guests will lick their fingers." She ended by telling me that she had made this dinner for my in-laws and they loved it. Another way in which I could learn; getting along with my mother-in-law was not my strong suit. I have to smile every time I make this dish and reread the letter; how clever and wise my mother was!

INGREDIENTS
2 lbs. flank steak
Two-egg omelet with parsley
Two carrots, cut length-wise
Two celery stalks
Six cornichons
Six pitted black olives
Three slices of "Jamón Serrano"
Salt and pepper

3 tablespoons olive oil
3 tablespoons unsalted butter

BAKED RICE
1½ cups Uncle Ben's Converted Rice
3 cups chicken broth

SAUCE
1 onion, chopped
2 carrots, sliced
3 ripe tomatoes, chopped
3 tablespoons olive oil
1 shot glass of dry sherry

METHOD
Cook the omelet with some parsley and set aside.
Peel carrots and slice thin length-wise, same with the celery, cornichons and olives.
Pound and roll out the steak until it is ¼ inch thick or less.
Arrange all the ingredients decoratively and evenly on the meat.
Roll it carefully, do not worry if some of the ingredients escape.
Tie the roll with cooking string.
Season with salt and pepper and set aside.
Warm up the olive oil to make the sauce. Sauté the vegetables until tender.
Add the butter and the rest of the oil until bubbly in a heavy Dutch oven casserole.
Sauté the meat carefully on all sides until browned evenly.
Turn heat down, cover and simmer until cooked through, for about half an hour.
Add the sherry to thin and flavor the sauce. Puree the sauce in a blender or a handheld mixer. Add broth and / or more sherry to reach the desired consistency.
Let the steak rest for fifteen minutes before cutting it in ½ inch slices.
In the meantime make the rice according to instructions on the box, using chicken broth instead of water. Finish cooking the rice in a 350-degree oven for 15 minutes.
Serve the baked white rice in the shape of balls with the ice-cream scooper.

Pour the sauce over one or two slices of the flank steak and the rice.

Serves 6–8 people.

"Rollitos;" Christmas Anisette Cookies

All the entries in my mother's recipe notebook are of desserts; there is not a single one of her savory dishes. The recipes are written neatly, underlined with red ink and they encompass a life trajectory of sorts. There are several from the old Alborg aunts, Isabel and Vicenta, some from her Spanish friends, all the way to my recipe for sherry cake and another for chocolate chip cookies, written in English! My mother never ceases to surprise me. It is interesting that she would take the time to write down these recipes, but not any of the meals she was best known for. It is as if she believed that cooking is an art and baking a science. She did not need to record her masterpieces, but needed the exact ingredients of the sweet treats, although she wrote "as much flour as needed" for the "rollitos."

Growing up we seldom had sweet desserts. Fruit was served at the end of each meal, but cakes and cookies were reserved for holidays, such as the Saints' Days and birthdays. Only at Christmas time did we have special treats of almond nougat and marzipan. "Meriendas" (a late afternoon or early evening snack) were usually made up of a sweet roll or a croissant, but those were store-bought. As children we usually had plain bread with some chocolate and a glass of milk, nothing more.

She made "rollitos" in early December for our Saint's Day on the 8th and the leftovers were reserved for Christmas. They were and still are my favorite cookies ever! Their liqueur smell permeated the house and when I was a little girl, I could smell them the minute I stepped out of the elevator. The recipe I have in my mother's handwriting with red ink on a 3 x 5 card is yellowed and stained, but I would never think of copying it anew.

I started making them as a young bride and continued doing so religiously after my daughters were born. I was glad that most of my friends and in-laws found them strong and strange and preferred the traditional American sugar cookies for Christmas, the more for me to savor. I know that making "rollitos" is a tedious job. They take a minimum of two hours and they are all rolled by hand in small donut-like circles the size of a ring. They are dipped in sugar, which makes one's hands sticky and you need to wash them often. When I was little, I liked them best eaten warm and I was supposed to wait until they cooled down or I would get a stomach ache. But I found out that it was not true, because once I ate at least a baker's dozen (an expression in English I love and we do not have in Spanish) when the "rollitos" had just come out of the oven and absolutely nothing happened to my stomach.

Diana, my oldest, learned to make them early and I thought she was a fan until the day that she took the dough and made one huge "rollitón" announcing: "Here, I'm done." Luckily, her sister was old enough to take over and, again, I thought she enjoyed the family tradition, only to find out that she hated making them too and did not like eating them, even if they were warm. When my daughters grew up and left the nest, I found friends and neighbors to join me making them. I soon got the feeling as soon as the first Christmas songs were heard, that no one wanted to see me, and they would disappear from my kitchen with the excuse of being really busy. My late husband Peter, despite his serious character faults, was very helpful in the kitchen and a fellow "rollito" lover and made them with me for years. In desperation, during my years as a widow, I have recruited unsuspecting boyfriends to bake with me with the expectation of perhaps winning my heart, which has not happened yet.

As we know, life can have very sweet surprises and now I have two lovely twin granddaughters who enjoy making "rollitos" with me, I think. At least they humor me as long as I make them a "tortilla de patatas" in return, a potato omelet, which they love. Having two helpers instead of one makes it more efficient. Actually, I have doubled the recipe since now the three grandchildren expect their own tin of "rollitos" to take home. The twins are amazing. They have figured out that one rolls out the dough and the other dips "rollitos" in sugar, which saves with the hand washing. They know how to charm me and speak Spanish during our baking day. One year, when they were in the "fighting-with-each-other phase," I allowed them to insult each other as much as they wanted as long as they used the affirmative and negative commands in Spanish, which are so tricky to learn. There is nothing like being a retired professor and a grandmother to come up with this trick!

Here is the recipe:

INGREDIENTS
1 cup virgin olive oil
1 cup anisette
1 cup sugar and more for dippin
2 eggs
1 teaspoon lemon zest
2 teaspoons baking powder
Flour, as much as needed (about six cups)

METHOD
In a large bowl, combine the oil, anisette, eggs and sugar. Add the lemon zest and the baking powder. Add the flour little by little until it becomes manageable and it can be kneaded on the counter.
Form rings of half an inch-size wide dough. Dip them in sugar before baking.
Bake in a 325-degree oven for 20 minutes. The bottom should be golden brown.
Makes about five dozen.

From the Old World to the New: "Cocido Madrileño" and Tortilla Soup
When I have traveled in Latin America, I often noticed how much their cuisine reminds me of the dishes my mother used to make, such as the flank steak recipe, which appears with a different name, "matahambre" (kill the hunger). One of those experiences is the typical Mexican tortilla soup that has many of the same ingredients as the traditional "Cocido Madrileño" (Madrilenian stew).

"Cocido Madrileño" is to Madrid what "Paella Valenciana" is to Valencia. Both dishes define their regions, but they are served all over Spain now. It has become trendy to eat "cocido" at fancy restaurants during the Christmas season and into the winter months. On my last trip to Madrid during the holidays, I had a chance to taste the Lhardy's "Cocido Madrileño" and it was memorable and not only because it cost almost $100 per person. The reservations had to be made weeks in advance and we were lucky to get a beautiful table in front of the fireplace on the second floor. Lhardy's version has the three traditional courses or "vuelcos:" a rich chicken broth soup with vermicelli, the vegetables and chickpeas dish and the diverse meats, including the meatball, served with a tomato sauce on the side. Dessert and coffee were extra, despite the hefty tab.

On the same trip, I was surprised by the menu when some sophisticated friends from the liberal Asamblea de Madrid (Madrid City Government) invited me for New Year's dinner and they served an impressive "cocido," proving how it has risen in popularity. They had gone to a lot of trouble to find authentic onion blood sausages — a treat for someone from Valencia like me — and they served it with cabbage and the meatball, something that my mother never made. She would have been equally surprised to find out that "cocido" has become fancy holiday fare; she used to serve it on a weekday and rarely on a Sunday.

The origin of the "cocido" can be traced all the way to medieval times when it was known as "olla podrida" (rotten pot). It used to be a simple stew of chicken and vegetables; other meats pork and sausages in particular, were added centuries later when the Jews were expelled from Spain at the end of the XV century. Conversos, the Jews who converted to Christianity, incorporated pork to show off their newly acquired faith. If Cervantes was a Converso Jew himself, as some scholars have concluded, no wonder then that his Don Quixote added as much pork as possible to the pot in order to save his skin.

My mother used to make "cocido" when someone had a cold. She used to say that it was the perfect healthy meal: lots of carbohydrates, fiber and protein. Her first course soup was made with rice instead of the Madrilenian vermicelli. It was not considered a fancy dish then, but it was a big meal, particularly because it provided menus for almost the entire week. On the day that the "cocido" was made, it was served in its traditional fashion, with the three "vuelcos" of soup, vegetables and meats. On following days, the soup with some of the vegetables became a puree for the first course, garnished with croutons. The second course was "ropa vieja" (old clothes, also found on Latin American menus), which was made by sautéing a tomato with some of the leftover "cocido" vegetables and the meats cut in small pieces. It is delicious and even more flavorful than the mild, original stewed "cocido."

On following days, the leftover "cocido" reappeared as croquettes, another Spanish staple. The croquettes are made by sautéing an onion with the meats that have been triturated in a meat mill (a Cuisinart nowadays), making a béchamel sauce (similar to the sauce for the cauliflower recipe). I have never figured out how Spanish couples stay married if they make croquettes together. My late husband and I would invariably have an argument every time we made croquettes. We agreed to let the béchamel cool in in the refrigerator for several hours and then shape the croquettes with a tablespoon. But we could never agree if it was best to roll them in egg whites or whole eggs, if it was best to roll them in breadcrumbs or leave them plain. Usually we ended up making separate batches — his and hers — and asking our guests which ones they preferred. The jury was still out when Peter was overtaken by cancer. What I can tell you for sure is that croquettes make a big mess in your kitchen no matter where you dip them; you are better off having them in any neighborhood restaurant.

I often make a "cocido madrileño" on January 6, because I still like to celebrate the arrival of the Three Wise Men. Growing up it was my favorite day of the entire holiday season. We used to leave straw for the camels and champagne for the Three Kings on the balcony, quite a long way from the American milk and cookies for Santa Claus! Naughty children could find coal in their shoes, which were also left on the balcony. I do not think I ever got coal or I would remember it. On January 6, whatever else is served for dinner, the dessert is a "Roscón de Reyes" (a Kings' Cake, something reminiscent of the Bouche de Noël). It is also similar to a challah bread, with a glass figurine hidden inside; whoever finds it, gets to wear the crown and be king for a day.

My "cocido" recipe, included here, has been adjusted to an American kitchen and palate. The chickpeas come from a can, the meats are as lean as possible and I skip the blood sausages, no matter how much I like them. A chorizo or pepperoni stick is also flavorful and a lot easier to find. It is important to skim the foam while the meats are cooking and to warn your guests to bring a big appetite.

I do not know how my mother would feel about turning a "cocido" into a Latin American tortilla soup recipe. Hopefully, she would think that I inherited the creative cooking gene from her. She would like that I do not waste any leftovers as she preached. The cilantro, the jalapeño peppers and the lime turn the mild "cocido" soup into a spicy, hearty broth anytime of the year. I discovered it on a trip to Puebla, in Mexico, with the exotic name of Tinga Poblana, and I remember thinking "Oh, my goodness, the 'cocido' has made it to the New World." These recipes serve as many guests as you have; just add more broth accordingly.

INGREDIENTS
MEATS
1 lb. meatloaf mix 1 egg, beaten
1 teaspoon dry mustard
3 tablespoons bread crumbs
1 tablespoon Worcestershire sauce
Paprika or Spanish "pimentón," salt and pepper
3 tablespoons olive oil
1 stick pepperoni or chorizo
3 veal shanks
6 chicken pieces, legs and thighs are best

VEGETABLES
3–4 carrots, peeled and cut in half
3–4 parsnips, peeled and cut in half
3–4 celery stalks, trimmed and cut same as above
3–4 potatoes, peeled and cut in half
1 white cabbage, trimmed and cut in half (optional)
1 can chickpeas, drained and rinsed well

BROTH
3 tablespoons olive oil
1 small tomato, chopped
3 cloves of garlic, pressed
¾ cup of rice
Saffron, salt, pepper, parsley
1 small can tomato sauce

"COCIDO"
Make one or two large balls with the meatloaf mix and your favorite ingredients. Mine has one beaten egg, Worcestershire sauce, dry mustard, salt, pepper and "pimentón" (Spanish paprika). Roll them in the bread crumbs. Brown the two balls in olive oil.

In a very large pot cover the meats and the meatballs with cold water. Simmer for about thirty minutes, skimming the foam as it forms.

Add the vegetables and cabbage (optional) and simmer for twenty minutes.

Add the chickpeas and cook for ten more minutes.

Always cook at low heat, do not overcook. Meats and vegetables should be tender but hold their form (the meatballs in particular!).

"COCIDO" SOUP

In a large pot sauté the tomato and garlic in olive oil. Add the rice and stir until coated. Add spices: saffron, salt, pepper and parsley to taste.

Cover with broth from the "cocido" pot. About two cups per person. Simmer for about twenty minutes, until the rice is cooked.

In the meantime warm up the tomato sauce.

Serve the rice soup as a first course.

Arrange the vegetables and chickpeas on a serving platter. Arrange the meats on another serving platter. Serve with the tomato sauce as an accompaniment.

TORTILLA SOUP
1 small tomato, chopped
3 jalapeño peppers, chopped
3 garlic cloves, pressed
3 tablespoons olive oil
Fresh cilantro, chopped
1 avocado, peeled and sliced thin
3 limes, sliced thi
1 bag tortilla strips
Sour cream or queso fresco

In a large soup pot sauté tomato, jalapeños and garlic in olive oil. Add "cocido" broth with leftover vegetables and meats cut into small pieces, skip the meatball, because it does not cut well.

Serve in large soup bowls with slices of avocado and lime. Top with cilantro, tortilla strips, and a dollop of sour cream or queso fresco.

Bibliography

Aciman, André. "Are you Listening? Conversations with My Deaf Mother." *The New Yorker* (2014) 3/17.

Alberdi Alonso, Inés. *Cartas a Alicia*. Madrid: Eila Editores, 2006.

———. *La nueva familia española*. Madrid: Taurus, 1999.

Alborg, Concha. *American in Translation: A Novel in Three Novellas*. Bloomington, Indiana: X Libris, 2011.

———. *Beyond Jet-Lag: Other Stories*. New Jersey: Ediciones Nuevo Espacio, 2000.

———. *Divorce After Death: A Widow's Memoir*. Charleston, South Carolina: Shorehouse Books, 2014.

———. "Falangismo y Feminismo: Mercedes Formica." *Modalidades de representación del sujeto auto/bio/gráfico femenino*. Eds. Magdalena Maíz and Luis H. Peña. UNAL: México, 187–198.

———. "Madres e hijas en la narrativa española contemporánea escrita por mujeres: ¿Mártires, monstruos o musas?" *Mujeres novelistas en el panorama literario del Siglo XX*. Ed. Marina Villalba Álvarez. Cuenca: Ediciones de la Universidad Castilla-La Mancha, 2000.

———. "*Una mujer por caminos de España*: la seudoautobiografía de María Martínez Sierra." *Revista de Estudios Hispánicos*, XXX (1996): 485–495.

———. *Una noche en casa*. Madrid: Huerga & Fierro, 1995.

Alborg, Juan Luis. *Historia de la literatura española. De Siglo a Siglo. Palacio Valdés y Blasco Ibáñez* (Vol. V, Parte III). Madrid: Gredos, 1999.

———. *Historia de la literatura española. Edad Media y Renacimiento*, (Vol. I). Madrid: Gredos, 1966 & 1970.

———. *Historia de la literatura española. Época Barroca*, (Vol. II). Gredos, 1967.

———. *Historia de la literatura española. Realismo y Naturalismo. Introducción. La novela, Fernán Caballero, Alarcón, Pereda* (Vol. V Parte I). Madrid: Gredos, 1996.

———. *Historia de la literatura española. El Romanticismo* (Vol. IV). Madrid: Gredos, 1980.

Bibliography

——. *Historia de la literatura española. Siglo XVIII* (Vol. III). Madrid: Gredos, 1972.

——. *Hora actual de la novela española,* Vols. I and II. Madrid: Taurus, 1958–1962.

——. *Manual de Historia Universal.* 2 vols. Madrid: Gredos, 1952.

——. *Sobre crítica y críticos.* Madrid: Gredos, 1991.

Arambarri, Ana. *Ataúlfo Argenta: Música interrumpida.* Barcelona: Galaxia Gutenberg, 2017.

Azcárate, Manuel. *Derrotas y esperanzas: La República, la Guerra Civil y la Resistencia.* Barcelona: Tusquets, 1994.

Baroja y Nessi, Carmen. *Recuerdos de una mujer de la Generación del 98.* Barcelona: Tusquets, 1998.

Bechdel, Alison. *Are You My Mother? A Comic Drama.* Boston: Houghton Mifflin, 2012.

Cercas, Javier. *El monarca de las sombras.* Barcelona: Literatura Random House, 2017.

Cerezales Laforet, Cristina. *Música blanca.* Barcelona: Ediciones Destino, 2009.

Colorado Castellary, Arturo. *El Museo del Prado y la Guerra Civil. Figueras-Ginebra, 1939.* Madrid: Museo del Prado, 1991.

Cura, Isabel del and Huertas, Rafael. "Public Health and Nutrition After the Spanish Civil War." *American Journal of Public Health,* Oct. 2009, Vol. 99, Issue 10, 1772–1779.

Diccionario Akal del español coloquial: 1492 expresiones y más. Eds. Alicia Ramos & Ana Serradilla. Madrid: Akal, 2000.

Domke, Joan. *Educación, Fascismo y la Iglesia Católica en la España de Franco 1939–1975.* Bloomington, Indiana: Author House, 2018.

Encarnación, Omar G. "Spain Exhumes Its Painful Past." *New York Review of Books* (2018) 8/24. 1–9.

Espina, Concha. *La esfinge maragata.* Ed. Carmen Díaz Castañón. Madrid: Castalia, 1989.

Formica, Mercedes. *Visto y vivido 1931–1937.* Barcelona: Planeta, 1982.

Fox, Soledad. *A Spanish Woman in Love and War. Constancia de la Mora.* Brighton: Sussex Academic Press, 2011.

Fraser, Ronald. *Blood of Spain: An Oral History of the Spanish Civil War.* New York: Pantheon Books, 1979.

García Nieto París, María del Carmen. "Trabajo y oposición popular de la mujer durante la dictadura franquista." *Historia de las mujeres: El Siglo XX.* Ed. Françoise Thébaud. Madrid: Taurus, 1993. 661–671.

Genevois, Daniéle Busey. "Mujeres de España: de la República al Franquismo." *Historia de las mujeres: El Siglo XX.* Ed. Françoise Thébaud. Madrid: Taurus, 1993. 203–221.

Gille, Élisabeth. *The Mirador. Dreamed Memories of Irène Némirovsky by*

Bibliography

Her Daughter. Trans. Marina Harss. New York: New York Review of Books, 2000.

Giralt Torrente, Marcos. *Tiempo de vida*. Barcelona, Anagrama, 2011.

González-Allende, Iker. "Las novias de Concha Espina: Amor durante la Guerra Civil Española." *Revista de Estudios Hispánicos* 45 (2011) 527–549.

Graham, Helen. *The War and Its Shadow. Spain's Civil War in Europe's Long Twentieth Century*. Brighton: Sussex Academic Press, 2015.

Hijas y padres. Ed. Alejandra Vallejo-Nágera. Barcelona: Ediciones Martínez Roca, 1999.

Historia de las mujeres: El Siglo XX. Ed. Françoise Thébaud. Madrid: Taurus, 1993.

Hochschild, Adam. *Spain in Our Hearts: Americans in the Spanish Civil War, 1936–1939*. Boston: Houghton Mifflin, 2017.

Hoeber, Francis W. *Against Time. Letters from Nazi Germany 1938–1939*. Philadelphia: American Philosophical Society, 2015.

Hood, Ann. *Kitchen Yarns. Notes on Life, Love, and Food*. New York: W. W. Norton & Company, 2019.

Huber, Lia. *Nourished. A Memoir of Food, Faith & Enduring Love (with Recipes)*. New York: Convergent, 2017.

Hughes, Kathryn. Review of *The Victorian and the Romantic. A Memoir, a Love Story, and a Friendship Across Time*. New York: Doubleday, 2018. *NYT Book Review* (2018) 9/23/18.

Introducción a la Historia de España. Eds. José María Jover, Juan Regla, Carlos Seco & Antonio Ubieto. New York: Las Américas, 1965.

Irujo, Xabier A. *Gernika: Genealogy of a Lie*. Brighton: Sussex Academic Press, 2019.

Iscla Rovira, Luis. *Spanish Proverbs: A Survey of Spanish Culture and Civilization (In 2850 Proverbs)*. Lanham, Maryland, University Press of America, 1984.

Karr, Mary. *The Art of Memoir*. New York: Harper, 2015.

Kaufman, Dan. "*La Despedida*: A Lost Memoir of the Spanish Civil War." *Autobiography and Memoir. Books & The Arts* (2009) 10/31.

Kephart, Beth. *Handling the Truth: On the Writing of Memoir*. New York: Goltham Books, 2013.

Kramer, Jane. *The Reporter's Kitchen. Essays*. New York, St. Martin's Press, 2017.

León, Víctor. *Diccionario de argot español*. Madrid: Alianza, 1986.

Letters of Transit. Reflections on Exile, Identity, Language, and Loss. Ed. André Aciman. New York: New York Public Library, 1999.

Lewis, Sinclair, *Arrowsmith*. London: Penny Books, 2010.

Lopate, Phillip. *A Mother's Tale*. Columbus, Ohio State U P, 2017.

——. *Portrait of My Body*. New York: Anchor Books, 1996.

Bibliography

Madres e hijas. Ed. Laura Freixas. Barcelona: Editorial Anagrama, 1996.

Mangini, Shirley. *Memories of Resistance. Women's Voices from the Spanish Civil War*. New Haven: Yale University Press, 1995.

Martín Gaite, Carmen. *Usos amorosos de la postguerra española*. Barcelona: Editorial Anagrama, 1987.

Martínez Sierra, María. *Una mujer por caminos de España*. Ed. Alda Blanco. Madrid: Editorial Castalia, 1989.

Mendelson, Jordana. "Learning from Guernica." *Teaching Representations of the Spanish Civil War*. Ed. Noël Valis. New York: The Modern Languages Association of America, 2007. 328–338.

Miller, Nancy K. "The Entangled Self: Genre Bondage in the Age of the Memoir." *Publications of the Modern Language Association* (2007) 122.3. 537–548.

Montero, Rosa. "Un trozo de cielo muy pequeño." *El País, Babelia* (2009) 1 /31.

Moradiellos García, Enrique. *Historia mínima de la Guerra Civil Española*. Madrid: Turner Publicaciones, 2016.

Nash, Mary. "Mujeres en España y en Hispanoamérica contemporánea." *Historia de las mujeres: El Siglo XX*. Ed. Françoise Thébaud. Madrid: Taurus, 1993. 619–625.

Orwell, George. *Homage to Catalonia*. London: Secker and Warburg, 1938.

Picasso: El Guernica. Ed. Miranda Harrison. London: Scala Publishers, 2008.

Pope, Randolph D. "Fighting the Long Battle of Memory: Autobiographical Writing about the Spanish Civil War." *Teaching Representations of the Spanish Civil War*. Ed. Noël Valis. New York: The Modern Languages Association of America, 2007. 398–405.

¿Por qué España? Memorias del hispanismo estadounidense. Eds. Anna Caballé Masforroll and Randolph D. Pope. Barcelona: Galaxia Guttenberg, 2014.

Prado, Benjamín. *Mala gente que camina*. Madrid: Punto de Lectura, 2006.

Preston, Paul. *¡Comrades! Portraits from the Spanish Civil War*. London: Harper Perennial, 2006.

——. *Doves of War: Four Women of Spain*. London: HarperCollins, 2016.

——. *La Guerra civil española: Reacción, revolución y venganza*. Barcelona: Penguin Random House Grupo Editorial, 2011.

——. *The Last Days of the Spanish Republic*. London: HarperCollins, 2016.

——. *The Spanish Civil War: An Illustrated Chronicle 1936–1939*. New York: Grove Press, 1986.

Bibliography

———. *The Spanish Holocaust. Inquisition and Extermination in Twentieth-Century Spain.* New York: W.W. Norton & Company, 2012.

Ramos, María Dolores. "¿Madres de la Revolución? Mujeres en los movimientos sociales españoles (1900–1930)." *Historia de las mujeres: El Siglo XX.* Ed. Françoise Thébaud. Madrid: Taurus, 1993. 647–659.

Rhodes, Richard. *Hell and Good Company: The Spanish Civil War and the World it Made.* New York: Simon & Schuster, 2015.

Ríos, Alicia and March, Lourdes. *The Heritage of Spanish Cooking.* New York: Random House, 1992.

Rodoreda, Mercé. *La Plaza del Diamante.* Trans. Enrique Sordo. Barcelona: Edhasa, 1983.

Ross, Christopher J. *Contemporary Spain. A Handbook.* Oxford University Press, 2002.

Sáez Buenaventura, Carmen. *¿La liberación era esto? Mujeres, vidas y crisis.* Madrid: Ediciones Temas de Hoy, 1993.

Salazar, Margaret Van Epp. "Personal Narrative: A Bridge in Time." *Teaching Representations of the Spanish Civil War.* Ed. Noël Valis. New York: The Modern Languages Association of America, 2007. 365–372.

Salidas de madre. Relatos. Ed. Alejandra Rojas. Santiago de Chile: Planeta, 1997.

Schiff, Stacy. "Making Herself the Subject." *The New York Review of Books.* (2018) 10/25.

Smyth, Katherine. *All the Lives We Ever Lived. Seeking Solace in Virginia Woolf.* New York: Crown, 2019.

Soler, Abel. *El poble de Salem i la goia de les fonts.* Salem: Ajuntament de Salem, 2007.

Stevens, Nell. *The Victorian and the Romantic. A Memoir, a Love Story, and a Friendship Across Time.* New York: Doubleday, 2018.

Teaching Representations of the Spanish Civil War. Ed. Noël Valis. New York: The Modern Languages Association of America, 2007.

Textos para la historia de las mujeres en España. Eds. Cándida Martínez & Mary Nash. Madrid: Cátedra, 1994.

Thomas, Abigail. *Safekeeping. Some True Stories from a Life.* New York, Anchor House, 2000.

Thomas, Hugh. *The Spanish Civil War.* New York: Touchstone, 1986.

Tusell, Javier. *Franco en la Guerra Civil: Una biografía política.* Barcelona: Tusquets, 1992.

Valis, Noël. "Civil War Ghosts Entombed: Lessons of the Valley of the Fallen." *Teaching Representations of the Spanish Civil War.* Ed. Noël Valis. New York: The Modern Languages Association of America, 2007. 425–435.

———. "Cuando mi madre leía *Ulises. ¿Por qué España? Memorias del hispanismo estadounidense.* Eds. Anna Caballé Masforroll and Randolph Pope. Barcelona: Galaxia Gutenberg, 2014. 625–652.

———. "'From the Face of Memory': How American Women Journalists Covered the Spanish Civil War." Soc (2017) 54: 549–559.

Warncke, Carsten-Peter. *Pablo Picasso.* Cologne: Borders Press, 1997.

Waxler, Jerry. *Memoir Revolution: Write Your Story. Change the World.* Quakertown, Pennsylvania: Neural Coach Press, 2013.

Willis, Liz. "Women in the Spanish Revolution. Solidarity." *Solidarity Pamphlet#48.* Libcom.org (2009) 11/6.

Women's Voices from the Spanish Civil War. Eds. Jim Fyrth and Sally Alexander. London: Lawrence & Wishart, 1991.

Woolsey, Gamel. *Malaga Burning. An American Woman's Eyewitness Account of the Spanish Civil War.* Paris: Pythia Press, 1998.

Index

Index

Index

Index

Index

Index

About the Author

Dr. Concha Alborg was born in Valencia, Spain, and grew up in Madrid. She has lived in the United States since the 1960s. More than any other event in her life, this move defines who she is, an immigrant living between two cultures. She may seem Americanized to her Spanish relatives, but she is from another country as far as her daughters are concerned. Although Concha fits well enough in both cultures, a tell-tale Spanish accent marks her speech as well as her writing.

She earned a Masters from Emory University (1977) and a Ph.D. from Temple University (1982). For over twenty years she was a professor of contemporary Spanish literature at Saint Joseph's University in Philadelphia, where she still resides.

Some of her academic publications include: *Cinco figuras en torno a la novela de posguerra: Galvarriato, Soriano, Formica, Boixadós y Aldecoa* (1993), a critical edition of *Caza menor* by Elena Soriano (1992), *Temas y técnicas en la narrativa de Jesús Fernández Santos* (1984) and numerous articles and reviews.

Since her retirement from teaching, she has dedicated herself to writing creative non-fiction. She has published a memoir, *Divorce after Death. A Widow's Memoir* (2014), a novel, *American in Translation: A Novel in Three Novellas* (2011) and two collections of short stories: *Beyond Jet-Lag. Other Stories* (2000) and *Una noche en casa* (1995).

More information on her career and publications is available at www.conchaalborg.com

The author with her mother's letters. Philadelphia, 2019.
Photograph by Jane Day Rasmussen.